NEWS, NEWSPAPERS AND TELEVISION

By the same author

GUARDIAN YEARS

NEWS, NEWSPAPERS AND TELEVISION

Alastair Hetherington

MACMILLAN
PRESS

First published 1985
Reprinted 1986, 1987

Published by
THE MACMILLAN PRESS LTD
Houndmills, Basingstoke, Hampshire RG21 2XS
and London
Companies and representatives
throughout the world

Printed in Hong Kong

British Library Cataloguing in Publication Data
Hetherington, Alastair
News, newspapers and television.
1. Journalism — Great Britain   2. Mass media—
Great Britain
I. Title
070.4'3   PN5118
ISBN 0-333-38605-1 hardcover
ISBN 0-333-38606-X paperback

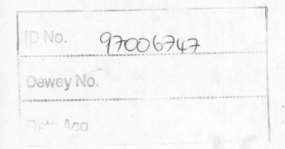

Contents

List of Tables

List of Charts

Preface

'It's like riding a bicycle: if you stop to think about it you'll fall off.' Thus the deputy editor, BBC television news, when interviewed by the author in December 1981 on his approach to news. As a former journalist, I could only agree. The pace of daily journalism leaves little time for introspective contemplation. Nevertheless, for many years I had felt that it would be useful to try to persuade journalists to explain how they reached their decisions – especially on what was or was not news, and on how it should be handled.

Sir Kenneth Alexander, an old friend, became Principal of Stirling University in 1980. Not long afterwards he suggested that a study of news could be undertaken from a base in Stirling. In December 1981 I carried out a small pilot study, to test what might be feasible. Together Sir Kenneth and I then secured grants from the BBC and from the Television Fund, which is financed by the independent television companies; and subsequently from the Social Science Research Council, now renamed the Economic and Social Research Council. In autumn of 1982 Stirling University appointed me as a research professor in media studies.

Without the funding from the ESRC, the Television Fund and the BBC – and the support of Stirling University – this study would not have been possible. I am most grateful to all of them.

Access to the newsrooms and news staff of the BBC and ITN was readily offered; so was access to the regional newsrooms of STV and BBC Scotland. Similarly the *Guardian,* the *Daily Mail*, the *Daily Mirror* and *The Times* all agreed to allow access; and they proved patient and tolerant of many fieldwork visits. (*The Times* deserves special thanks for admitting a former editor of the *Guardian* who still had close connections with that paper.) The *Daily Telegraph, Daily Express* and *Sun* refused access – though the editors of the *Telegraph* and the *Express* individually offered to be interviewed. At the *Express* Sir Larry Lamb explained that, since he had only recently arrived and there were tensions within in the 'Lubianka', the presence of outside observers in the newsroom might be misunderstood. The *Sun* simply turned down two requests.

Lack of access to any of the most strident popular papers leaves a serious gap in this study. The *Mail* and *Mirror* are consequently the only 'popular' papers covered here; and they too were always open and friendly in allowing observation of their daily work. So was the Scottish *Daily Record* during our brief visits there.

The ESRC believed that a sociologist should work with me, and Mr Howard Tumber was appointed to do so. His background was in the study of television, and he is associated with the City University. For a year he gave me much valuable help. He undertook the primary fieldwork at the *Guardian,* the *Mirror* and BBC television news, while I observed in parallel at *The Times,* the *Mail* and ITN.

It was always our intention to complete most of the fieldwork in the winter of 1983–4, as we did, and then to finish by studying coverage of one major event. The NUM–NCB dispute, starting in March 1984, was an obvious choice – but it lasted much longer than we or others had foreseen. Howard Tumber had to move to other commitments at the end of his year. For a short period therefore, with the approval of the ESRC, I recruited Mr Innis Macbeath. He had lately retired after many years as labour editor and an assistant editor of *The Times,* and then as professor of industrial relations at the London Business School. In the end he wrote the chapter on newspaper coverage of the coal dispute – and it appears under his name in this book – while I wrote the chapter on television coverage.

One regret was that, because space in a single book prevents it, we were unable to include most of the tables of content analysis prepared at each stage. They are, however, being lodged in a more extensive report with the British Library and the library of the ESRC.

Thanks are due also to my wife, a constantly constructive critic; to other members of the family who helped in various ways; and to colleagues and students at Stirling University. Their assistance and advice is acknowledged more fully at the end of this book.

Alastair Hetherington

Stirling

1 What's News? Who Makes the News?

News is what someone wants to stop you printing: all the rest is ads.

> William Randolph Hearst (US newspaper proprietor, 1863–1951)

It's all lies and trash, anyway.

> Arran ferryman, watching that day's supply of newspapers sinking into the sea, having been accidentally dropped between ship and pier (Summer, 1947)

Both comments contain an element of truth, though neither tells the whole truth. Hearst's quip highlights one point: that obtaining news is often a struggle, with participants in the event trying to prevent publication. But the same people, as frequently, may seek publicity for actions or decisions favourable to them – especially if they are politicians or industrialists. What they say may well be worth printing, though journalists must be wary about the motives and reliability of such sources.

As for the Arran ferryman, the papers that he was prepared to let sink included the *Glasgow Herald*s on which I had worked hard the previous night, for I was then the late duty sub-editor and in charge of the final edition. What he said about lies and trash might well have been true of the *Daily Express* or *Daily Sketch*, but not of the *Glasgow Herald*. My feelings were saved, however, by another seaman who fished the packages out of the water and stood them to dry in the morning sun.

After some forty years of active journalism, my perspective is that of a journalist. In spite of that, in this book I have tried to take a detached look at the work of journalists. Herbert Gans, one of the shrewdest of American sociologists who have studied the press and broadcasting, said (1980) that the hardest

1

thing 'is to study people who are politically and culturally akin
to the fieldworker and who take the same things for granted'.
If Gans found it hard, so have I. But there are some
advantages, not least in being familiar with the fast-moving
routine of a newsroom and with the kind of verbal shorthand
that journalists use in talking to each other.

What is news? More than thirty years ago the first Royal
Commission on the Press (the Ross Commission of 1947–9)
said this:

> The idea of what constitutes news varies from office to
> office: a paper's standard of news values is one of the most
> distinctive facets of its personality. There are, however,
> certain elements common to all conceptions of news. To be
> news an event must first be interesting to the public, and the
> public for this purpose means for each paper the people who
> read that paper and others like them. Second, and equally
> important, it must be new, and newness is measured in
> newspaper offices in terms of minutes.

Ross thereby accepted that news judgements must be conditioned both by the audience – or at least by a journalist's
estimate of his or her audience – and by a judgement of what
will interest that audience. Thus we already have two partly
speculative elements: (1) who are the audience? and (2) what
will interest them?

The Ross Report goes on (paras 373–5) to set out the
interests of an average British audience in 1948, as revealed by
a survey which it undertook among newspaper proprietors,
managements and journalists. This put sport top of the list,
followed by 'news about people, news of strange or amusing
adventures, tragedies, accidents, and crimes – news, that is,
whose sentiment or excitement brings some colour into life'.
The replies, the Royal Commission says, 'did not rate interest
in public affairs very high'. It adds, however, that many replies
suggested that interest was increasing because of education and
because of 'the increased impact of politics, and particularly of
Government activity, on the lives of ordinary people'.

A reader's taste in political news is affected by his or her own
political opinions, the report says, and supporters of one party
are more interested in the speeches of its leaders than in those

of an opposing party. (The weekend or midweek speeches of politicians were still important in 1948 and 1949.) One newspaper company, in its reply, noted that if its papers did not reflect 'the limitations and prejudices' of at least a considerable section of the public 'it will cease to exist, for it will find no buyers'.

The report complains (para 553) that the press is too ready to publish 'what at best corresponds only roughly to the truth' and is ready to make statements on inadequate evidence. It complains also of triviality and sensationalism. It accepts that in a country with a partisan political machinery a partisan press must be expected, but it says that this leads to 'a degree of selection and colouring of the news which can only be regarded as excessive'. It pays a tribute to the quality papers and the non-metropolitan morning papers, but says this of popular news values (para 559):

> In the popular papers, consideration of news value acts as a distorting medium even apart from any political considerations. It attaches supreme importance to the new, the exceptional, and the 'human' and it emphasises these elements in the news to the detriment or even the exclusion of the normal and the continuing. Consequently the picture is always out of focus.

The Royal Commission's most stinging conclusion comes near the end (para 572). 'In our opinion the newspapers, with few exceptions, fail to supply the electorate with adequate materials for sound political judgment.' In a liberal democracy, at that time dependent primarily on the press for the dissemination of information, that must rank as the Commission's significant finding. Unfortunately the Ross Report failed to recommend any substantial remedies. It called for better education and training of journalists, the creation of a General Council of the Press to encourage a sense of public responsibility in the press and promote professional standards, and the ending of 'non-journalistic forms of competition' in the industry. The National Council for the Training of Journalists and the Press Council came into being as a result of that report, though by the 1980s the NCTJ was in decline and the Press Council had never proved more than a forum for hearing

complaints from the public. As for 'non-journalistic competition', that has moved onwards to the millionaire realms of
bingo.

The first Royal Commission nevertheless provides a useful
starting point for the study of news values. To summarise, it
found that these were the categories then in common use:

Sport
News about people
Strange or amusing adventures
Tragedies, accidents
Crime
and (bottom) public affairs.

These were the criteria, of course, resulting from replies by
publishers, managements and journalists in 1948.

The second Royal Commission, chaired by Lord Shawcross
in 1961–2, was concerned exclusively with economics. The
third – chaired in 1974–7 by Lord McGregor of Durris, a
sociologist of wide experience – had a much broader remit. It
dealt with finance, ownership, performance, the closed shop,
industrial relations within the newspaper industry, and other
issues. It was less critical of the performance of the press, for
there had been evident improvement since the late 1940s.

It undertook a detailed analysis of coverage of three
subjects – industrial relations, social welfare and foreign
affairs – and found (paras 10.38 to 10.71) that on all three the
reporting was 'highly factual' and 'devoid of any overt bias'.
More generally it examined bias against the political Left and
against trade unions. While it found that editorial support for
the Conservative party had been consistently higher than for
the Labour and Liberal parties – and at general elections much
higher than the popular vote – it concluded that on 'agenda
setting' (the choice of subjects to be reported and discussed)
the balance against Labour was not strong. On trade union
affairs it drew attention to failings because non-specialist sub-
editors were handling the copy of specialist reporters; and to
an 'unsatisfactory mosaic' produced by ignorance of industrial
relations (para 10.128). It was critical of continuing invasions
of privacy, cheque-book journalism and lack of background
information.

Two members wrote a minority report which spoke of 'complacency' in the main report, especially (p. 243) on the polarisation of the press between 'the excellence of some of our quality newspapers and at the other edge the vacuity and irresponsibility of some of our popular newspapers'.

Neither the main report nor the minority one makes much of radio and television news as an influence on the performance of the press, though both touch on it briefly. My own view, based both on years of working journalism and on the fieldwork for this study, is that broadcast news has been and is a powerful influence. A popular newspaper today can no longer ignore a topic or a political issue that is taken up by radio and television news, and gross distortion of the kind that was common in the 1940s is more readily detected by readers, almost all of whom are seeing or hearing broadcast bulletins. In every newspaper office today, as will emerge later, the early morning radio news and the midday and early evening television news are closely monitored.

On news values as such, the third Royal Commission did not follow the Ross Commission with its own survey. But its Working Paper Number 2, prepared by Professor Denis McQuail (and published by HMSO in 1976), offers a useful guide to the work of sociologists from the 1920s to the 1970s. McQuail draws attention in particular (pp. 45–8) to the distortions that may occur because of journalists' 'unformulated criteria'

through primary emphasis on action, personality and conflict;

through the snowball effect when one newspaper follows another, and a dominant 'news angle' is established (sometimes influencing broadcast coverage, too);

through selective emphasis on themes such as disorder among immigrant communities, soccer hooliganism and types of crime;

and through 'stereotyping' which may affect the reporting of women, minority groups (ethnic or other), juveniles, and deviants.

These are common causes of distortion. It is as well, nevertheless, to remember two comments from the 1920s –

Walter Lippmann's, that without standardising, stereotypes and routine judgements to help him, an editor would go mad with excitement every day; and Max Weber's, that good journalism requires at least as much 'genius' as any scholarly accomplishment, and that the sense of responsibility of every honourable journalist 'is, on average, not a bit lower than that of a scholar'.

More specifically, let us look at the projections of news values by the Swedish sociologists Galtung and Ruge (1965 and 1973) and by the American Herbert Gans (1980). Galtung and Ruge base their analysis on the reporting in four countries of the crises in the Congo, Cuba and Cyprus. They systematically formulate a list of twelve factors (three with subfactors) which must be satisfied before an event is likely to become news.

The elements in summary are (1) *frequency*, or timing – 'a murder takes little time and the event takes place between the publication of two successive issues of a daily', so a meaningful story can be told, whereas events over a longer timespan are likely to go unrecorded. (2) *Threshold,* or the size of an event – for if too small it will pass unreported. (3) *Unambiguity* – the clearer the meaning of the event the more probably will it become news. (4) *Meaningfulness* – this can be subdivided into 'cultural proximity', which implies, for example, that Islamic or oriental events are less likely to be reported in the West than those in Europe or America, and 'relevance', which means that anything impinging on the news gatherers' home culture is likely to be reported. (5) *Consonance* – or the existence of a mental 'pre-image' or expectation, for unless there is some previous knowledge or expectation, the event will not readily register in the mind. (6) *Unexpectedness* – this is linked with consonance, in that if the event has crossed the threshold of consonance then the more unpredictable, rare or unexpected it is, the stronger its prospects of being reported.

(7) *Continuity* – or the 'running story' which, once established, will continue to run. (8) *Composition* – or the demand of news editors and programme editors for a mixed diet, to entertain and hold the audience. (9) *Élite nations* – or the more an event concerns the USA, the Soviet Union or another leading nation, the stronger the interest in it. (10) *Élite people* – kings, praesidium members, trade union leaders, TV personalities and others who are easily photographed. (11)

Personal – people as individuals whether used to 'personify' a force or institution (in 1984, for instance, Mgr Bruce Kent for the CND or Mr Arthur Scargill for the striking miners) or because an event can be attributed to them as named individuals. (12) *Something negative* – the more negative the consequences of the event the more probable that it will become a news item.

Galtung and Ruge regard the first six factors as almost essential before an event becomes news anywhere in the world; the last four factors, they suggest, are of particular importance in the north-western corner (extending, by implication, from Moscow and Athens to California and Alaska), though they apply to some extent throughout the world. The Swedish authors also qualify factors 9 to 12 by saying that while in socialist countries élite nations and élite people will be reported, under factor 11 structures rather than persons may be featured and under factor 12 positive rather than negative happenings. In the developing countries, they say, the positive is also more likely than the negative; and, of course, there is much less concentration on the élite nations.[1]

None of this will come as any great surprise to journalists in the West, though most journalists, in my experience, will resist formalised 'news values' lest these cramp their freedom of decision. McQuail reports that many fieldworkers have encountered comparable reactions in their questioning of journalists, and he sums up by saying that journalists believe their professional expertise rests on their ability to 'know news when they see it'. Obviously journalists working at speed against edition times or programme 'on air' times do not go through any mental checklist of factors such as Galtung and Ruge have listed. As will become clear through the case studies in later chapters, the night editors or programme editors talk to the reporters if there is time, read the copy or view the rough-cut film or tape, discuss with one or two others if in doubt, and then make up their minds quickly and decisively. They must, if they are to do their jobs properly.

Their resistance to codified news values has another reason. Each newspaper believes itself to be distinct from other papers, with its own character and values, and probably every experienced executive in Fleet Street believes that his promotion came at least partly through his personal flair and originality. In television and radio newsrooms, too – even in the BBC's, where the institutional ideology is most clearly evident – the freedom to make or change decisions hour by hour and night by night is prized, as is the freedom to try a fresh approach or new style. Routine is essential; so is inventiveness. 'Flair' was accepted by the McGregor Commission (para 9.3) as one of the factors in competitive editorial success.

Before I had encountered either Galtung and Ruge's formula or the wider sweep of the Gans classification, reported below, I had devised my own 'seismic scale'. It was drawn up before I embarked on the fieldwork and mainly based on my own instinct about the factors likely to influence news editors, night editors and the editors themselves. It had only seven categories:

Significance: social, economic, political, human.
Drama: the excitement, action and entertainment in the event.
Surprise: the freshness, newness, unpredictability.
Personalities: royal, political, 'showbiz', others.
Sex, scandal, crime: popular ingredients.
Numbers: the scale of the event, numbers of people affected.
Proximity: on our doorsteps, or 10 000 miles away.

It was derived partly from the *Guardian*'s 'Advice' to new staff, prepared in 1961 before the paper started printing in London – the only attempt by a major newspaper, so far as I know, to set out its news priorities in writing and a risky thing just because it might inhibit freedom.[2] It leaves open, of course, the daily interpretation of words such as 'significance'.

For television news there must be an extra factor: pictures, or visual attractiveness. Although not essential, colourful or active pictures bring extra points to an item, promoting it in television news priorities. Geoffrey Cox, editor of ITN from 1956 to 1968 and creator of News at Ten, writes of the need to 'thrust cameras into the heart of the news', and he regards the searing pictures of October 1956 – from the Anglo-French invasion at Suez and the Soviet invasion of Hungary – as the 'crucible' which shaped the future of television news. He also describes how competition from ITN radically changed the anonymous, respectful and uninquisitive approach of BBC television news.³

In 1984 I tried out my seven-point seismic scale on journalists at *The Times,* the *Daily Mail* and ITN. I suggested that, to analyse one's own thinking, one might award points on a scale of 1 to 10 to individual reports and thus determine in aggregate which came top in one's priorities. How far, if at all, did this match a journalist's quick decision-making? The replies were cautious but interesting. They are reported more fully in later chapters. Here, however, are two – starting with a senior executive at *The Times.*

If a computer could analyse my mind better than I can, it might come up with something like that. I have never stopped to think about those elements, but they seem eminently sensible. My instinctive reactions, I hope, are an unconscious disposition in any decision or judgment. The element of flair and originality ought to be there, and the other element not there is the style and quality of writing. I should like to get on every one of our pages just one little oasis of truly good, enjoyable writing . . .

It's largely instinct, and a certain amount of tuition – and from the editor. The most important factor is the continuum of experience and knowledge, with a good grasp of *The Times,* its readers, and its editor's notions.

The second response comes from a senior man at the *Daily Mail.*

Of course significance comes first – and prominent personalities. There's only one acid test: does it interest me? My old man taught me my first lesson in journalism: tell it as you'd tell it in the pub. Simple and conversational.

No abstract theorising there. These indications of senior Fleet Street thinking mark, among other things, a considerable change from the response that the first Royal Commission received in 1948. Public affairs are now at the top of the list, instead of the bottom, even in some though not all of the popular papers. The proviso must be added that, when there is no strong topic of 'significance', the populars will go for something of more direct human interest for the sake of variety and entertainment. So will ITN, and sometimes the BBC. These points are also well illustrated in the case studies which follow.

As to what constitutes 'significance' – social, economic, political or human – that is another area which will be explored more fully later. It is one of the areas where journalists depend heavily on unspoken or unarticulated assumptions. My conclusions, however, can be stated briefly. First, in estimating significance most journalists in national newspapers or broadcasting are concerned with events or decisions which may affect the world's peace, the prosperity or welfare of people in Britain and abroad, and the environment in which we live. They are therefore concerned both with events such as a big strike which may upset British trade and economic prospects and with the policy-making of governments, industry and local authorities.

Secondly, their foremost unstated assumption is that we live in a liberal democracy and want to secure its continuity and harmony so far as possible. Consequently anything which upsets that harmony, whether through government action or from other quarters, tends to be treated as important but unwelcome news. Thirdly, the combined effect of these priorities is to reinforce the status quo, regardless of whether or not it will in the end be beneficial to the community as a whole. On occasions the tenor may be towards reform – for example, in the general concern shown for civil liberties – but these are exceptional.

Fourth, the British perspective is generally parochial – at least to the extent that British interests and British home news normally come first. Television has broadened horizons, because dramatic pictures come from the Middle East, Africa and other remote places. A striking example in the autumn of 1984 was the huge publicity for the famine in Ethiopia. It had been reported in newspapers months earlier, but with little public response. When starving children were shown on television, thanks to a BBC-Visnews crew, the topic became second only to the NCB–NUM dispute in intensity of coverage. Such attention to events 3000 miles away, with no direct British involvement at first, is again exceptional.

Parochialism is, of course, in line with the Galtung and Ruge factor 4, 'meaningfulness', for Ethiopia is a long way from Britain's home culture. It is in line also with my seventh factor, proximity. It further fits the analysis offered by Herbert Gans, who shows that normally foreign news can achieve sustained attention in the United States only if it is regarded as 'American' news – as over Vietnam during US involvement in the war there.

The Gans study (1980) was based on prolonged observation of the networked early evening news from CBS and NBC – starting in the late 1960s and continuing intermittently until 1978 – and on observation of the magazines *Time* and *Newsweek*. It is a comprehensive and revealing work, though it contains few case studies. Gans is professor of Sociology at Columbia University in New York.

It begins with a statistical demonstration that 'known' people receive three times the attention of 'unknowns' in the news. 'Knowns' include the President of the United States, presidential candidates, leading federal officials (with the Secretary of State, Henry Kissinger during much of the 1970s, top of the list), state and local officials, and a quite different group 'alleged and actual violators of the laws and mores'. Gans notes that many of the economically most powerful people, such as executives of large corporations and holders of great wealth, appear only rarely in the news. The 'unknowns' in the news include protestors, 'rioters', strikers, victims, some of the alleged or actual violators of the laws or mores until they become well known and 'participants in unusual activities' such as people in man-bites-dog stories.

All this may be fairly predictable – the 'knowns', after all, are mostly exercising governmental powers and their actions are therefore of general concern – but it has not often been as thoroughly documented as by Gans. He goes on, however, among other things to list the 'enduring values in the news' and the functions of journalists in American society, and here we again encounter the unintended tendency to sustain the status quo. His grouping of the enduring values is this: ethnocentrism (one's own nation and its affairs coming first), altruistic democracy, responsible capitalism, small-town pastoralism, individualism and moderatism, social order and national leadership. Within ethnocentrism, he says, many news stories are critical of domestic conditions and he includes reports such as those on the Watergate scandals, 'which were usually ascribed to a small group of power-hungry politicians'. Altruistic democracy implies through the news that politics should follow a course based on public interest and public service, while waste and corruption are treated as evil. Underlying the responsible capitalism is 'an optimistic faith in the good society'. Small-town pastoralism indicates the virtues of smallness, including small communities within big cities, and of nearness to nature. It is against Big Government, Big Labour and Big Business. And so on. Gans remarks that the news 'often supports the kinds of values sometimes unfairly belittled as "motherhood values" '.[4]

These American values cannot, of course, be transported wholesale across the Atlantic and applied in Britain. Apart from history, there are two simple reasons. One is that in Britain capitalism has been modified more extensively than in the United States – through public ownership, the National Health Service and social security provision. In the mid-1980s 'privatisation' and other Conservative measures are taking Britain towards the American pattern, but some of the 'enduring values' of the Attlee era (1945–51) continue to influence British life and journalism. The second is that the United States has no equivalent to Fleet Street's competitive popular press, which can reach the whole of England and much of Wales and Scotland every morning. The US is too big and too diverse, so that there is no real equivalent of UK 'national' news.

The effect of competition in Britain, according to the minority report of the third Royal Commission, has been to encourage bad and shoddy journalism and to drive out the good and responsible. The majority report took a less gloomy view. Whichever is correct, popular television news – BBC and ITN – has maintained standards that make it a counter-vailing force. While accepting, therefore, that we cannot precisely apply in Britain such of Gans's values as responsible capitalism and small-town parochialism, we are likely to find sociocentralist equivalents to them here. The media do on the whole reinforce the established society, uphold law and order, and accept social reform only gradually.

The evidence exists first in the attention given to government ministers – to Labour no less than Conservative ministers –

just because they exercise decisive authority; to Parliament, the Courts, major industrial and trading companies when they are accessible, and to others with economic or social power. Since few of them are radical reformers, the media must tend to reinforce the status quo.

Secondly, consider the treatment of crime and the police. Cases where the police have brought a criminal or suspect to trial almost inevitably receive more publicity than cases which remain unresolved, and in the latter category the reporting of police investigations is more often favourable than unfavourable. Where major police operations are mounted, as in dealing with the 1984–5 mining dispute, reporting of police action is generally sympathetic – even if with occasional questioning of particular incidents or tactics. Sometimes, as over the Yorkshire Ripper's murders in 1979–80 until Sutcliffe was arrested, there is adverse publicity for the police. Sometimes, also, the media may alarm old people or other groups by emphasis on particular crimes. The overall effect, nevertheless, is to create a reassuring impression that order is being maintained – whether or not journalists have had any intention of creating that impression. Mostly they have not thought about it in such terms.

A third element is publicity for the Royal family, almost always favourable and containing a British variant of the American 'motherhood values'. They are treated as symbols of continuing stability. A fourth element is the prominence given to television and entertainment personalities, perhaps the nearest thing to a late twentieth-century 'opium of the people'.[5] In this respect popular television and the popular press feed off each other.

A seriously misleading impression is given, however, if we leave the analysis there. During the fieldwork for this study we frequently observed ('we' being the author and others working with him) the dispassionate and open-minded approach of reporters, sub-editors, night editors, programme editors and other journalists, regardless of their personal opinions. We observed also the care and thought that went into coverage of controversial issues. We noted the value of disclosures through 'exclusives' – a suspect category because of extravagant claims and fabricated falsehoods in some papers, but genuine and important in others.

A few examples are worth mentioning now, though they are more fully recorded in later chapters. These are not in any sense a comprehensive catalogue: they are no more than a handful of instances which occurred during our fieldwork, and indicative of the daily activity of responsible journalists.

Times reporting of the **GCHQ** affair in February 1984, after Mrs Thatcher had banned trade unions at the secret communications headquarters in Cheltenham. This involved both fact and inference, and was far from favourable to the government. It included a notable exclusive on a possible compromise then being discussed privately by the Cabinet Secretary and trade union leaders, though rejected by the Prime Minister when she returned from a visit to Moscow (pp. 155, 162–5, 168–9).

Guardian coverage of two government reports in February 1984 on the discharge of radioactive waste into the sea from the **Sellafield** nuclear plant in Cumbria. It was the most extensive coverage, apart from the earlier Yorkshire Television programme which had provoked the inquiries, and it was given prominence because of the news editor's belief that after previous official concealment the 'appalling' findings must be made plain (pp. 160–1, 174).

ITN reporting from **Grenada** and **Cuba** after the American invasion of Grenada in October 1983. The work of ITN staff men in St George's (Grenada), Havana and Washington was notable for its factual care and cool detachment. The Cuban aspect of the crisis was handled without prejudice, indicating that the Cuban workers in Grenada were not all armed and were not an effective military force (pp. 88–9, 93–8, 100–1).

The reporting by ITN and BBC in November 1983 of preparations for the arrival of **Cruise missiles** at Greenham Common. Much care went into drawing the elements together – the Commons debate, Defence Ministry briefings, the arrival of the first Galaxy transports, and the Greenham women's reactions. The ITN reporter's concern to portray the women 'as they wish to be portrayed', not as fanatics, is of interest (pp. 89–100).

The heartsearching in Scottish newspapers in April 1983 over how to handle reporting of the **Falklands families,** the visit by wives and other relatives to the graves of men killed in the Falklands. The newspapers were conscious of government manipulation of the event, in advance of the general election, and therefore cautious.

A *Daily Mail* exclusive in January 1984 on a proposal by the Howard League for **Penal Reform** that criminals should be made to pay compensation for the damage they had done or injury they had caused. It had been obtained privately by the *Mail's* chief crime reporter and was followed up next day by other papers (pp. 127–8).

Times and *Guardian* coverage of **Mr Chernenko's** accession to the Soviet presidency and their differing ways of treating his opening moves (pp. 152–60).

On the political front, as an indication of how controversial topics are handled, three further examples follow. These, too, are simply evidence from events that happened during the days of our study.

1. The **Chesterfield by-election,** with Mr Tony Benn as Labour candidate. The campaign began in the week of our *Times–Guardian* fieldwork. Both on the opening day and next day Mr Benn condemned *The Times,* saying that it 'very often tells lies', and on the second day also the BBC, saying that its man was playing the role of SDP candidate. On the evidence of the coverage from Chesterfield, neither attack was justified. After Mr Benn's own role in dividing the Labour Party in preceding years, there was legitimate interest in how he would perform as the official Labour candidate and in what he would say about policy on defence and the Common Market. Reporting in the *Guardian* was more extensive than in *The Times,* both being partly factual and partly atmospheric; both reported Mr Benn's criticisms. The BBC's coverage in *Newsnight* was greater than in any newspaper, though cover in news bulletins was short (pp. 169, 173–9).

2. **Heath's 'treachery'.** That was the *Daily Mail's* front-page 'splash' headline one day in the week of our *Mail–Mirror* fieldwork. Mr Edward Heath had led a revolt with 12 other

Conservative MPs, some of them former ministers, against the government's legislation to restrict rate increases by local authorities. It was the first time in this century that a former Prime Minister had voted against his own party in the House of Commons. The event was reported on the front page of almost every newspaper, though with the word 'rebellion' or 'rebels' in the headline rather than 'treachery'. Mr Heath's protest was politically important, and indeed there would have been cause for complaint if it had not been given prominence. Whether the *Mail* transgressed the boundary of fairness is a matter of individual judgement. The reasoning of the assistant editor who wrote the headline is reported later (pp. 126–32).

3. **Bone marrow transplants** – a less dramatic event, but of human significance, in the week of our BBC–ITN fieldwork. It was an ITN item about children who were being refused treatment because of a lack of resources, with death inevitably following within a few years, and was exclusive in the detail it contained. It included a short interview with the Health Minister, Mr Kenneth Clarke. The programme editor that night rigorously cross-examined the reporter less than half an hour before 'on air' time before she accepted the item for transmission. It was nevertheless the subject of a mild and informal complaint by telephone from the Health Minister to ITN's editor next day (pp. 101–3).

To revert to some of the criteria mentioned earlier: on *significance,* an area of particular concern to sociologists because of its unstated assumptions, every one of the ten events or episodes listed above is, to journalists, self-evidently important. That is to say, each has some bearing on public policy, directly affects a number of people in Britain (apart from Grenada, which affects Britain only indirectly through relations with the United States and the Commonwealth), and contains an element of the new or unexpected. At the same time, each qualifies as news within the first six criteria laid down by Galtung and Ruge – with all well above the 'threshold', unambiguous, meaningful, and so on. As a means to understanding journalists' news values, however, my primitive 'seismic scale' appears to offer a quicker and more directly relevant guide.

As to Gans's 'enduring values', four or five of the ten appear to run counter to them. The GCHQ affair shows a democratic government acting in an arbitrary and authoritarian way, not practising 'altruistic democracy' – though since Gans says that reports of deviant behaviour can serve to reinforce the norm, it might be argued that reports of Mrs Thatcher's behaviour will in the long run strengthen British democracy. At the time of writing (early 1985) we are too close to the event to judge. Similarly the Sellafield affair does not show 'responsible capitalism' at work but rather the reverse, though again it can be said that reporting of such deviant action as the release of radioactive waste on to the Cumbrian and Scottish beaches may serve to reinforce a sense of responsibility elsewhere. That would be pleasing, but we cannot count on it. Gans points out that the enduring values such as 'altruistic democracy' can have an anti-government and anti-status quo aspect: to that extent their sociocentralism must be qualified. In the US, he says, the notion of an 'adversarial relationship' beween journalists and government has become a cliche, even if the journalists 'are not always as adversarial as one might want them to be'.[6]

There is ambiguity in the way any of the ten events can be interpreted in terms of reinforcing or undermining the status quo. They were given prominence partly because of their unusual character, and it remains plausible – even probable – that the overall effect of current British news values is still to create a sense of stability and order. The ten do, however, in my view show two things unambiguously. One is that every item among the ten was worthy of reporting and of the prominence it was given; and, with the possible exception of 'Heath's treachery', each was treated responsibly. The other is that the journalists working on them were careful, thorough and open-minded in their approach to deciding what is news and how to handle it. That applies, most probably, to the great majority of journalists in Britain; though that is not a view which will be universally shared ('Politicians and journalists are held in much the same public esteem as thieves and prostitutes' – Rt. Hon. Norman Tebbit MP, February 1985).

Thus far we have set out some concepts of what is news, drawing on the findings of two Royal Commissions, studies by sociologists, the writings and comments of some journalists and my own experience. The importance or significance of an event remains the first consideration, except in the most popular of dailies, and working journalists must also keep in mind some notion of the audience for whom they are writing or broadcasting. Their unstated assumptions about significance have been explored above – particularly the concern with world peace, the prosperity and welfare of people in Britain, and our environment – and these will be explored further in the case studies. The unstated assumptions about audience will be discussed in the next chapter.

There is, however, a gulf between the way journalists look at their work and the way sociologists see it. That is unfortunate for both, for if sociologists were to write in plainer language, and if journalists were less distrustful of sociologists, both sides would benefit.[7] The rift is widened by conflicting use of words, by what may seem to journalists tortuous explanations of simple procedures, and by the Marxist background of some sociological studies. Let us look at each of these phenomena.

Words such as 'story', 'encode' and 'myth' can have a multiplicity of meanings. To most journalists a 'story' is verbal shorthand for any item being prepared for printing or news broadcasting, and the word carries no implication of fictitious invention. To some sociologists, perhaps because they have legitimately compared the narrative styles of fiction and news, the word has come to connote distortion or untruth in the way news is written. (That has been aggravated by the falsehoods and fabrications perpetrated by the *Sun, Daily Express, News of the World,* and others in that class.[8]) To 'encode', according to the Concise Oxford and Penguin Dictionaries, is to write in code or cipher – a secretive process, the opposite of what journalists are trying to do – whereas to media academics it commonly means no more than to translate into a system of signals for fast communication. Similarly, 'myth' can mean the primitive creation of mythical legends or widespread falsehoods, which is its first dictionary meaning, or it can be used (as by Barthes) to mean a chain of concepts widely accepted in a particular culture.[9]

Journalists generally want to tell a 'story' as simply, clearly and accurately as they can. That is what they are trained to do. Consequently it appears professionally insulting to them when anyone suggests that they are producing fictitious stories, encoding their messages obscurely or secretively, or creating false myths. Misunderstanding may come also through the use

of such words as ideology, ikon, rhetoric and sign, unless the
intended meaning is clearly defined.

That, however, is only one crack in the crevasse. The
projections and conclusions are sometimes even more mystify-
ing. Fiske and Hartley, for example, in analysing an item about
Northern Ireland in News at Ten in January 1976 say that the
images of soldiers on patrol, sandbagged positions and
armoured troop-carriers were all intended to trigger the 'myth'
of 'our lads out there, professional, well equipped'.[10] Possibly,
but it is far more likely that the reporter in London and the film
editor simply took the best library film available to them to
illustrate a government decision announced by the Prime
Minister in the Commons to send extra troops to South
Armagh after 15 people (5 Catholics, 10 Protestants) had been
murdered near the border in two days. What is more, for those
of the audience already sceptical about the effectiveness of
military operations in Northern Ireland or antagonistic to the
use of British troops, those images would do nothing to
diminish their scepticism or antagonism.

The authors reach a number of other conclusions, no less
questionable, about the reporter's 'naturalising' of the presence
of the troops and offering an 'alibi' for their deployment in
South Armagh. Again, it seems an overstretching of the evidence. The reporter, Peter Snow, is not likely to have thought
the audience gullible or to have been trying, consciously or
unconsciously, to create an 'alibi' for anyone.

Another example is taken from the categorising of news
values by O'Sullivan and others – in general a sensible listing,
but sometimes reaching realms of unreality.[11] Here is one of
their criteria:

(6) Stories must be compatible with *institutional* routines, so
events must be diary events (party conferences, anniversar-
ies, annual reports, and so on) or already covered in another
news outlet, in press releases or in agency reports.

The first few words are valid in that no event on which the facts
cannot be assembled and reported by edition time or 'on air'
time stands any chance; the rest, regrettably, is bunkum.
Neither the Harrods bombing at Christmas 1983 nor the
Brighton bombing in October 1984 was in anyone's diary,

though of course the Conservative conference in Brighton was, but both made big news. Of the ten items in my list above, only six or seven can be counted as in any sense 'diary events'. *The Times* on GCHQ, the *Mail* on penal reform and ITN on bone marrow transplants were neither in anyone's diary nor indicated anywhere else beforehand; and as for Mr Heath's rebellion, the debate had been signalled beforehand, as had Mr Heath's objection to Mrs Thatcher's policy, but even in the *Mail* office, until the vote came at about 10.15 p.m., senior executives simply did not believe that he would go into the lobbies against the government.

On the Marxist tendency in some work, it is neither surprising nor in itself offensive, but when cloaked in pseudo-scientific objectivity it is misleading. The Glasgow University Media Group is the most obvious case. Having scored something of a bull's-eye with *Bad News* – causing a review among broadcasters of their reporting of industrial disputes – they threw away their advantage in their next two books by offering prejudiced evidence and suspect statistics.[12] While accusing others of bias, they were apparently unable to see it in themselves.

To gather, select and present the news requires a team of journalists. Each member of the team must take a series of individual decisions during the day's or night's work – the news editor on where to send his or her reporters and what suggestions to make to his or her specialists; the reporter or specialist on what questions to ask, what aspect of the event to put first in his/her account of it and how much to write or record; the sub-editor or scriptwriter on whether to insert any news agency material or revise the copy or videotape; and the night editor or programme editor on any final instructions to reporters and writers, on any changes in manner of presentation and on the final order of priorities. Within parallel frameworks groups will be working on the home news, foreign news, pictures, sport, finance and features. For television the cameraman, sound recordist, film editor and videotape editor are also taking individual decisions that affect the way the news is presented – camera angles, lighting, what to cut and whether to use library film.

All must work within the timetable set by 'off stone' schedules for newspapers or 'on air' for programmes. Chat and consultation between individuals and groups is frequent though not always harmonious. Often reporters or camera crews must work on their own, using individual initiative, though for the larger events there is a tendency to work in 'packs'. Some reporters prefer the security of comparing notes with those from other organisations, while some prefer to operate alone. The result can be the 'lies and trash' mentioned at the start of this chapter. Outside the most popular newspapers, however, that is rare and exceptional.

The news is not a series of 'almost random reactions to random events', to use a much misused phrase.[13] It is a highly-organised, systematic response based on years of personal experience among senior journalists. It is of course 'an artificial human construct', because there are no God-given, ultimate, objective means of measuring news priorities. But it is one to which most journalists and most broadcasters bring a strong sense of public responsibility.

Journalists may often be unaware of the way their own social or personal background affects their judgements or their phrasing. Consciously or unconsciously, however, they generally base their choice and treatment of news on two criteria: (1) what is the political, social, economic and human importance of the event? And (2) will it interest, excite and entertain our audience? The first takes precedence over the second, but both matter. No newspaper or broadcasting unit can succeed unless it strikes a chord with its audience and keeps in tune with them.

The influences upon working journalists through owners and institutions (BBC and IBA), editors and perceptions of the audiences are discussed next. The influence of sources, also important, will be discussed later.

2 Owners, Editors and Audiences

Historically the most notable of British newspaper proprietors have been Lord Northcliffe of the *Daily Mail*, Lord Beaverbrook of the *Daily Express*, John Walter of *The Times* and C. P. Scott of the *Manchester Guardian*. The public service philosophy of John Walter and C. P. Scott lives on in their papers; it is echoed in the surviving ethos of John Reith's BBC and in the news output of British independent television. Northcliffe and Beaverbrook by contrast were commercial profit-seekers, politically partisan, original in their journalism, and immensely powerful individuals.

Northcliffe probably did more to change British journalism than any other single person. He was the chief creator of twentieth-century popular journalism in this country. In 1888, at the age of 23, he started a weekly aimed at a new class – those who had learned to read as a result of the 1870 Education Act. His paper used short sentences, short paragraphs and short articles; and he introduced a prize – a pound a week for life for guessing the value of gold in the Bank of England on a given day.[1] In 1894 he bought the *Evening News,* modelling it upon the American 'yellow' press; and in 1896 he started the *Daily Mail,* which within three years was selling over half a million copies, more than twice the figure reached by any other paper until then. The *Mail* was sensational and unscrupulous, relying on the likelihood that when its inventions and inaccuracies were revealed its readers would have forgotten. Northcliffe introduced also the function of the sub-editor who rewrites stories, makes them spicier and adds lurid headlines.

At a later stage Northcliffe became proprietor of the *Daily Mirror* from 1903 to 1913, when he sold it to his brother; of *The Times* from 1908 until his death in 1922; and of the *Observer* also from 1905 until his death. But it is for the *Daily Mail,* and his concept of popular journalism, that he remains most memorable.[2] He was an interventionist proprietor, giving constant direction to his staff on policy, politics, style, news and anything else, and firing off notes and telegrams signed 'Chief' even to the editor of *The Times*.[3]

Beaverbrook was in much the same mould but more impish. He was a creative journalist, full of energy, politically active and eventually a millionaire. Charles Wintour, one of his editors, says 'he was arrogant, malicious, cruel, unforgiving', but Wintour also writes with great admiration of his handling of his newspapers and his stimulating leadership.[4] The *Daily Express* and the *Sunday Express* became his prime political weapons, as well as great money-makers, but some of his cherished causes failed. The Empire, his strongest theme, was doomed, for the British Empire was already in decline. 'There will be no war', his hope and belief in 1938–9, was no less doomed for like many others he had misread Hitler's character and intentions. His opposition to British involvement in Europe was another failure, for Britain eventually entered the Common Market – and under a Conservative government. Nevertheless his papers prospered while he was there to guide them.

Beaverbrook was candid about his approach. 'I run the paper purely for the purpose of making propaganda and with no other motive', he told the first Royal Commission. That propaganda, he added, was to support the policies which he himself thought important rather than supporting any one party. 'You must give your editors, if you are going to make a successful paper, a great deal of latitude; you must not coerce them; you must carry them along with you', he said. But when asked what happened when one of his editors took a divergent view, for example on an Empire matter, Lord Beaverbrook replied 'I talked them out of it.'[5]

Beaverbrook had three newspapers, which he watched closely. Rupert Murdoch today – proprietor of *The Times*, the *Sunday Times,* the *Sun* and the *News of the World* in this country – has dozens of newspapers spread over three continents, as well as an airline and television companies. Normally he is in London only for two or three days a month, and even with vastly improved communications he cannot monitor his British papers or British politics and public affairs as closely as Beaverbrook did. Robert Maxwell, having acquired the *Mirror* group in 1984 after years of trying to become a Fleet Street proprietor, still has extensive interests in printing and publishing. He cannot neglect these without risking the financial base of his whole operation. Although trying to be a left-of-centre Beaverbrook, he may find that his commitments are too many and too diverse.

The long traditions of *The Times* and the *Guardian* – still an important influence in their daily work – differ from those of the popular papers. Although *The Times* was once owned and dominated by Lord Northcliffe and is today in Mr Rupert Murdoch's hands, it retains respect for the standards of public service set by three generations of the Walter family. So, too, does the *Guardian* for the fair and open-minded style set by three generations of Scotts.

Founded in 1785, *The Times* was at first mainly concerned with commercial and shipping news. Its aim was to provide rapid and reliable information for the City's businessmen. It extended into political news some years later – with, it must be admitted, the backing of government money. But it soon established its independence and its concern for parliamentary reform.[6] Its reporting of the Peterloo massacre of 1819, when troops killed 11 people at a political gathering in Manchester and wounded hundreds, was uncompromising. Thirty years later it was explicit and damning in its reporting of the Crimean War. Editorially, over the years, it was guilty of some gross errors of judgement – supporting the South in the American Civil War, being duped into printing forged letters supposed to have been written by the Irish leader Charles Parnell, suppressing news of casualties in the 1914–18 war, approving of the appeasement of Hitler in the late 1930s, and supporting the Anglo-French invasion of Egypt in 1956 until the last moment. Throughout, however, its strength and prosperity were built on a generally reliable service of daily news. Except in the Northcliffe period, its editors enjoyed freedom from management control or political interference.

The *Manchester Guardian* also had its roots in the reform movement and was founded soon after the Peterloo massacre.[7] Until the end of the nineteenth century, however, it remained no more than a local newspaper, Whig and nonconformist in outlook and at times struggling for survival in a competitive field. In 1872 C. P. Scott was appointed editor at the age of 25 and remained editor for over 57 years, becoming also the principal proprietor in 1907. In his later years one of his sons became managing director and another followed him as editor. It was C. P. Scott who raised the *Manchester Guardian* from a local paper to one with national and international influence, although still based in Manchester. The third generation of Scotts, by starting to print the paper in London from 1961, provided it with a national distribution as well as a national reputation. By then I was editor, having been appointed in 1956.

C. P. Scott kept the *Guardian* on a radical course – he was a Liberal and for a short time also an MP, on the left of the party and with much sympathy for the young Labour movement – but throughout his time and afterwards the paper was scrupulous in its reporting. At its centenary he wrote about the functions of a newspaper in words often quoted since then. 'Its primary office is the gathering of news. At the peril of its soul it must see that the supply is not tainted. Comment is free but facts are sacred . . .' Those last words have been misinterpreted almost as often as they have been quoted. Scott well knew that reporting must frequently involve analysis and interpretation, and he encouraged his staff to explain and illuminate, most notably in their work from Russia after the revolution and in Ireland during and after the troubles leading to independence. But he insisted that, whatever the interpretation, the basic facts must be stated as plainly as possible – which was not always easy.[8]

After C. P.'s death the Scott family did something that is so far unique in newspaper history. They divested themselves of all beneficial ownership in the company – then the Manchester Guardian and Evening News Ltd – transferring the whole of the ordinary shareholding to the Scott Trust. A very small preference shareholding was allowed to continue, to avoid difficulties in buying it out. Today the Trust remains the holder of all ordinary shares, and the eight trustees as individuals draw no income or dividends whatever, apart from three who draw salaries as employees of the company and one as a non-executive director. All profits are ploughed back into the company. The Trust deed requires them to carry on the business 'on the same lines and in the same spirit as heretofore' but leaves them almost complete freedom in deciding how to conduct their affairs.[9]

The trustees appoint the editors and managing directors of the group's two principal newspapers and the other group directors. The only instruction given to the editor of the *Guardian* on appointment is to 'carry on the paper in the same spirit as before'. Editorial policy is discussed by the trustees only infrequently, and then generally on the initiative of the editor. The trustees also choose new members of the Trust. Creation of that Trust was a remarkable act of generosity and public responsibility by the Scotts. It has in practice secured the continuity of the *Guardian* and the independence of its editor.

The Scott Trust is worth attention both because it provides a greater guarantee of editorial freedom than any other and because it aims to maintain journalism with a high standard of accuracy and impartiality, as well as an open-minded approach. While the Astors owned *The Times* between 1922 and 1966, and again under Lord Thomson of Fleet (Roy Thomson) between 1966 and his death ten years later, there was little or no intervention by the proprietors apart from choosing their editors and setting financial targets. The present position at *The Times* is rather different.

Mr Rupert Murdoch bought *The Times* and the *Sunday Times* from the Thomsons in 1981. He transferred the highly successful editor of the Sunday paper, Harold Evans, to the daily but a year later dismissed him. Instead the more conservative deputy editor, Charles Douglas-Home, took over. Evans's book *Good Times, Bad Times* gives a graphic account of relations with the new proprietor.[10] Evans alleges that the rift grew because Murdoch complained about critical reporting of Mrs Thatcher's monetarist policy, that there was trouble over other issues such as the reporting of the rail dispute in January 1982 (when *The Times* gave space to the ASLEF leader, Ray Buckton, to state his union's case), and that Murdoch consulted the Prime Minister before dismissing him. Murdoch, having stayed silent for over a year, replied briefly in a television programme with the words 'rubbish' and 'a lie' to the charges that he had put pressure on Evans to move to the right.[11] Douglas-Home, in the same programme, declared himself 'firmly to the right', but said that there had never been any discussion between him and the proprietor about his political position. A former *Times* leader writer of long standing, who had stayed with the paper through nearly three years of Murdoch's ownership, had this to say:

> The political line came to be the line which reflected the known views of Rupert Murdoch, and I found those views impossible to follow or even at times to respect, and it was therefore impossible to write leaders for the paper.[12]

Here, however, we are chiefly concerned with the way owners influence the gathering and presentation of the news, not with their effect on leading articles or features; and evidence on this is hard to secure. Indeed, as will be seen later in this book, my own fieldwork at *The Times* uncovered no evidence of any political slant or perspective being imparted to the news – rather the reverse, apart from a possible lack of interest in economic news that might reflect adversely on the government, and apart also from one worrying aberration over the BBC (see Chapter 12). There is less news space than *The Times* used to carry, with sometimes only two home news pages inside the paper, so that the coverage is inevitably more compressed and less complete. The reporting, however, is generally factual and news priorities are not evidently prejudiced. *The Times* continues to provide a responsible news service.

The *Daily Mail* is a case not of a dominant proprietor but of a dominant editor. After years of success, rescuing a paper that seemed near collapse, Sir David English is in a strong position. His proprietor, the third Lord Rothermere, now lives in France and appears in London only infrequently. It was Lord Rothermere – then the Hon. Vere Harmsworth – who chose English to edit the *Mail* after its merger with the *Daily Sketch* in 1971. In the previous 21 years the editor had been changed six times, a sure sign of weak and uncertain management.[13] (The *Express* changed its editor eight times in 18 years, before the arrival of Sir Larry Lamb in 1983.)

English, however, has not only survived but produced a solid and profitable newspaper with more readers in the A-B socioeconomic groups than any other popular paper. Its sale is steady at about 1 850 000 copies, which is around 200 000 more than after the merger in 1971. Only a brief period of observation is needed in the *Mail* office to recognise that English is an extremely active editor, a strong leader of his team, and the most powerful force in shaping his paper's character and conduct. It is a partisan newspaper, appealing to middle-class Conservatives though inclined to take an occasional swipe at Mrs Thatcher's ministers – 'Pathetic' was its one-word front-page headline, in heavy type on a day in January 1985, reporting on the Chancellor's fumbling over a sinking pound. There have been serious misjudgements in English's time, the worst being in 1977 when it published an entirely false story about a British Leyland 'slush fund', leading to an expensive libel settlement. The *Mail*'s news desk is regarded as one of the toughest in Fleet Street, an aspect of the newspaper in which some of its reporters glory. Most of the staff, so far as can be seen, are proud of their paper's professional competence and of their editor.

The *Daily Mirror,* while no less partisan politically, is on Labour's side: on the side, that is, of the centre left and not of the hard left. Its proprietor since the summer of 1984 has been Mr Robert Maxwell, once a Labour MP but better known as a flamboyant and prosperous book publisher, as well as chairman of Oxford City football club. Interventionist owners are not new to the *Mirror*. Mr Cecil King, a nephew of Northcliffe, was its chairman from 1951 to 1968 and for many years commercially effective, taking the *Mirror*'s sales to above 5 million in the mid-1960s. He overstretched himself, however, in 1968 by ordering his papers to carry a front-page article saying that the Prime Minister, Harold Wilson, must be removed. The *Mirror*'s editor and political editor were not consulted. It was King himself who was removed by his fellow directors a few days later.[14]

Soon afterwards the *Mirror* group became a subsidiary of Reed International, which had many trading interests outside newspapers. There was less intervention in that period, but also a loss of sales and vitality. Reed's directors eventually grew tired of the troubles in the newspaper industry and sold the *Mirror* group to Maxwell, though before doing so they had tried to promote a scheme which would have given the staffs of the newspapers a stake in ownership. Immediately after taking over, Maxwell projected himself constantly through his papers with personal publicity such as no other proprietor had sought in recent years, if ever. He was in the office almost every night, telephoning as often as six times in an evening to staff who were working on political reports, and calling specialists for consultation or revision of their writing. 'I've shaken this place up and I sure as hell have got control, and everybody knows it', he told a reporter from another paper.[15]

Particular attention has been given here to the ownership and control of the *Guardian, The Times, Mail* and *Mirror* because those were the papers where fieldwork was possible. As noted earlier, the *Telegraph, Sun* and *Express* were not willing to let us watch their journalists at work. At the *Daily Telegraph* Lord Hartwell is the only surviving proprietor whose newspapers – the *Daily* and the *Sunday Telegraph* – are his single major interest, and at the age of 74 (in 1985) he continues as editor-in-chief of both. Mr William Deedes, editor of the *Daily Telegraph*, says 'I see him every day'.[16]

Lord Matthews at the *Express* came from a City background after the diverse conglomerate Trafalgar House (property developers, construction, Cunard shipping, the Ritz Hotel) bought the *Express* group in 1977; at that time, he knew little about newspapers or journalism. Although at first he tried to exercise editorial control – and showed himself liable to react to random comments from friends and acquaintances – he later took a less active part. But, having taken the *Express* down market from the middle ground that it had shared with the *Mail,* in 1978 he started the *Daily Star* aiming at the lowest end of the market with nudes, gossip and sensation. No reader, of course, could long confuse that newspaper with the *Morning Star,* organ of the Communist party and provider of a quite different dimension in journalism, especially in its reporting of industrial relations. It too, however, was riven by disputes between the Eurocommunists and others in 1984 and although owned by a cooperative saw its editor sacked.

Details of the owners, editors, average sales, politics and other aspects of the UK national newspapers and the Scottish morning papers are in Appendix A, pp. 299–302.

Structurally, the BBC and ITV differ from each other and from the newspapers. The BBC is a single programme-making body, ruled by part-time Governors and a full-time Board of Management, and subdivided into television, radio and external directorates. It employs more journalists than any other group in Britain. Independent television and radio are controlled by the Independent Broadcasting Authority, which awards franchises to 15 regional television companies and at present to 38 independent local radio stations. Both BBC and IBA are designed to provide an 'arm's-length' relationship – or insulation from direct influence – between the government and broadcasters. To a large extent they do so, even though the Governors of the BBC and the board members of the IBA are themselves appointed by the government. Although far from perfect, this system seems to work better than any other so far devised. That is to say, the BBC and ITV have shown themselves capable of withstanding government pressure, open or concealed, and of exercising independent judgement. That is vital to the impartiality and reliability of their news and current affairs programmes.

Direct pressure has been applied by government only infrequently – on no more than five occasions, so far as is known, in the 40 post-war years – and it was resisted in most of those. In any event, discreet government pressure or informal persuasion is more likely to succeed, and sensitivity to official attitudes must at times have influenced internal decisions. That has been particularly evident when the BBC's licence fee, its main source of revenue, is about to be settled. The mood of caution in the nine months before the 1977 settlement – never made explicit but amounting to 'don't upset Downing Street' – was something that I experienced within the BBC at the time. Those of the IBA's staff who are charged with monitoring company programme plans seem also to have periods when they suffer from a nervous twitch.

Of the known occasions of direct pressure on the BBC, the first was the least important. In 1950 some ministers in the Labour Government took offence at a comic play and let it be known. The chairman of the BBC's Governors ordered cancellation of a repeat performance, overriding the Director-General; later he apologised publicly for what he had done, adding that he had not foreseen the 'hurricane' of public protest. (There are indications that the episode strengthened Conservative determination to end the BBC's monopoly of broadcasting, although it was a Labour Government which had been upset.)[17]

In 1953 there was trouble over Central Africa, though the precise nature of intervention is not clear. The dilemma is well illustrated by Grace Wyndham Goldie, who was producer of

the programme, in her book on television and politics.[18] On
the eve of a major negotiating conference, three conflicting
views were to be presented on the future of the Central African
Federation – then white ruled but since 1963 split into the
separate nations of Zimbabwe, Zambia and Malawi – but at
the last minute senior BBC management cancelled the transmission. She indicates that there was government pressure but
she does not know what form it took. She acquits her superiors,
although she disagreed with their decision, saying that it was
extremely difficult to determine whether the broadcast might
diminish the chances of agreement on a serious matter where
disagreement could lead to bloodshed.

In 1956, with the onset of the Suez crisis, there was a much
more serious risk. The Prime Minister, Sir Anthony Eden, was
infuriated by the BBC's attention to opposition views, object-
ing both to the reporting in overseas broadcasts of what was
said by the Labour leader, Hugh Gaitskell, and to the quoting
of *Manchester Guardian* leaders. He instructed the Lord
Chancellor to prepare an instrument to take over the BBC,
putting it under direct government control. The BBC held its
ground, continuing to broadcast as before. Fortunately the
legal measure was not ready when the crisis reached its climax,
and Eden retired soon afterwards.[19] The BBC's chairman at
that time was a retired head of the diplomatic service, Sir
Alexander Cadogan, and its Director-General a retired general,
Sir Ian Jacob.

More recently, from 1969 onwards, each party in turn has
put pressure on the BBC over the reporting of Northern
Ireland; and in 1982 Mrs Thatcher did so over reporting of the
Falklands War. An adequate account of the conflicts over
Ireland would require a chapter in itself – and more will be
said towards the end of this book (Chapter 11) – but three
episodes may be mentioned briefly here. In December 1971
BBC television planned 'a long cool programme of talk, not
action' to complement the day-to-day news of violence and
disorder. It aimed at examining the seven or eight policy
options conceivably available to the government. Three weeks
before the proposed transmission the Prime Minister of
Northern Ireland, Brian Faulkner, told the Director-General
that it was unwise to broadcast the programme while people
were being killed. Some days later the Home Secretary,

Reginal Maudling, asked the BBC's chairman and Director-General to call on him and said much the same thing. Later he publicly urged the BBC not to transmit the programme. Nevertheless *The Question of Ulster* was broadcast in early January, lasting three hours, and at the time was generally thought by the press to have been valuable and informative.[20] The BBC's chairman was Lord Hill, who had been appointed by the previous government in the expectation that he would subdue it; the Director-General was Sir Charles Curran.

In 1976 the BBC's Governors held a dinner party in Belfast which, with Labour back in office, was attended by the Northern Ireland Secretary, Roy Mason. He astonished his hosts by telling them that the BBC was disloyal, purveying terrorist propaganda, and reminding them that the BBC's Charter and licence were soon due for renewal. Although the BBC has never published any account of the affair, it probably contributed to the mood of caution before the licence settlement of 1977. Three years later there was an eruption over filming by *Panorama* of IRA activity in Carrickmore, South Armagh, leading to public condemnation by the Prime Minister, Mrs Thatcher – although the film had not been and never was transmitted. Afterwards a senior BBC producer was transferred to other work, unjustly in the opinion of his colleagues, but his real sin in the BBC's eyes had been in failing to tell the BBC's Controller, Northern Ireland, what he was doing. Months later the Attorney-General told the BBC that in his view the filming at Carrickmore had been a breach of the Prevention of Terrorism Act. That was never tested in court, but the threat was plain.

Over the Falklands campaign in 1982, Mrs Thatcher let her views be known both publicly and privately. She too regarded the BBC as disloyal because it sought to present a balanced view of attitudes both at home and abroad. She took particular exception to its reporting from Argentina, saying in the Commons on 6 May 1982 that while she had little time to watch television or listen to the radio she understood that 'there are times when we and the Argentines are being treated almost as equals'. The BBC's chairman, George Howard, in a speech later that day, said that the corporation was not and could not be neutral 'between our own country and the aggressor', but was no less determined that 'in war truth shall not be the first casualty'. The public, he said, 'in this democracy deserves to be given as much information as possible'. The verbal conflict grew in the following days, particularly because of a *Panorama* programme on opposition to the war in the UK. Again in the Commons, after a barrage of comments from MPs hostile to the BBC, Mrs Thatcher said she knew how strongly many people felt 'that the case for our country is not being put with sufficient vigour in certain – I do not say all – BBC programmes'. She hoped that people would make their views known to the BBC by letter and telephone.

Again, the BBC stood its ground. The chairman and the Director-General designate, George Howard and Alasdair Milne, attended in mid-May a crowded meeting of the Conservative Media Committee.[21] It was described as violently hostile. Sir Hector Monro, a former minister, said it was 'the ugliest meeting I have ever attended in my years as an MP'. The Conservative chairman of the meeting, himself a former broadcaster, thought afterwards that Milne was 'profoundly unimpressed with the intellectual calibre of the arguments put up against him'. No concessions and no apologies were offered by either Howard or Milne. Given the emotional tension of the time, after the sinking of the *Belgrano* and the *Sheffield* and with the task force known to be nearing the Falklands, the BBC's stand required determination.

One caveat must be entered here. Dr Philip Schlesinger, author of a perceptive study of the BBC newsrooms at work, treats the 1972 *Question of Ulster* as 'a success story in the midst of a general defeat'.[22] His thesis is that because the government applied direct pressure, the BBC had to resist; and that the BBC had already limited its own impartiality by accepting, in Lord Hill's words, that it must report with revulsion the IRA's campaign of murder. Schlesinger's book was written before the Falklands War, but a similar argument might be used in that context.

My own view, discussed further in Chapter 11, is that although over Northern Ireland the BBC has generally stood up well to pressure, it has been too cautious about interviews with the IRA, INLA and to an extent with militant loyalists; and programmes such as *The Question of Ulster* have been too few and far between. Its news coverage, however, has been extensive and normally reliable, even if the background to the long crisis has been inadequate. Over the Falklands even such secondary criticism does not apply. It was often extremely difficult for journalists – whether in the battle area or in London, Washington or Buenos Aires – to discern the truth about the campaign or about the diplomatic moves because information was fragmentary or withheld. But the BBC's news services maintained their effort to provide factual information, leaving listeners and viewers to make up their own minds. As an example of the value in a democracy of an 'arm's-length' relationship between government and broadcasters, the Falklands period is compelling evidence. The public was not treated to the propagandist coverage that the government and much of the Conservative party appeared to want.[23]

The BBC is big – the biggest employer of journalists in Britain, and one of the biggest targets for politicians. ITV's current affairs programmes can be as controversial as *Panorama* – Granada's *World in Action,* Thames's *TV Eye* and LWT's *Weekend World* – but they are less likely to draw fire either on the ITV network as a whole or on ITN's news services. Similarly over YTV's documentary on radioactive pollution from Sellafield – which probably caused nervous anxiety at the IBA – it was Yorkshire who took the initial criticism and the ultimate praise. BBC television news and BBC radio news have been involved in fewer controversies than *Panorama, Tonight* or *Nationwide,* but to the public they are or were all parts of the BBC.

That bigness has two other consequences. Because of the sheer size of the BBC, its editor television news and its editor radio news and current affairs do not rank in the top 40 executives of the corporation. They come about equal fiftieth along with the heads of network production centres in Birmingham, Bristol and Manchester. They are, as a result, compelled to spend much more of their time attending meetings with higher management than are their counterparts at ITN. The BBC's editor television news cannot keep as close to his journalists, specialists and programme editors as does the editor at ITN. Secondly, because of the sheer weight of Reithian tradition – a healthy tradition, though in some ways inhibiting – BBC journalists, in Schlesinger's phrase, carry with them their own 'evaluative baggage'.[24] With distinguished exceptions, they tend to be more cautious and conformist than the staff at ITN.

The healthy part of the Reith tradition – John Reith was the BBC's first Director-General, from 1927 to 1938, and he set standards which have influenced all British broadcasting and much in other countries ever since – is its insistence on objectivity and accuracy, so far as is humanly possible. 'It's bad to miss a deadline', in the words of a senior newsman, 'but worse not to have checked the story properly.' BBC staff are trained from the beginning to set aside their personal beliefs and to try to achieve political and social neutrality. Human feelings are acceptable in their reports only where joy or sorrow is an integral part of the event. To an extent such requirements apply also in ITN and in ITV's regional news. In the smaller BBC units – local radio and regional television news – there is often a more informal atmosphere. But because of the institutional character of the BBC, its size, the remoteness of its senior management and the formality of its training (professionally excellent though it is), there is a heavy emphasis on conformity. The foremost BBC journalists are first-class professionals who have retained their originality. The average staff member keeps within the predetermined framework. The oppressive effect of size can be seen in the organisation charts at the end of this chapter.

The Governors of the BBC, part time, meet fortnightly for a whole day. The Board of Management, full time, meets weekly. The three principal directorates – television, radio and external – have their own weekly management meetings, as well as weekly programme review boards which serve both as a channel of information and as an opportunity for pro-gramme heads to savage or praise each other's output. The lesser directorates – engineering, finance, personnel and public affairs (including regions) – have their own gatherings. Minutes, sometimes many pages long, flow from these and other meetings. (In 1976 I got into trouble with the hierarchy because I mentioned to the Annan Committee, in an aside, that BBC Scotland had to send southwards 62 copies of a financial proposal to spend about £800 of its own money on a new typeface for television captions.)

There is also a weekly news and current affairs meeting, which used to be chaired by the Director-General and could last as much as three hours but is now chaired by the Assistant Director-General and usually shorter. The BBC's editor television news is likely to be involved in major meetings on at least three or four mornings each week. His immediate superior since a structural change in 1982 is the managing director television, though when something has to be 'referred upwards' he may have to deal with any of four or five people above him.

ITN's environment is less complex. The company, Independent Television News, was created in 1955 by agreement between the ITA (forerunner of the IBA) and the programme companies. It exists to provide the regional companies with national and international news, and they are its shareholders. Its profits are ploughed back into the business. The chairman at present (1985) is Lord Buxton, of Anglia Television; eight other directors are drawn from the programme companies and five from ITN's full-time staff. The latter group include David Nicholas, editor and chief executive; Paul McKee, deputy chief executive; and Sir Alastair Burnet, one of the leading broadcasters. The Director-General of the IBA has the right to attend all ITN board meetings and is normally there. Board meetings are monthly and rarely last more than two hours, unlike the BBC's fortnightly all-day sessions.

The sole purpose of ITN is the provision of news, and its senior staff can therefore concentrate on that. The IBA occasionally calls the editor or his deputy for consultation, and one or other will attend some committee meetings of the IBA or ITCA (the Independent Television Companies Association). Trade union matters, negotiation of new contracts such as with Channel Four and fresh projects such as a possible 24-hour news service by satellite take up some of their time. But ITN's daily output is their primary concern. They are the sole providers of national and international news for the regional companies. Only TV-am, with the early morning franchise for the whole of the UK, does not rely on ITN – a decision which both the IBA and TV-am have probably regretted, for compared with ITN's service TV-am's is flimsy. ITN has fewer reporters permanently abroad or in the regions than the BBC, but it can draw on the regional companies for contributions.

David Nicholas, as editor, is convinced that the compact

nature of the organisation is important to its success. Also important is the policy of giving young news editors authority to make quick decisions and if necessary spend large sums of money.

> If an oil rig has gone down and the only way to get there is a four-engined jet, and if there's no way of getting to the governor [Nicholas himself], then I say: 'Your reputation is at stake and you get the VC or you get burned . . .' I mean, I want decisive people who are going to make the right judgements when the occasion requires it. It's mainly money and coverage, but it can be a delicate political point.[25]

In practice Nicholas carries a 'bleep' even when off duty or on holiday. He keeps in close touch with his deputies and the programme editors, as will be seen in a later chapter, and regards the whole ITN company as 'editorially-orientated'. Recruitment of all but the senior staff is left to others, and there is no requirement of security vetting, as there is at the BBC. Nevertheless, Nicholas appears to know all his journalists, which is more than can be said for most newspaper editors.

What of the audiences, both for newspapers and for television news? Another paradox: readership surveys and audience research can and do provide much detail of income, social groupings, interests and political opinions – yet very few journalists have more than a hazy personal view of their public. Even at the highest levels concepts are not always clear. Asa Briggs notes a meeting of the BBC's Governors in 1943 of which Harold Nicolson (a governor) wrote: 'There is no consensus of opinion even as to the target audience. Do we, for instance, aim mainly at the educated, the half-educated or the uneducated?'[26] Schlesinger is surely correct in pointing to this as a 'missing link' between journalists and their audiences, with no systematic feedback.[27] Gans equally finds that neither print nor television staffs know much about their audiences, and he quotes a top American magazine editor as saying: 'If we had to think about how our readers feel, all twenty million of them, we'd freeze.'[28]

Family and friends, pub and telephone – these are the most common contacts between the journalists and their public.

Like Gans, Schlesinger and others, in our fieldwork we found the most frequent response was that the staff were writing for their editors, their wives or themselves – in that order. Some sample replies:

Oh, we're writing for the editor of course. He's the audience.

My wife, she's the critic.

Will it get people talking over the breakfast table or in the pub? That's what I ask myself.

If I like it, that's the only quotient I put on it. I reckon that I'm an average reader.

A reporter at the *Guardian,* having taken many telephone calls from *Guardian* readers, had convinced himself that a majority must be members of CND. Readership research does not bear that out. His problem was in having to explain to callers who expected the paper to report every movement of Cruise launcher convoys on training in Wiltshire that such exercises had become routine, and that only something exceptional would find space in the paper. News desks have to remain attentive to calls from readers or viewers, which often bring valuable tips, but these are probably not a true cross-section of the audience.

In thinking of their audiences, both BBC and ITN see their main evening news as able to carry more demanding material than their early evening bulletins – though since the autumn of 1984 the BBC have taken the risk of carrying solid content in their half-hour programme at six p.m. At both times of day ITN staff see themselves as aiming for an audience nearer to the *Mail–Express* level than to a *Guardian–Times* profile. Numerically, of course, they must be correct. The main evening news attracts big audiences. Whereas in the 1970s there tended to be a drop in viewing figures when the news came on, in the mid-1980s an increase in viewing has been more common. In the first week of November 1983 (the week of our fieldwork at BBC Nine o'clock News and ITN's News at Ten) the audience increased at 9 p.m. on BBC1 on four of the five nights, dropping only on the night when the Nine o'clock News followed *Dallas*. It was measured at levels between 6½ million individual viewers – the lowest figure, on the Friday – and nearly 9 million on one night midweek. ITN's News at Ten maintained a steady audience of 7 million to 8 million, giving a slightly higher total for the week than the BBC's. But because ITV1 as a channel enjoyed larger audiences than BBC1, there was a slight decline in viewing at 10 p.m. on three of the five nights. After peak programmes such as *The Outsider* and *Rumpole* it was harder to hold an eight-figure audience. A year later the BBC's aggregate audience had overtaken ITN's, with the 9 p.m. bulletin reaching a peak of 9½ millions, though generally the two were running neck and neck.

As to newspaper sales, the details are in Appendix A. In the autumn of 1984 the *Sun* remained the most popular daily with average sales of over 4 million and thus an estimated readership of above 8 million. The *Daily Mirror* held at sales of just under 3½ million, the *Express* at just under 2 million, the *Mail* at 1.85 million, and the *Telegraph* at 1.25 million. The *Guardian* and *The Times* were neck and neck at around 466,000, and the *Financial Times* stood at 215,000 including its Frankfurt printing.

No newspaper can achieve adequate sales and survive unless it has a clear concept of what will interest its readers, both in news and in features. BBC and ITV enjoy a near monopoly, but they too must try to gauge the interests of their audiences if viewing figures are to be maintained. Newspaper journalism and broadcast journalism have to start from common ground with their public – from the knowledge acquired by their audiences through previous reading and viewing; from the concern or curiosity among that audience about events affecting their daily lives, especially their jobs, income, health and families; and from the social or political environment in which they live. The daily paper or news bulletin must be packaged or presented in ways that will attract attention and hold its audience. It must strike a responsive chord in the minds of viewers and readers. A newspaper must have a distinctive character; from the broadcasters, talking to a wider audience and committed to neutrality, it calls for a friendly and informal style if they are to succeed. Without all this, communication is not achieved.

From the need to share a common background with the audiences comes the sociocentralist aspect of much news judgement and presentation. Almost inevitably, anything that threatens people's peace, prosperity or well-being is news and likely to make headlines. It is also likely to be seen as unwelcome news unless there is already a tide of reform. Public outrage over the Peterloo massacre in 1819 gave impetus to *The Times* and contributed to the birth of the *Manchester Guardian*. But most people most of the time want peace and quiet. As a result, news judgements and the presentation of news will generally tend to reinforce the established state of society. That follows from the wish to share a common background with readers.

Treatment of the police illustrates this. Because crime threatens citizens with injury, theft of their property and other harm, it is news; those responsible for crime are generally seen as hostile to public well-being, and the police are presented as protectors of the public. But when policemen misbehave, using unjustified force, that in turn becomes a threat and is widely reported. Two comparatively minor but worrying incidents in 1959, one in the north of Scotland and the other in London, were reported by press and broadcasters and contributed materially to the appointment of the 1959–62 Royal Commission on the Police. In 1981 the Brixton and Toxteth riots were perceived as a sign of social upheaval, and because police forces endeavoured to contain the threat their action met with much public approval, irrespective of the part that police methods may have played in sparking off the trouble. For most journalists the actual riots and the containment of them at first ranked higher, as news, than examination of the causes. But the examination followed, retrospectively. During the 1984–5 coal dispute, which will be discussed more fully in Chapter 12, the police were commonly perceived as maintaining order in the face of mass picketing. But their tactics were sometimes provocative and often controversial, and were reported as such.

The endeavour to embark from common ground with the audience and the sociocentralist tendency that follows from it create two problems for thoughtful journalists. One is how to make sure that legitimate claims of social reform are given adequate publicity; the other is how to break through with fresh ideas, new areas of concern and unfamiliar perspectives. Both problems are easier to solve through features and special articles or through current affairs programmes than through news columns or news bulletins. But the gradual acceptance in the 1960s of environmental conservation as a front-page topic, of news about the issues of birth control and news of the women's movement are examples of what can be done. The 'heavy' newspapers gave a lead in these areas, and it was followed by the popular papers and by broadcasting. Latterly the arrival of Channel Four has brought a wider range of views in television, together with a more regular 'right of reply'; and through Channel Four News there has been an extension of the news agenda into science, the Arts and an analytical approach to economic news.

This chapter has been about the influence on news of the national newspaper owners and of the BBC and ITV as institutions; and about the influence of editors, about perceptions among journalists of their audiences and about the tendency to uphold the established society. A Marxist interpretation would probably find that the influence of commercial competition and of capitalist proprietors leads to distortion and prejudice in the reporting of events, and that the BBC and ITN are so institutionally conditioned that they have become agents of government ideology and of the ruling class. The evidence is rather different – that in this country the broadcasters are independent of direct government influence and use their independence, and that in the serious newspapers reporting is generally impartial, responsible and reliable.

At times of major crisis, as at Suez in 1956 and over the Falklands in 1982, the broadcasters and the 'heavy' newspapers have retained their freedom. They were able to report dissenting views and to present a picture of the 'enemy' side, in spite of government pressure against it. Not all of them have always used their freedom – in 1956 *The Times* knew more than any other news channel about Eden's preparations to invade Egypt and told its readers next to nothing – and neither newspapers nor broadcasters have been as thorough as they should have been in reporting from Ireland. Nor have they always given adequate attention to social evils such as poverty, bad housing and poor health in the inner cities.

Before coming to a final judgement about their daily

performance, however, readers may prefer to consider the chapters on our fieldwork. Among the popular press we cover only the *Daily Mail* and the *Daily Mirror* because we could not gain access to the *Sun* or the *Express*. On news coverage, in spite of their partisan characters, both *Mail* and *Mirror* are found more often than not to report all sides of controversial events; the brevity of their reporting is a greater hazard, starving readers of information. But a more nourishing diet is available for anyone who wants it, through the broadcasters and the 'heavy' newspapers. Because substantial audiences in this country want to be well informed, and because broadcasting has built on the best of the Reith tradition, reliable information is available to those who want it.

CHART 2.1 *Management structure, ITN*

Note: Links with a solid line are those where an operational instruction can be given from above to below.

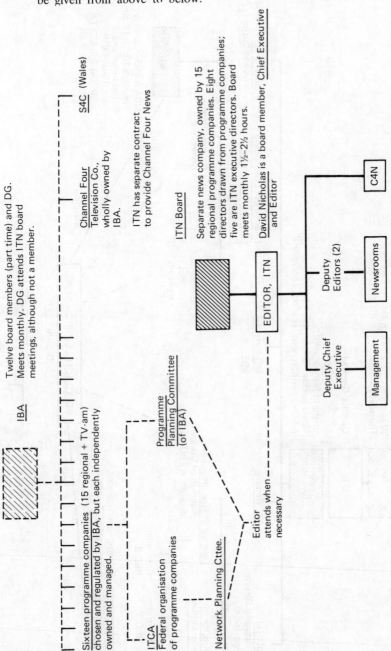

IBA

Twelve board members (part time) and DG. Meets monthly. DG attends ITN board meetings, although not a member.

S4C (Wales)

Channel Four Television Co., wholly owned by IBA.

ITN has separate contract to provide Channel Four News

ITN Board

Separate news company, owned by 15 regional programme companies. Eight directors drawn from programme companies; five are ITN executive directors. Board meets monthly 1½–2½ hours.

David Nicholas is a board member, Chief Executive and Editor

EDITOR, ITN

Deputy Editors (2)

C4N

Newsrooms

Deputy Chief Executive

Management

Sixteen programme companies (15 regional + TV-am) chosen and regulated by IBA, but each independently owned and managed.

Programme Planning Committee (of IBA)

ITCA
Federal organisation of programme companies

Network Planning Cttee.

Editor attends when necessary

CHART 2.2 *Management structure, BBC*
Note: Links with a solid line are those where an operational instruction can be given from above to below.

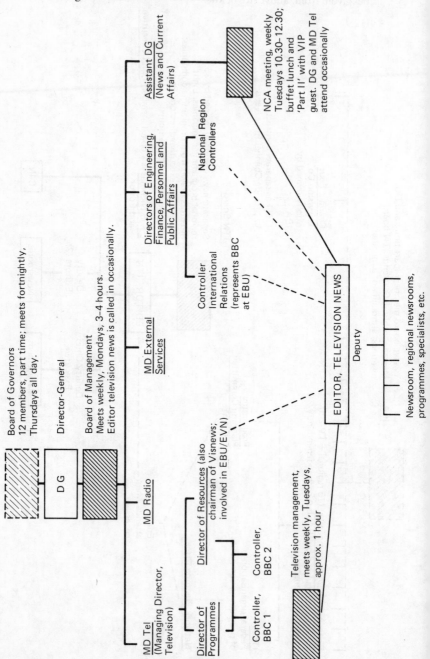

CHART 2.3 *Management structure, the* Guardian

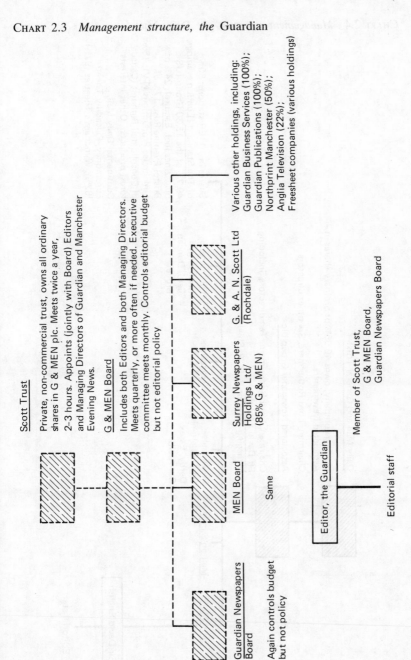

Scott Trust

Private, non-commercial trust, owns all ordinary shares in G & MEN plc. Meets twice a year, 2–3 hours. Appoints (jointly with Board) Editors and Managing Directors of Guardian and Manchester Evening News.

G & MEN Board

Includes both Editors and both Managing Directors. Meets quarterly, or more often if needed. Executive committee meets monthly. Controls editorial budget but not editorial policy

Various other holdings, including:
Guardian Business Services (100%);
Guardian Publications (100%);
Northprint Manchester (50%);
Anglia Television (22%);
Freesheet companies (various holdings)

G. & A. N. Scott Ltd
(Rochdale)

Surrey Newspapers
Holdings Ltd/
(85% G & MEN)

MEN Board

Same

Guardian Newspapers
Board

Again controls budget
but not policy

Editor, the Guardian

Member of Scott Trust,
G & MEN Board,
Guardian Newspapers Board

Editorial staff

CHART 2.4   *Management structure, the* Daily Mail

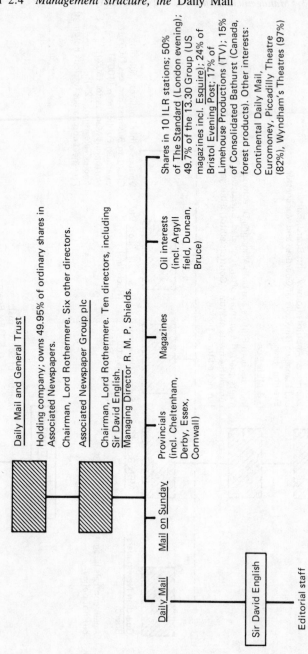

Daily Mail and General Trust

Holding company; owns 49.95% of ordinary shares in Associated Newspapers.

Chairman, Lord Rothermere. Six other directors.

Associated Newspaper Group plc

Chairman, Lord Rothermere. Ten directors, including Sir David English.
Managing Director R. M. P. Shields.

Daily Mail

Mail on Sunday

Provincials (incl. Cheltenham, Derby, Essex, Cornwall)

Magazines

Oil interests (incl. Argyll field, Duncan, Bruce)

Shares in 10 ILR stations; 50% of The Standard (London evening); 49.7% of the 13.30 Group (US magazines incl. Esquire); 24% of Bristol Evening Post; 17% of Limehouse Productions (TV); 15% of Consolidated Bathurst (Canada, forest products). Other interests: Continental Daily Mail, Euromoney, Piccadilly Theatre (82%), Wyndham's Theatres (97%).

Sir David English

Editorial staff

CHART 2.5 *The flow of news – inside the office*

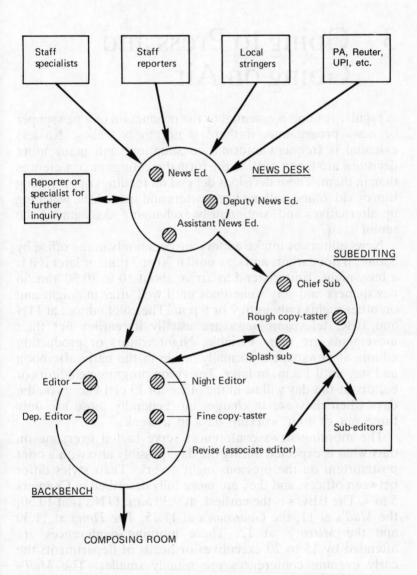

3 Going to Press and Going on Air

A regular routine is essential to the production of a newspaper or news programme, if there is not to be chaos. No less essential is frequent informal consultation, and many more decisions are taken outside the formal meetings or conferences than in them. These decisions depend on reading copy, viewing film or videotape, talking to reporters and specialists, weighing up alternatives and continuously exchanging ideas among the senior staff.

News editors or intake editors are commonly in the office by 8 a.m., if not earlier, and stay until 6.30 or 7 p.m. or later if it is a busy night. Editors tend to arrive about 10 to 10.30 a.m. in newspapers and stay sometimes until well after midnight and on other nights only until 7 or 8 p.m. The chief editors at ITN and BBC television news are usually in earlier but their movements are more variable. Night editors or production editors at newspapers normally arrive in the early afternoon and stay until 1 a.m. or later. Television programme editors or editors-of-the-day will be in the office for 13 or 14 hours on the days when they are in charge, but generally those are only three out of four working days in a week.

The morning news conferences serve to tell everyone on duty what is expected during the day, possibly also with a brief postmortem on the previous night's work. Their styles differ between offices, and they are more fully described in Chapters 5 to 7. The BBC's is the earliest, at 9.30 a.m. ITN's is at 10.30, the *Mail*'s at 11, the *Guardian*'s at 11.15, *The Times* at 11.30 and the *Mirror*'s at 12. These morning conferences are attended by 15 to 20 executives or heads of department; the early evening conferences are usually smaller. The *Mail*'s conference is the longest, lasting about 40 minutes, and it is also, for me, the most entertaining of the ones that we were able to observe – no coincidence, since it leaves scope for argument

48

and opinion, though it also eats up a lot of executive time. ITN's is next longest and next liveliest, and *The Times* a close third. (My own conferences, when running the *Guardian,* were notoriously brief and probably dull or unintelligible to a visitor.)

Mid-afternoon most offices have some kind of informal gathering, to brief night staff, scriptwriters and others. Both News at Ten and the BBC's Nine o'clock News have theirs at 3 p.m.; the *Mirror*'s also is at 3; the *Guardian* and *Mail* have no fixed time.

The main evening conferences, chaired by the editors, are at 3.50 for the BBC's Nine o'clock News, 4 p.m. for *The Times,* 5 p.m. for the *Mail,* 5.15 for the *Mirror* and News at Ten and 6.15 at the *Guardian. The Times* has an informal gathering in its newsroom, with the editor, somewhere about 6.10 to 6.30 p.m. at which most of the final decisions are made. All the news channels, however, remain as flexible as they can to allow for late changes to page one make-up or programme running orders. Paradoxically, the newspaper timings are all much earlier than they were ten years ago. *The Guardian* used to hold a formal 'front-page conference' at 8.10, but that was before the illusory benefits of 'new technology'. (It is not the technology itself which is at fault, but the high cost of union agreements for operating the new equipment, which have forced a shortening of hours and reduction of typesetting and page make-up capacity on Fleet Street.)

At the *Mail* and *Guardian,* the editor or his deputy will be on the 'back bench' with the production editor from 6.30 onwards; at *The Times* and the *Mirror* the editor is seen less often. At ITN the editor, David Nicholas, is likely to look into the news-room either shortly before the programme editor's decisive 7 p.m. gathering or soon after it; at the BBC the deputy editor Robin Walsh, is usually available for consultation.

News lists are produced for the main conferences. Generally they are no more than a recital of engagements to which reporters are assigned. The *Mail*'s is the most informative, because the news editor is expected to offer a short summary of each item and his assessment of priorities. The BBC also summarises the main items for its 9.30 meeting. ITN tables no more than a bare list such as the *Guardian* and *Mirror* employ. An unusual feature at *The Times* is that the editor's secretary sits in at the morning conference, making notes. Soon afterwards she circulates a cryptic memo of the editor's comments, which is a reminder that action is expected on these points. An example is reproduced here.

TABLE 3.1 The Times: *home news schedule for Monay, 13 February 1984 (11.30)*

A. MAIN ITEMS

1. LABOUR
   - (a) GCHQ developments (x ref Whitehall Brief) — Felton
   - (b) Scott-Lithgow: Parly Cttee visit yard — Faux
   - (c) Threat to Scottish coal field — PA/Lab Staff
   - (d) Strike at BL Cowley plant — PA

2. POLITICS
   - (a) Shore attacks Thatcher over Mark deal
   - (b) Chesterfield by-election — Bevins
   - (c) Opposition at entry ban on East-Bloc delegates

3. Whitehall Brief: Cabinet moves to solve GCHQ row — Hennessy

B. MUST
4. Wormwood Scrubs redevelopment (B. Page) — R. Drinkwater
5. Law Society statement on house buyers' bill — Gibb
6. GLC Tories attack £900m Livingstone budget — Clayton
8. Civil servants union on NHS staffing levels — Timmins
9. Midlands diplomat under developments — Seton

C. ON MERIT
10. Sellafield radioactive mud-dumping charge — FSNA
11. Greenham women on runway damage charges — PA/Corr

TABLE 3.1—*continued*

12.	Gypsy council condemns 'criminals'	Altheer
13.	Cuts at Epsom psychiatric hospital 'unsafe'	Samstag
14.	World Bank man shot in Uganada – inquest	Steed
15.	PAC report on Forestry Commission accounts	PA/Staff
16.	Two Scottish castles auctioned	PA
17.	Libel: Derek Jameson v. BBC	MacMillan
18.	Man charged with murder 13 years ago	Jones

19. RE-SUBMIT
    (a) Garden shed used as jobs centre for
        executives   R. Evans
    (b) Land prices cheap in Falklands   Cowton

TABLE 3.2 The Times: *foreign news schedule for Monday, 13 February 1984 (11.30)*

ANDROPOV

1.	MOSCOW:	Chernenko chosen as Andropov's successor.
2.	MOSCOW:	Man in news profile (600 by 1600)
3.	MOSCOW:	Three categories of Soviet power (panel) (in hand)
4.	WASHINGTON:	Reactions to Chernenko's appointment (600 by 1700)
5.	VARIOUS:	World reactions
6.	LUXEMBOURG:	Bush press conference

MIDDLE EAST

8.	BEIRUT:	The effects of the New Jersey shelling / Saudi peace initiative
9.	WASHINGTON:	Reagan meets Husain (300 by 1700)
10.	NEW YORK:	Britain's Lebanon initiative (300 by 1700)
11.	JERUSALEM:	Sharp drop in Shamir's popularity
12.	PORT OF SPAIN:	Britain's docile Caribbean colonies (in type) (with map)
13.	PARIS:	Row over Louvre pyramid plans (? illustration) (450 by 1430)
14.	UNDATED:	Prisoner of conscience: Kenya (Moorhead) (WITH LOGO) (in type)

TABLE 3.3   The Times: *memo after 11.30 conference*
32pp   Monday 13 February 1984   11.30 Conference
Taken by the Editor

Not on schedule – *Prin of Wales* expecting 2nd baby
P Hennessy to be asked re 1974 Cyprus – *Cheltenham story*
  Editor would like measurement of acceptances of £1000
  Will money be taxed?
  Editor wants more background to this story
Chesterfield sociologically? P Stothard to look at
Try F Emery for comments on *BBC/MPs* row
Editor asks why no Crufts story on Court page today
Obits need, if poss, 3 cols a day for this week as large backlog
R Owen to be thanked
Editor wants box of previous 5 Sov leaders since Lenin and length of
  tenures
Wants story on kidney specialists in Eur and USA
N Ashford to be thanked for series last week
Pres Reagans 8 yers in California – go back
Her Trib story last week – China and nuclear waste in Gobi – we did
  not have, go back
Editor would like Moscow back page letter if poss for tomorrow
Business – rework B Cal snatch and grab raid
Editor wants childs guide to A320 ingreds, funding, may be ref. back
  to joint ventures
Hennessy and Miller to be thanked for sports stories
Scott-Lithgow – Editor wants map of yard, also when stories of
  Israel's position in Lebanon, often need single col map
Features – 1200 by R Owen, B Walden and R North

TABLE 3.4   *BBC: proposed home news diary, television news –
Monday, 31 October 1984 (9.30 a.m.)*

CORRS & REPS: *Andrew Taylor, Clive Ferguson, Mike McKay,
                  Neil Bennett
TONIGHT: Michael Sullivan
ASST NEWS ED: Bob Barton
TONIGHT: Steve Selman
SPUR OB: Not available

NILSEN   The Old Bailey trial of the   ENG FOR 1230
1000   former civil servant continues.
            It's expected to end tomorrow.
            REPORTER: KATE ADIE

TABLE 3.4—*continued*

MERCURY	Mercury Communications are hoping for a hearing at the Court of Appeal today. They're fighting the Telephone Engineer's refusal to connect its new service to the public telephone network. REPORTER: JOHN FRYER	ENG
MINERS	The National Union of Mineworkers overtime ban starts today.	INDUSTRIAL STAFF TO ADVISE
FIREWORKS 1030	A group from the British Safety Council hand in a petition to Number 10 Downing Street asking for a ban on all fireworks sales to the general public. Among those present will be children who've been injured by fireworks. REPORTER:	ENG FOR 1230
P.A.C.E. 1100	A police monitoring group funded by Islington Council is launched. Called Police Accountability for Community Service, it's one of number of groups set up in London to advise the public on their rights in making complaints to the police force. Roy Hattersley is one of the speakers at the launch. REPORTER:	ENG FOR 1230
CSV 1800	The Queen and Prince Philip host a reception for 1000 people to mark the 21st anniversary of the Community Service Volunteers. The Prime Minister, MPs, full-time volunteers and young unemployed people on the Community Service Volunteers training schemes will attend.	ENG FOR NEWSROUND

Table 3.4—*continued*

OLD VIC 1100	The Old Vic reopens after a £2 million refit. The first production a new Tim Rice musical 'Blondel' starts tonight. We look at the transformation of the theatre and watch the final rehearsals.	POSS SPUR OB FOR NEWSNIGHT & 0700
ACC	The Association of County Councils hold their annual conference in Cardiff. It's a chance to hear their views of the local government shake up.	CARDIFF WATCHING
ENERGY 1130	Peter Walker launches the Energy Efficiency Office. It's planned as a 'Save It' Mark II to encourage the public to use energy more efficiently. REPORTER:	COVERAGE TO BE DECIDED

Last copy from the newsrooms must normally be with the composing room at 8.15 p.m. for the first edition of *The Times*, at 8.40 for the *Guardian* and at 9.05 for the *Mail*. Completion of page make-up is supposed to be by 9.10 at *The Times*, 9.40 at the *Guardian* and 10 p.m. at the *Mail*. No more than 18 or 20 pages are 'live' on the night; all others have to be made up the previous evening. The earliest 'live' pages go to press at intervals of about ten minutes, from 7.30 onwards; the last eight pages (or pairs of pages with the tabloid papers) are supposed to go at five-minute intervals up to the final deadline. The *Mail* and *Mirror* have on the whole a better record of timekeeping than *The Times* or *Guardian*, where for a variety of reasons late running has been an endemic disease in the last few years.

All papers aim to have a second edition about 45 or 50 minutes after the first, though with changes on only a few pages. Provided there have been no hitches or hold-ups in the composing room or machine room, two or three further editions follow later – the main London edition being about midnight and the final edition about 3 a.m. Distribution in a city the size of London has to start early, and the last papers to be printed are as likely to arrive in Cambridge or Reading as in Westminster or the City. (At Heathrow or Gatwick you are likely to get an early first edition.)

Some newspapers print all their copies in London – *The Times, Financial Times* and *Sun* among them – and some print in both London and Manchester. Until the 1960s the *Express* and *Mail* printed also in Scotland, but neither does so now. The *Mail, Mirror* and *Telegraph* transmit all copy between London and Manchester by 'doxfax' or teleprinter, and it is then reset as necessary in the second centre. The *Guardian* alone uses facsimile transmission of whole pages – a system invented and tested by the old *Manchester Guardian (MG)* in 1951, but because of trade union problems brought into use only in 1976.[1] The system had meanwhile been used extensively and profitably in Japan, the United States and many other countries. (The *MG's* prototype machines, developed with Muirhead and Co., had been sold in 1957 to the Japanese publishers of *Asahi,* which had a joint morning and evening sale of 6 million copies.) Apart from management caution and union resistance, there is no reason today why UK national newspapers should not publish in five or six centres, cutting production and distribution costs – and supplying readers more reliably with later editions. Both Mr Rupert Murdoch and Mr Eddie Shah are planning operations on these lines.[2]

Newspaper conference times and indeed the whole editorial operation have to be geared to the production schedule. Much the same is true of television news, though it has had fewer hang-ups over new technology.[3] For the BBC's Nine o'clock News, a running order begins to take shape at the 3 p.m. informal gathering chaired by the editor-of-the-day. The 3.50 formal conference with the editor brings further discussion but counts for less than ITN's 5.15 meeting with its editor. (The BBC's changeover in the spring of 1985 from Peter Woon as editor to Ron Neil could make a difference, for Neil has a reputation for being active and interventionist; but the organisational structure already described will always make it more difficult for the BBC's editor to keep close to news output.) The Nine o'clock group gathers again at the end of transmission of the early evening news, and item lengths are then allocated. The headlines have to be devised if possible by

7 p.m., and there ought to be a studio rehearsal starting about 8.35, though it must often be truncated.

The routine at News at Ten effectively starts at 3 p.m. with an informal group chaired by the programme editor, with the news editors, presenters, director, scriptwriters and film librarian present. For the 5.15 meeting with the editor (Nicholas) a preliminary running order is presented – though headed 'line-up at 5.30' as if anticipating Nicholas's approval – and three or four of the items are usually discussed. At 7 p.m. the whole team gathers again round the programme editor's desk in the newsroom, and after further exchanges a final running order is drawn up. It can still be revised, of course, up to about 9.50 or even when the programme is on air. The tensions in the last three hours and the interplay of influences are described in Chapter 5.

Here, however, let us look at how far the final output – in print or on screen – coincides with conference expectations. Taking four of the fieldwork days at the *Mail*, the eventual front-page 'splash' was listed top on only one occasion at the morning conference and on two at the 5 p.m. meeting; but on two of those four days the item that became the splash had not yet been heard of at 5 p.m., and on one it was a *Mail* 'exclusive' that was being held in reserve for use on a night when there was a shortage of strong news. Also on the one day when the item was listed first in the morning, its character and strength changed greatly in the evening, for it was the day of 'Heath's treachery', as the splash headline put it; in the morning it had simply been listed as a controversial parliamentary debate on rate-capping. In practice, nevertheless, the news editor's top three or four choices were always well placed in the paper, often as the lead to an inside page.

Looking at the list for 8 March, the 'Raffles escape', which was placed first at 5 p.m., became the second story on page one, having been displaced as lead by a speech from Mrs Thatcher critical of the EEC – 'Maggie mauls the market'. The development of that splash, on the editor's initiative, is described in Chapter 6 (pp. 119–23). Even that, however, was displaced in the final edition by the first sortie from Greenham Common of a Cruise missile convoy, on an exercise about midnight.

Choice of items for the front page is more volatile at the *Mail* than at *The Times,* and late changes are more frequent. An analysis on three nights at *The Times* shows few major changes from the priorities stated by the editor at his 4 p.m. conference. On one night, when at 4 p.m. he had resisted prominent placing for the pregnancy of the Princess of Wales – for reasons reported in Chapter 7 – he was persuaded by 6.30 to allow it second place on the front page as a more cheerful offset to the messages from Moscow about Mr Chernenko's succession to the Soviet presidency. On another night the Olympic gold medal won by the ice skaters Torvill and Dean was no more than a possibility at the 4 p.m. meeting but was given second place on the front page when it happened. On the third night the probable appointment of Mr Cecil Parkinson as an EEC commissioner in Brussels, listed fourth at 4 p.m., went to an inside page – which was perhaps just as well, since the appointment was never made. Similarly, the fifth choice that night at 4 p.m., another row between the BBC and the Conservative party, was dropped completely.

At the *Guardian* even at 6.15 the news priorities are left more loosely undetermined than they are at 4 p.m. at *The Times*. That is largely because of the different personal styles of the two editors. Charles Douglas-Home at 4 p.m. lays down his preferences in a fairly precise way, though his chief night editor says that he does not regard them as binding:

> The editor's view at 4 is a photo of the situation then, but situations change. He would not want me to take it as binding. If he's in the office and I contemplate a change of 'splash' I'd consult him. If he wasn't I'd go ahead and change it. We do so fairly regularly. He's never said 'you've made a mistake' though he may have thought it . . . It's a good paper: people don't get officious.

Towards the end of the 6.15 meeting at the *Guardian* the editor, Peter Preston, usually invites his night editor to comment on the prospects and then adds a marginal note or two of his own. It is no more than a loose indication of preferences, however, and Preston himself is frequently in the newsroom later in the evening. He differs from Douglas-Home in being actively engaged in later decisions on many nights each week; he differs also from Sir David English at the *Mail* in that he rarely takes over the actual design of the front-page layout. Mike Molloy's style at the *Mirror* is different again, for although he is not often in the newsroom he is acknowledged as a master of design and quite frequently draws the page plan for the front.

Douglas-Home remains mostly in the background, apart from his early evening visit to the newsroom. Preston, in his own words, likes to 'potter' out from his office beside the newsroom and chat to the backbench (night executives) and read as much copy as possible, sometimes sub-editing it himself. Molloy is little seen but still significant in the evening's decisions. English is the most active and interventionist of all, designing layouts and writing headlines and giving directions. Of the newspaper conferences, therefore, those at *The Times* are the nearest to decision-making; elsewhere they are no more than a useful exchange and sharing of ideas.

At ITN, as already indicated, Nicholas takes part at 5.15 in discussion of the main items listed by then and normally has a further consultation with the programme editor of News at Ten later. At the BBC while Woon was editor he left most of the night-by-night supervision to his deputy. The lists at the BBC are no more than a useful guide.

Among the ITN 'line-ups' presented at the 5.15 conference on four days of our fieldwork, the item listed top remained top on transmission of News at Ten on only two nights. On the third, the videotape of the intended first item was only coming in from Newcastle as the programme went on air, having been delayed by late developments in shipyard negotiations, so it had to be run later; and on the fourth the report on a major murder trial (Nilsen's) was relegated because the jury had not reached a verdict as expected. There were a number of other variations in the running order on each of the three nights, though virtually all the items discussed at 5.15 went on air. As one of the programme editors remarked, the precise placing is probably less important than the choice of a newspaper's 'splash', provided the three or four most significant or attractive items come at the beginning of the programme and provided there is rhythm and balance in the way the programme is paced.

From these findings three points emerge. (1) Although pre-planning, news lists and conferences are important to all the media, they are decisive in none. An item well placed on a news list is likely to reach print or broadcasting, but events reported after a list has been drawn up are being assessed all the time. Informal talk among news teams is the most common route to a decision to publish. (2) *The Times* is the nearest to having a conclusive conference, but even there informal discussion is at least as important in shaping news judgements. It is probably no coincidence that the listings and conference indications at the 'heavy' newspapers correspond most nearly to the published result, because they are principally concerned with the political, social and economic events which they regard as significant. That gives stability in their choice of content (or monotony, some journalists will say), whereas the popular papers and television news place greater emphasis on a varied diet and surprise.

(3) Some academic analysts (O'Sullivan and others, Hartley, the Glasgow Media Group) overstate the importance of news lists or diaries, whether compiled within an office or from news agencies. It is an error to suppose that items not listed stand little chance of publication; that will apply only if they are of a minor character. It may be said that there is a circular argument here, since the journalists themselves decide what is minor. The evidence above, however, points to a readiness to make full use of items that were unscheduled or unpredicted.

Sources are another matter worth explanation before we start on the detail of case studies. Sources are many and various – some routine and open, others irregular and confidential. Much news is gathered as a result of routine telephoning to the police, the fire brigades, British Rail, bus stations, airports or airlines and shipping or ferry terminals. The telephone call by itself is not enough: the initial information that it provides must often be followed up. For local newspapers and local broadcasting these are important contacts, worth ringing two or three times each day; for national newspapers or network news, the routine calls tend to be restricted to New Scotland Yard, possibly the City police (who specialise in fraud cases, the diamond and related trades and such City affairs) and Heathrow and Gatwick airports. All these fields are also covered by local 'stringers' or freelance journalists. Financial, diplomatic and sports staffs will make their regular calls, too.

It is chiefly in the higher political, governmental and industrial areas that the pattern is more complex. To chart even the Whitehall and Westminster connections produces an extraordinary spider's web, and similar patterns exist in the reporting of industry and company affairs, trade union and related areas, local government and the law. They are a matrix of open and private information – from open press conferences called by ministers or officials to strictly confidential briefings in which a journalist learns the background to government or other actions and decisions. In either case, the greater the journalist's knowledge beforehand, and the shrewder his questioning, the more information he will obtain.

For a journalist it is as well to be clear from the start on the terms of a meeting – all for publication, with sources stated; or 'off the record' to the extent of being intended for publication but without attribution as to source; or totally off the record, and ostensibly designed only to make an action or decision more intelligible. The last category is the most fraught, because the briefing may really be intended to silence the journalist by telling him too much. It may on the other hand be a genuine and valuable attempt to explain an intricate situation so that when news eventually breaks in the open the writer or broadcaster can fill in the background.

The middle category – off the record but for unattributable use – is sometimes called 'on Lobby terms'. That derives from the work of accredited Lobby correspondents (approved, that is, by the Sergeant at Arms at the House of Commons). For many years the Lobby worked in pseudo-secrecy, but more recently its rules have been revised. The Lobby is briefed by the Prime Minister's press secretary twice a day when Parliament is sitting and once a day at other times, almost always off the record; the Leader of the House usually talks to it once a week, as occasionally do other ministers and shadow ministers. But 'Annie's Bar', a popular meeting place in the Palace of Westminster, is also much used for passing on unattributable information.

For political correspondents the most important single source is the PM's press secretary – currently (1985) Mr Bernard Ingham, a tough and effective operator on Mrs Thatcher's behalf. He is a Yorkshireman, trained on the *Hebden Bridge Times* and with experience on the *Yorkshire*

Post and the *Guardian* before he joined the civil service. Mrs Thatcher picked him for his present post after winning the 1979 election. While he has been an accomplished political operator, he is generally trusted and respected, and during the Falklands War he was instrumental in improving the flow of reliable news. But it is an old principle of experienced Lobby journalists that they should still check information with a second source, and when that is not possible, as must frequently happen, they must be cautious about accepting it as the whole truth.

The Prime Minister herself, like her predecessors, talks privately to editors from time to time – more often to those who support her than to those who do not. Occasionally she gives 'on the record' interviews to particular papers or television programmes, including television news. Other ministers follow a similar pattern. Some are readily accessible – Mr Peter Walker at the Energy Department and Mr Patrick Jenkin at Environment, for example – while others are not. It was much the same when Mr Harold Wilson (now Lord Wilson of Rievaulx) was Prime Minister, though the longer ministers were in office the more aloof they tended to become. It is mainly a matter of the minister's own wish. Such informal contacts are more likely to be away from Parliament or their offices, being instead in clubs or restaurants or at home. In much the same way there are contacts between senior civil servants and senior journalists in places such as the Reform Club or the Travellers' Club.

Such contacts can be criticised as corrupting. Sometimes they may be, but there is no reason why they should be. It depends on the integrity of both sides. Sir William Haley, a wise if austere editor, used to say that journalists must talk to people in authority.[4] A newspaper, he said, could not be well informed unless its senior editors were able to look into the minds of those who were taking the great decisions of public policy (my paraphrase, but others who knew Haley confirm it). Haley, though, was as clear as anyone about the hazards. There was to be no 'truckling' to ministers, and he delivered a stinging rebuke to one who thought that *The Times* might like to anticipate a parliamentary reply.[5] He knew that the most valuable conversations were a two-way flow – such as he had had at times with Harold Macmillan and I had with Wilson in his early days as Prime Minister, with the PM listening as well as talking – but there was always a risk of getting too close. It was a trap, unfortunately, which both he and *The Times* fell into with Eden before Suez.

To conclude the discussion of routine, deadlines and sources – and to put all three into perspective – here is the reply from the *Guardian*'s political editor, Ian Aitken, to a question during our pilot study in December 1982. The previous day he had written the paper's front-page lead on Mr Michael Foot's demand, as leader of the Labour party, for an inquiry by the party into the Militant Tendency movement. In his opening he had said that the battle lines were drawn between those in the party committed to parliamentary democracy and those who believed that British society could be transformed only by extra-parliamentary methods. The question: was not the use of the word 'only' an oversimplification? His reply, verbatim:

> Yes, I think probably it was. Had I not been dictating straight down a telephone without having written it down I might have left the word 'only' out. You witnessed me tonight [in the Commons gallery] tumbling into a telephone box and pouring it all out as quickly as I can; and that's what happens almost every night.
>
> The exact choice of any given word? I get resentful of the number of people who pick you up on the exact choice of a word, because they've never seen a reporter working in this place. You come out of a room, you have just got a great long spiel perhaps at a press conference, or you come out of a bar where a chap – out of the side of his mouth – has been telling you what's been happening at a private meeting; and you've got a quarter of an hour to get on the telephone with your stuff.
>
> You don't even have time to write it down. You go into the phone box, you phone 'Copy' and you hope that by the time 'Copy' has answered you've thought of the intro. That's actually the way it works.

It is a salutary reminder from one of the most conscientious and competent of political reporters. Edition deadlines and 'on air' times have to be met.

4 Decisions (1): A Cross-section

Take an average week and look at news priorities. We did so in July 1983, barely a month after the general election that put Mrs Thatcher back in power with a big majority of Conservative MPs. In this chapter we hear from night editors, programme editors and others why they gave priority to particular topics. They articulate what are normally unstated assumptions about 'significance'.

It was a week when the new Chancellor of the Exchequer, without warning, announced a package of economies – some in the health service, although the Conservatives had campaigned with promises to protect the NHS. At Greenham Common, where the first Cruise missiles were expected before midwinter, the 'peace women' held a special week of protest. At Britain's top-ranking soap opera, *Coronation Street,* the star Len Fairclough left. The weather was hot and much of the nation on holiday.

Average sales for the *Daily Mirror* were then about 3 242 000, for the *Daily Mail* 1 802 000 copies, for the *Guardian* 487 000 and for *The Times* about 382 000. The Nine o'clock News then had an audience varying between 6½ million and 8 million nightly, and News at Ten between 6½ million and 9 million. Only seven months after the start of Channel Four News, it was being watched by 250 000 to 350 000 – figures much increased since then. Its bulletin, at a duration of fifty minutes, was by far the longest, and its format had been changed at the end of June to provide deeper coverage of a few topics each night, the remainder being reported in brief summary.

Some conclusions may be summarised. (1) On some days there was near unanimity about news priorities, on others there was not. All three television bulletins led with the same topic on the evening of Thursday 7 July – the £1 billion economies announced by the Chancellor, Mr Nigel Lawson. Next morning, three of the four newspapers also led with the Chancellor's cuts, while the *Mirror* concentrated on Len Fairclough leaving *Coronation Street*. Its choice was shared by the *Sun*, Britain's most popular daily. (2) The week began and ended with 'difficult' days when 'hard' news was scarce, and those days produced the widest diversity in news priorities. On the Monday morning, 4 July, each of the four newspapers chose a different lead, and few items were common to more than one or two front pages. Friday evening's television news displayed as much diversity, with little common ground either about leading topics or about secondary events.

(3) Logistic and technical difficulties affected news priorities, as frequently they do. Monday's BBC Nine o'clock News had to lead with an item previously placed fifth because neither of its two top items was ready for transmission in time; conversely Friday's News at Ten solved its problem over lack of a lead by using colourful pictures from Washington which came in at 9.45 p.m. Because of mechanical troubles *The Times* on the Monday told only a tiny fraction of its readers about the burning in Belfast by the IRA of the house of Gerry Fitt, a leading Catholic politician; whereas the *Mail* on the Thursday achieved a greater 'scoop' over the decision of the Liberal leader, David Steel, to take a long sabbatical because late running in its machine room prevented other papers from seeing its front page.

(4) In terms of creative journalism, where interpretation brings out the political or social context of an event, the week included a number of examples: Monday's Channel Four News on the political influence of the big trade union conferences and their implications for the Labour party after the election; Tuesday's News at Ten on the annual report of the Commission on Racial Equality; Wednesday's *Times* and *Guardian* highlighting the excessive money supply figures and perceiving that these could lead to early cuts in government spending (the figures having been available to the television bulletins which failed to see their possible consequence); and notable contributions to Channel Four News from Lebanon, both on a likely Israeli withdrawal from the Beirut area and on the 'insiders' who had blown up the US Embassy in Beirut.

(5) Whom do you love and whom do you hate? The

revulsion factor was at work in decisions on reporting Mr Arthur Scargill at the NUM conference. (This was nine months before the start of the 1984–5 NCB–NUM dispute.) The varying judgements on how to handle the Greenham 'peace' women's week of demonstrations also make interesting reading.

Monday Morning, 4 July

Sunday night in newsrooms was generally seen as a typical 'summer Sunday' – no dramatic news, but a wide choice of topics. *The Times* led with the continuing dispute between Mr Michael Foot, then leader of the Opposition, and Mrs Thatcher over dissolution honours. The *Mail* picked a story of its own about 'video nasties', developing a campaign. The *Mirror* carried pictures from the final day at Wimbledon, as did nearly everyone else. The *Guardian* chose the Middle East, with the Syrians rejecting overtures from the Palestinian leader, Yasser Arafat. Common to all the papers was a late report from Belfast on the burning of the home of ex-MP Gerry Fitt.

The Times report on peerages for the first time named two of the disputed names. The topic had been running for some days; the paper's executive editor, Charles Wilson, said that the story was chosen as the lead because it named names. The *Guardian's* assistant editor, Geoffrey Taylor, said that the peerages were considered – as was a hint by the Chancellor that unemployment benefit might be cut – but both were relegated in favour of the Syrian snub to Arafat. That was chiefly because the paper's Middle East specialist was in Damascus and able to give a deeper explanation of the troubles among the Palestinian guerrillas. Both papers were evidently influenced by extra elements which their specialists could offer. Taylor at the *Guardian* added that since the Middle East was an area of overt hostility between the superpowers and was being visited by the US Secretary of State, that made it the more worth attention.

The *Mail's* decision to lead with 'Video share deal shock' – revealing that the NUM's pension fund held thousands of shares in a company distributing sadistic cassettes – was also taken for lack of anything stronger. Peter Grover, the deputy editor, said that the campaign on 'video nasties' had begun more than 12 months earlier:

> We started it not as a specific campaign but because readers wrote to us – getting worried about their kids, who can go into shops and hire them and play them when the parents aren't there . . . A campaign like this is self-generating in stories. We had a story about a car company; companies buy up another company and don't always realise what's involved in the woodwork. The NUM story was self-generated, arising from the campaign . . .

The *Mail* report was picked up in later editions of the *Telegraph* and *Mirror* – and next day at the NUM conference Arthur Scargill said that 'pin-striped smoothies' had made this investment on behalf of the NUM pension fund and that the union had refused to sign the fund's annual accounts.

The *Mirror* gave greatest prominence on its front page to a promotional display, with the promise of £20 000 bingo prizes, plus Mini cars for lucky numbers, as well as trailers for articles on inside pages. (This was in the early stages of the Fleet Street bingo war.) The night editor, John Parker, explained that this was part of the marketing strategy introduced in April – as a result of which the nightly print had been increased by 350 000 copies and sales were up by about 250 000. Market research, he said, had shown that this form of promotion paid. Of the prominent Wimbledon pictures he said: 'we've actually got a Brit who's won a trophy for the first time since 1936.' They were 'happy pictures', which was important. Other papers went for Wimbledon pictures for similar reasons.

Among secondary stories there were wide divergencies. Most, however, carried reports of Arthur Scargill's press conference before the NUM annual conference. Only *The Times* thought it worth the front page. 'He never makes a speech which is not extravagant', Geoffrey Taylor (*Guardian*) said, 'and he consequently devalues the currency of his own speeches.' When Scargill spoke on miners' pay or pit closures, he had to be reported. 'But when he calls for the overthrow of a government elected only three weeks ago, I'd have thought readers of most papers would quickly tire of this.' As already noted, this was nine months before the strike.

Monday Evening, 4 July

Three events dominated the evening television news – the apparent illness of Mr Andropov, the annual conferences of the miners' union and the transport union, and a siege in Cornwall where a man with a shotgun was holding councillors hostage. The siege came too late for Channel Four News but was a 'live' story for the BBC at 9.00 and ITN's News at Ten. It made a dramatic element in both bulletins, including the gunman's reported surrender just at the end of News at Ten.

For an outside observer, however, the most striking point about the three bulletins was the length and vigour of Channel Four's treatment of the union conferences. The T & G and NUM conferences were put squarely into the context of the Labour party's future, with a plain indication that both were taking the party further away from being a credible alternative government. By contrast, the main BBC and ITN bulletins treated the union conferences blandly and without any political pointers.

Altogether Channel Four News gave just over 13 minutes to the union conferences, 4 minutes to Andropov's illness, and almost 12 minutes to a special report from the Lebanon on a possible Israeli withdrawal to south of the Awali River (confirmed by the Israeli Cabinet a fortnight later). The BBC's Nine o'clock News treated the T & G and NUM conferences separately, spacing them out quite low in its running order – because neither was ready, following line failures – and giving them 3½ and 2 minutes respectively; and it allowed 1 minute and 50 seconds to Mr Andropov as third item in its bulletin. The siege in Cornwall came near the start and at the end, totalling 1 minute, 20 seconds. ITN's News at Ten led with Andropov, at 3 minutes; the T & G as third item received 2 minutes, followed by the NUM at just under 2 minutes.

The Union Conferences

Something of the flavour of treatment can be tasted from the opening of the union items in each bulletin:

Channel Four News. [Peter Sissons to camera] It's just over three weeks since the Labour party's most calamitous showing ever in a general election. The shock was as great for the trade unions as anybody. They founded the party and they largely finance it. More important, no significant changes in the party are possible without their consent. On top of that, they will have more say than anyone else in choosing the party leader.

So as the Labour party begins another four or five years in opposition, with the political pendulum by no means certain to return to its familiar grooves, the unions could make or break the prospects for the party in being able to assemble again the credentials of a credible alternative.

Two of the most important unions this week provide us with clues as to how they plan to use their influence over the next crucial years . . . Both are set to make major reaffirmations of left-wing policies. Their leaders and the majority of their delegates are convinced that the policies on which Labour fought the last election are largely right.

BBC Nine o'clock News. [Eighth item in bulletin: John Humphrys to camera] Miners' leader Arthur Scargill has again called on trade unionists to take direct action to fight Mrs Thatcher's new government. He's warned of social destruction on a truly horrific scale unless people resist with extra-parliamentary action. Mr Scargill predicted that eight million people would be out of work by the 1990s . . .

ITN's News at Ten. [Third item: Martyn Lewis to camera] Britain's biggest union, the Transport and General Workers, has decided to back Mr Neil Kinnock in the race for the leadership of the Labour party. The union conference in the Isle of Man threw their one and a half million votes behind Mr Kinnock after rejecting a call for a postal ballot of members.

The NUM conference report followed, introduced by Alastair Burnet: 'Miners' president Mr Arthur Scargill says he's not prepared to accept the policies of a government elected by a minority of the electorate . . .'
Channel Four News, in setting the union conferences in the context of the future of the Labour party, illustrated the degree

of subjective personal judgement implicit in putting together any news bulletin or newspaper. At the same time, however, it can be said to have shown a sense of responsibility in making the significance of the union conference plain. The blander treatment in the Nine o'clock News and News at Ten left viewers to draw their own conclusions, but failed to alert them to the direction that union influence in the Labour party was taking. (With hindsight a year later, though, the BBC's highlighting of Mr Scargill's militancy had more force.)

The second point is that the episodic treatment of the Nine o'clock News and News at Ten – perhaps less demanding and more digestible on a hot summer evening – conveys less information though it covers more topics. The BBC's Nine o'clock News covered 19 items, the largest at 3½ minutes; ITN's News at Ten covered 24 items, the largest also just over 3½ minutes. Channel Four News covered 22 items in a programme twice the length of the others, its two largest items being respectively just over 14 minutes and just over 12 minutes.

The Hostages in Cornwall

The BBC first heard of the trouble in the council chamber at Liskeard at 8.25 p.m. through Radio Cornwall. ITN had confirmation through a Press Association 'snap' at 9.15, just six minutes after BBC television had broadcast its first report. The Nine o'clock News depended mainly on a voice report, relayed by Radio Cornwall, from a local newspaper reporter who had escaped from the council meeting and raised the alarm. ITN relied on a telephone interview with a detective inspector at Devon and Cornwall police headquarters who provided a clear and graphic account of what was happening. Elwyn Evans, editor of the Nine o'clock News that night:

I'm always wary of late stories, so I sat on it at first. Then we heard from Radio Cornwall that they had an interview with a witness who was extremely good. After I'd heard it, I thought it should go higher in the programme. Then we heard that they were holding 20 councillors hostage at gunpoint, so I thought 'a good second story for the Nine o'clock News'.

At ITN the news desk started trying for telephone interviews immediately after the PA snap at 9.15. It received the first with the detective inspector at 9.30 but arranged to speak to him again a little later. Jill Chisholm, programme editor that night:

> We ran the second interview. He was amazingly articulate and fluent. We couldn't stop him, really. We got that just before going on air.
>
> I was a little worried. I hesitated about whether that should go up to the lead. It could have – if the man had been really disturbed and started shooting . . . On the other hand in this country these things tend to boil down. They just do. We haven't had the sort of incident where someone has done the American thing and shot everyone in sight. And therefore I thought it better to play it slightly down.

She was also concerned about possible contempt of court, but decided that it did not prevent reporting of the current siege.

Andropov's Absence

President Andropov failed to greet Chancellor Kohl at Moscow airport – the first Western head of government to visit the Soviet Union since his election – and at the opening banquet his speech, a singularly tough one about Soviet reaction to Cruise and Pershing missiles, was read for him. Was his 'illness' a diplomatic snub or real, and what did it imply?

Channel Four News regarded it as a major story and would have been willing to lead with it. But their diplomatic editor was taken up with the Middle East. So an interview was arranged with the ITN Channel 1 diplomatic editor, together with the pictures from Moscow. No studio was available for an interview from Moscow, because all had been booked long beforehand by German television.

Elwyn Evans at BBC television news had thought of Andropov as a possible lead, but at their 4 p.m. meeting the editor and deputy editor had both been against it on the ground that Andropov was quite likely to turn up next day, as he did.

Other Topics

Trevor McDonald's report from the Lebanon, run for nearly 12 minutes after the midway break on Channel Four, clearly indicated that an Israeli withdrawal from the vicinity of Beirut was imminent – and that as a result the British, French and US troops in the international force could find themselves in the firing line. Although newspaper reports in previous days had touched on the Israeli debate on redeployment, McDonald's film report provided a clear and graphic account of Israeli thinking, the conflicts within the PLO, and the position of the international force. A shortened version was used in News at Ten. Paul McKee, deputy chief executive of ITN and temporarily in charge of Channel Four News:

> Trevor was away thirteen days in which he provided six reports. It was a deliberate attempt to pull together and set out what was happening, in a strategic way; and that requires a lot of time (on the ground) and some length on air. It's unusual for a television news programme.

Falklands Family

News at Ten, near the end of the programme, carried two minutes of a family returning disillusioned from the Falklands, having put £20 000 of their own money into trying to set up a fish-and-chip business in Stanley. The BBC was envious of the story, having tried to locate them but failed. 'We got to them quicker and kept them to ourselves', Jill Chisholm said. But there was no question of 'buying them up'. The ITN reporter had made contact by radio telephone when they were still at sea and had arranged the interview. Once it was recorded they went their way.

Tuesday Morning, 5 July

As in television newsrooms on Monday evening, so in newspaper offices: the choice lay between Andropov's illness and the trade union conferences. In later editions the story of the hostage Cornish councillors came as an alternative – and was 'splashed' by the *Mirror, Express* and *Sun*. The *Mail* went its own way all night, with the whole front page given to a picture of Gerry Fitt standing in the wrecked sitting room of his West Belfast home: 'an extremely evocative picture', according to Peter Grover, deputy editor of the *Daily Mail*. 'Gerry Fitt is the only Northern Irish politician who rings any sort of bell with the English public. People like him and can identify with him.'

At *The Times* David Hopkinson as night editor was undecided between Andropov and the NUM. The miners had the attraction of a big pay claim, backed by the threat of strike action, coming soon after the general election. But Colin Webb, the deputy editor, took the view that 'Scargill is always yelling and screaming about strikes and massive pay increases', and he felt that the story from Moscow was newer and fresher. David Hopkinson was somewhat concerned that the 'illness' of Andropov might prove to be diplomatic, but was persuaded that his frail health was a more likely explanation. In simple terms, why did it matter?

> What made it a strong *Times* lead story is the consequences in the Soviet Union if Andropov, so soon after the death of Brezhnev, is unable to carry on – whether he is incapacitated or whether he is dead. It wasn't so much the Kohl talks as the suggestion that Andropov might no longer be president in a matter of days or weeks or months . . . They've barely settled down after Brezhnev's death. To have another death or incapacitation so soon could be quite catastrophic for this group of old men.

Of the secondary stories, in David Hopkinson's view only the BL settlement at Cowley could have made a front-page lead. It mattered because it was the first major victory for the new BL management after Michael Edwardes. At the *Guardian* similar preference was given to Andropov.

At the *Mirror* John Parker, as associate night editor, dismissed the Moscow story as 'not particularly important for Mirror readers'. It was to have been carried on page 2 but became a casualty during rapid changes after the reports from Cornwall started to come 40 minutes before off-stone time.

The previously planned lead, on petrol prices, went on to page 2, dislodging Andropov.

In the end the *Daily Mail* had the greatest detail both of events in the council chambers at Liskeard and of the background, including the reasons why the council had rejected the aggrieved man's applications for further development of his holiday hotel – once the house of Lord Cornwallis. It was the work of the *Mail*'s man in the West Country, backed by two reporters telephoning from London. The *Guardian* got much of its detail through telephoning the council chairman's wife.

In every office the risk of contempt of court was considered, but all the newspapers named the arrested man and described how he had held the councillors hostage for two hours. 'If we had consulted the lawyers', one executive said, 'they would have told us "No, you cannot use it".' But since the man had been arrested in the council chambers 'he canot deny that he was there'. What was more, he had presumably done it partly for publicity, and there were plenty of witnesses. So the risk was taken.

Pictorially, a minor scoop was enjoyed by *The Times* which juxtaposed on its back page a group of the Queen's Own Highlanders perched on an observation post at Greenham Common and some women demonstrators outside the air base. This was the first photograph of the troops in position at Greenham Common, and David Hopkinson said it had 'a certain East European feel about it'.

Tuesday Evening, 5 July

Andropov, a kidnap, petrol prices, the impending Commons debate on hanging; these were the common topics. Channel Four, in addition, had a major exclusive about insiders being responsible for the bombing of the US Embassy in Beirut in April.

On the choice of priorities, views diverged. At BBC television news Rick Thompson, assistant editor in charge that night, put the kidnap of a schoolboy first because of its 'immediacy'. It started to come in at 7.30 when the BBC's Newcastle newsroom notified a big police operation. It was 'a straightforward, interesting story, on a day when not a lot had grabbed us'.

Jill Chisholm at ITN put the kidnap well down in her running order, at fifteenth place, near the end. According to the police briefing, she said, it had happened before and the boy had been returned safely. The police believed the kidnapper was the same man again, well known to them, and with the mental age of a child. Although the police were seriously concerned and mounting a big operation, the danger did not seem great. The boy was located shortly afterwards and returned home.

On hanging, reverse views applied. Jill Chisholm placed it top in her programme because ITN's political correspondent was certain that the Commons debate and vote were coming on Wednesday 13 July, and the script was written to indicate that the government wanted the issue out of the way quickly, to minimise Conservative divisions. In her view, the vote was of 'huge public importance'. Rick Thompson, on the other hand, although offered a report from Westminster, judged that a vote 'probably next Wednesday' was not much of a story, and he felt that the publicity over the hanging debate had been 'hyped' in American style.

Both recognised the importance of the Moscow news, which both placed as their second main item. Andropov was back, Jill Chisholm said, and there was a duty to report that. The meeting itself was important, at a time when Cruise and Pershing missiles were about to be deployed. There was evidence of intransigence on both sides.

Rick Thompson similarly regarded the health aspect as less significant than what was being said in the talks – though the BBC report by Tim Sebastian said at the start that Andropov was 'frail' but showing no signs of mental strain. The main emphasis again was on the Soviet warnings of no concessions after deployment of Cruise and Pershing. Rick Thompson's team went to some trouble in preparing a graph of missile deployment, a sensitive matter.

How far back do you go? If you start off with the deployment of the SS20s – if you have a map showing East and West, and you first put up the SS20s, and then you put up the Cruise and Pershings, and then the new missiles that the Soviets are intending to deploy, visually you have suggested that *they* started it. Equally if you start with the Cruise and Pershing and then say they intend to match them, that suggests that they are the ones catching up with the West.

What the script and graphics did was to show first the 572 Cruise and Pershings due to come in December and then to say (and illustrate) that these were a response to the 240+ Soviet missiles already in place; and finally the script spoke of the Russians possibly deploying 'their own Cruise system' and other new missiles in Eastern Europe. 'It was as fair as we could get', Rick Thompson said.

The women's 'blockade' at Greenham Common – in its second day – went without mention in the BBC's Nine o'clock News. ITN's News at Ten reported it, but quite late in the programme, with only a brief mention of the 14 arrests; most of the item was given to a film report by John Suchet from the United States on the Seneca Falls women's camp, a feminist attempt to follow the Greenham women's lead.

Wednesday Morning, 6 July

The money supply figures, neglected by television at night apart from Channel Four, were extensively treated on Wednesday morning. The *Guardian* on its front page projected the likely consequences as 'a tough new Government line on public spending, including a package of cuts in the autumn review'. In practice the cuts came within 48 hours and were to make the biggest news of the week. *The Times* dealt with the money supply extensively on its first financial page, saying 'it has brought closer the possibility of hefty cuts in state spending this year'. Its front page led with the government's curb on high-spending councils, as did the *Express* ('Not a penny' for Red Ken and Co.), and the *Morning Star* (savage cuts in councils' cash).

The *Mail* and *Telegraph* led on petrol prices: 'Defeat for BP' in the *Mail*. The *Mirror*, with the headline 'It ain't half hot, Mum!', splashed a big picture of Prince William in his pushchair in Kew Gardens, bare-legged and wearing a sun hat.

On the money supply – the June figures being twice as high as expected – at the *Guardian* the story was at first being handled by the City office. But the home news desk became interested, and a decision was reached to bring it on to page 1. *The Times* chose the curb on council spending because, according to the night editor, David Hopkinson, 'It seemed to us that during the lifetime of this government there's going to be a major confrontation between the rate-collecting bigger councils and the government – and more centralisation of spending in Whitehall.'

Of the *Mirror*'s picture of Prince William, the associate night editor said that it came late from a freelance photographer specialising in royal pictures. It was pleasing, he said, with the one-year-old looking 'bonny and brown' in the 82-degree heat.

Wednesday Evening, 6 July

Redundancies at British Aerospace, the Defence White Paper and the hanging debate – or, to put it in headlines, thousands of jobs lost at a 'privatised' company; the Cruise missiles that will roam around Britain; and the Archbishops are against hanging. These three topics held the main places on all the major television bulletins – showing that the top priorities were common to all, even though there were differences of order, emphasis and style. None of the television bulletins carried any indication of the coming cuts in government spending, which were the lead stories in *The Times, Guardian* and *Telegraph* next morning – though Channel Four News had apparently heard a whisper of the Chancellor's decision, but could not verify it in time.

On British Aerospace, as in Monday's vigorous approach to the trade unions and the Labour party, Channel Four News did not muffle its message. Sarah Hogg's opening words: 'The canker of redundancies is now reaching even profitable companies.' In spite of a 25 per cent increase in sales and a pre-tax profit of £84 millions, British Aerospace was making 3500 redundant, of which 2000 were at Hurn.

BBC television news, in putting the Aerospace redundancies first, spoke of them as a 'shock'. John Fryer began by saying that British Aerospace was in the high technology business, making satellites and Harrier warplanes as well as the world's quietest passenger jet. 'But even jet-setting industries can't escape the recession.' John Anderson, assistant editor, judged this 'more dramatic, more newsy', than any of the alternatives. Only the cost aspects were new in the Defence White Paper; and on hanging, though there was important material, very little was fresh.

ITN's News at Ten placed Aerospace second, after hanging, with the shortest of the three reports. Jill Chisholm had in fact planned it as the lead until the Archbishop of Canterbury's strong words on hanging came; she then switched the positions.

Runcie's intervention was amazing. He was making his position known well in advance of the hanging debate, and the fact that he was calling the Synod into session the day before the vote was expected was important . . . And Glyn Mathias [ITN political correspondent] said he had the full terms of the Commons motion, and how it was going to work – that the government were now unlikely to put through a Government Bill, that it was more and more likely that they'd put through a private member's if it was passed . . . We had the motion and amendments, Runcie and Habgood, Brittan's first interview as Home Secretary, clear guidance from the Whips that their count was showing a small majority against reintroduction. It was a strong story, extremely strong.

On the Defence White Paper, the variations of emphasis were most marked. News at Ten concentrated almost wholly on 'Cruising round Britain' – Mr Heseltine's insistence that the US Cruise missiles must be free to exercise beyond their main bases. The BBC's Nine o'clock News devoted most of its 3 minutes to costs – 'where the money goes'. Channel Four News used 4½ of its 7½ minutes to showing Britain's defence commitments, as set out in the White Paper; then to a comparison of conventional forces in Eastern and Western Europe, with graphics devised from the White Paper. The remaining 3 minutes were used for an interview with Mr Heseltine, in which he was asked to justify the 13 per cent increase in defence spending.

To the criticism that the Channel Four presentation represented only the government view, Paul McKee replied that in the past television news had tended to devote too much time to comment without adequately explaining what the Defence

White Paper was about. 'We set out to give a clear but short exposition of where the money is going and why – and to that extent it had to be an exposition of what the government proposes. I thought it worked all right.'

Thursday Morning, 7 July

The night that produced Thursday morning's papers saw rapid change in many offices. New lead stories appeared in later editions of the *Mail, Mirror, Sun* and *Guardian* – on the *Mail*'s front page, indeed, nothing was left of its first edition contents. In *The Times* there were fewer changes, because it began the night with one of the most powerful reports of the week: 'Lawson demands £500m cut in public spending.' The *Mail* from its third edition splashed a scoop of its own: 'David Steel drops out.' The *Mirror* and the *Sun* at that point were remaking their front pages to lead with a horrifying story from South London of muggers who slashed a baby's face with broken glass when her mother refused to hand over money and jewellery.

On the Chancellor's cuts, at first *The Times* had the report to itself, though the *Guardian* followed on with a similar story from midnight. For both it was a sequel to the previous night's analysis of the June money supply being nearly double the expected figure. Neither, however, had expected such abrupt Treasury action – nor had Mr Lawson's Cabinet colleagues, who were also taken by surprise when they read their *Times* or *Guardian* that morning, as emerged from briefings later in the day. Both papers had some detail of the expected economies.

David Hopkinson, *Times* night editor:

It was all hotly denied by Whitehall sources on Thursday morning, but of course it all happened. It was basically the enterprise of Frances Williams, our economics correspondent, backed up by the political people. The story developed late in the evening; it wasn't showing as good as that until after Frances had talked to one or two of her particular contacts . . . Why did it matter? Here's a government, a month old, already running into the old familiar troubles of overspending or being unable to control its spending, so soon in its life. Plus the politically highly-charged fact that the National Health Service was going to come in for the chop at a fairly early stage. That sold it instantly to everybody as the most important story of the night.

At the *Guardian* Ian Wright, deputy editor, readily admitted that *The Times* had a very good story. His first edition was carrying on City pages a further analysis of the aftermath of the June money figures. They saw *The Times* at about 10.45. Their man on duty at Westminster, Colin Brown, had confirmed the main points by 11.00 and was on the telephone dictating copy. Confirmed how? 'I think through the Treasury, but I'm not certain', Ian Wright replied. Some of the analysis from City pages was added to Colin Brown's copy for the front page.

Thursday afternoon brought the Chancellor's statement in the House of Commons. As will be noted later, that had been preceded by some sharp words in the Cabinet about the way the news had been fed to *The Times*.

The *Mail*'s lead in later editions had the stark headline 'David Steel drops out', with the secondary heading 'Tired and dejected, he plans long break'. It reported that he was about to take a break from politics – being depressed by the result after a gruelling election campaign and upset that negotiations about the future of the Liberal–SDP Alliance were not running smoothly. No other paper had anything on the subject. Peter Grover, deputy editor, described it as 'the best political scoop we've had for a long time – they're not so easy to come by.'

The *Guardian* knew but carried nothing, because they were not surprised that he wanted a holiday. David Hopkinson said *The Times* 'never got a whiff of it'. He thought the *Mail* had got it right – Steel was 'taking his bat home'.

On Andropov and Kohl, both *The Times* and the *Guardian* ran substantial stories reinterpreting the implications of Chancellor Kohl's talks in Moscow. David Hopkinson said that their foreign desk accepted that there had been a change of view, with the Russian interpretation overtaking the earlier German briefings. The headlines embodied it: 'Soviet mood hardens after Kohl's visit.' And Ian Wright, deputy editor at the *Guardian*:

As so frequently happens in big negotiations involving the

Russians, more comes out subsequently – the day after or the day after that – than on the day. It's always a problem for newspapers. Do you have the courage of your convictions to go back on what many people regard as old news because you think you've got the thing straight? We were very impressed with Jonathan Steele's story. It put Kohl's mission into context. The thing had been a failure . . .

On the Defence White Paper, as with television, there was differing emphasis – *The Times* mainly giving details of the naval aspects, the *Guardian* the financial and the *Mail* the Falklands costs. The *Mirror* gave only a few lines to its report.

Thursday Evening, 7 July

The Chancellor's 'cuts' were the chief topic, beyond any doubt – 14 minutes on Channel Four News, 4¾ on the BBC's Nine o'clock News, and 3¼ minutes on News at Ten. All three were long items by normal standards.

Channel Four News provided not only the most thorough cover but also the most forceful, describing the measures as 'amounting to an emergency budget'. The Channel Four News political correspondent said that ministers 'complained that they'd been "bounced" by the Treasury'. The report in *The Times* 'left them no choice but to accept if they were to avoid a panic in the City'. Mr Lawson was interviewed, replying with a smoothness that amounted to disdain. For example, had he 'bounced' the Cabinet? No: there had been a lively discussion today. Were more draconian cuts coming next year? It was too soon to say. Tight control was essential; and he would call today's prudent savings, not draconian cuts. Was room left for tax cuts? He hoped so. And so on.

The annoyance of Cabinet ministers at being 'bounced' rumbled on through the newspapers on Friday, Saturday and Sunday – though the papers also noted that the City saw the measures as inadequate.

Among comments from those in charge, Paul McKee at Channel Four News thought their 'hard' treatment came because their economics and political correspondents – Sarah Hogg and Eleanor Goodman – both came from senior positions in print journalism. 'We could be harder, spikier, than others.' At the BBC John Anderson had no doubt about the significance of the event 'largely because it was in the aftermath of the election'. There had already been much concern over the future of health, education and other areas, and there was an obligation to tell what was happening.

At News at Ten Sue Tinson thought 3¼ minutes was 'quite long' for her programme. She had reservations also because she thought the measures were 'tinkering with the economy'. She thought that the ITN package was as long as their audience were likely to take in, rather than going off to boil a kettle. Especially after a heavy diet during the election, she believed the item could not be allowed to run too long.

Friday Morning, 8 July

This morning there was a clear dichotomy – all the 'heavies' and the *Mail* leading on Lawson's cuts, while all the populars except the *Mail* led on what the *Mirror*'s headlines called 'Len sacking riddle' (Len of *Coronation Street*). The essentials of the 'cuts' story were the same in all newspapers, though the treatment differed. Under its headlines *The Times* carried six short paragraphs in bold type, summarising the measures and the reaction. A combined report by the political and economics correspondents followed.

The *Guardian,* under its headlines, went at once into its political editor's report, whose second paragraph noted that Mr Lawson's move, 'taken four weeks after a general election campaign fought largely on pledges to maintain spending on matters like the National Health Service', had outraged Labour MPs 'and stunned many Tory backbenchers'. It said also that Cabinet ministers 'received virtually no notice before they met at Downing Street yesterday'.

The *Daily Mail* splashed a report by its political editor, which also said that Mr Lawson's Cabinet colleagues were 'stunned' and that the Chancellor's proposals were circulated only on Wednesday night – 'a classic Treasury tactic which always works, as the rest of Whitehall have no time to organise'.

The *Daily Mirror* carried nothing on its front page but summarised the measures on page 2.

Both Peter Preston at the *Guardian* and Charles Wilson at *The Times* said that there was no real choice about the lead – it had to be the Chancellor's cuts, coming so soon after the election. Peter Preston added:

The spending departments did not expect it; it was literally a twenty-four-hour alert job and there was therefore a good element of surprise . . . To see the surprise, there's Heseltine geting up one day and boasting about the burgeoning nature of the defence budget, and then having to lop off £250m the following day.

Both papers turned many reporters to work on inquiring into the likely consequences.

Friday Evening, 8 July

This Friday was universally agreed to be 'a poor day for news'. Greenham Common led Channel Four News; News at Ten placed that third and the BBC fourth in its order of major items. ITN had tried all day to secure detail of the Cabinet row over the spending cuts but failed; so News at Ten led with a late item from Washington, with the President – open-necked in a summer shirt – instructing his staff to 'tell all' to a congressional inquiry.

The comments on Greenham coverage revealed a common concern about the women's exploitation of television for publicity, combined with a common belief that the nuclear debate remained a high priority. All three channels carried pictures of the carnival atmosphere among the women early in the day, with singing and dancing; and then of two mounted policemen riding up to the women who were starting to lie in the road, though carefully going round them; of the contract workers' buses going through the gates, with a protective police cordon, after the road had been cleared and some women arrested; and of another group of women trying to break through the fence on the far side of the base, leading to more arrests.

Channel Four News, however, included three optimistic interviews – direct to camera – in which women said that the week had been a success even though the 'blockade' had only delayed the arrival of workers at the base each day. Mike Sheppard, programme editor:

> We wanted the women's reaction. All the press coverage was saying it was all over, it had failed. We wanted to see whether the women agreed with that. We found that they didn't, that morale was surprisingly high . . .

And Paul McKee, in charge of Channel Four News:

> We're acutely conscious that the Greenham group are attempting to use us, and television in particular, as a propaganda vehicle. On the other hand it's quite clear that they are an enthusiastic and dedicated group of people . . . If you have that feeling about being used for propaganda purposes, then rather than doing a commentary over the event – which is essentially what happened on other pro- grammes – it is a valuable addition to reflect through their own voices what they are trying to do and what they feel about it . . .

It may be argued that there is a logical flaw in what both Sheppard and McKee say, in that the reports never stated that the Greenham women created the event as political propa- ganda or persuasion. But most viewers probably knew enough of the background to sense that, without having to be told explicitly.

At the BBC John Anderson thought it a legitimate story at the end of the women's week of protest. Two reporters were there, and he saw no problems over it; the nuclear debate was a fascinating issue, but in the news the 'peace women' could now do with a rest. Asked about the concluding sentence of the BBC report – 'as the demonstrators headed home, local resi- dents were hoping for peace and quiet' – Anderson laughed and replied: 'It's absolutely fair.'

At ITN Sue Tinson said that she had begun by being extremely sympathetic to the women, but now found them 'extremely boring'. That night's was a good story with great pictures; but 'they've been at it a long time and the voters of this country showed they weren't terribly sympathetic to the unilateralist approach'. Therefore it was not something at which to keep hammering. The 'mainstream view', she concluded, was important.

CONCLUSION

This chapter began by noting that news priorities converge on days when there is, in the judgement of journalists, plenty of 'hard' news. Priorities diverge on days when such news is scarce. This implies that there is a common perception of what constitutes 'hard' news; and that the 'hardest' news of the week, in almost every news desk's eyes, lay in the cuts in public spending imposed by the Chancellor of the Exchequer. Only the *Mail* and the *Sun* preferred the entertainment value of *Coronation Street* to that.

It could be argued that this simply shows journalists to be sharing a common myopia. If so, it is a failure of vision shared by most citizens, whatever their political persuasions. The Chancellor's action, coming so soon after the general election, mattered to many people and deserved prominent reporting. How else can the electorate in a democracy be adequately informed?

We also noted at the start that comments on the treatment of the Greenham peace women were of interest. Channel Four News can be seen to have taken a pluralist approach and News at Ten a sociocentralist one (both being ITN productions); the BBC's Nine o'clock News gave it a lower priority and treated it in a detached way.

As a sample of content analysis, comparing newspaper and television priorities, see Table 4.1 for 5–6 July. A more extended analysis has been lodged with the Economic and Social Research Council as part of a larger report and with the British Library.

TABLE 4.1 *Priorities: TV and newspapers*

Story	Tuesday evening, 5 July — Place in running order and duration (min, secs)			Wednesday morning, 6 July — Placings and text measurement (page number/col. cm)			
	Channel 4 News	BBC Nine o'clock	ITN News at Ten	Times	Guardian	Mail	Mirror
Andropov warns Kohl on missiles	H	2/2.58	2/2.45	1/22	1/33 +28/8	4/14	—
Petrol prices up and down	H	4/0.53	3/0.30	1/14	1/23	1/18 +3/13	—
Big-spending town halls hit	H	10/3.04	—	1/42	28/33	2/38	2/1
Money supply up	3/1.14	—	—	19/30	1/40 +28/12	17/5	—
Beirut Embassy bombing	1/5.00	—	9/1.53	—	6/23	—	2/13
Thatcher hedges on dole cut	—	—	—	2/12 +4/67	—	9/16	—
Stockton schoolboy kidnapped	—	1/1.34	15/0.34	2/7	28/1	2/15	5/13
Hanging vote next week	H	—	1/1.46	1/15 +2/24	1/15	11/8	—
Foot concedes on peerages	H	—	4/0.31	2/16	1/15	2/18	2/3
Hattersley attacks 'sectarian' Left	—	—	—	1/23 +5/18	2/27	—	2/7
NUM big pay claim	H	5/2.22	6/1.52	2/22	1/2 +2/20	—	—
T & G rejects incomes policy	H	—	7/1.45	2/20	2/18	—	—
Sunday Standard to close	H	—	—	1/3 +2/15	2/25	—	—

TABLE 4.1—*continued*

| Tuesday evening, 5 July Place in running order and duration (min, secs) | | | | Wednesday morning, 6 July Placings and text measurement (page number/col. cm) | | | |
Channel 4 News	BBC Nine o'clock	ITN News at Ten		Times	Guardian	Mail	Mirror
2/6.54	—	11/1.52	Greenham Common/Seneca Falls	—	4/1	—	—
—	—	—	Hong Kong; Mrs T, briefed	—	—	17/3	—
—	18/0.25	—	Hot weather (+ Prince William)	1/pic +32/3	28/14 +pic	2/20	1/4 +pic
—	—	a	Topless sunbathers controversy	32/35	—	10/20	—

H = in headlines, or brief summary
a Pictures in Thursday's News at Ten; also Friday's papers

5 Decisions (2): Television News

From the cross-section of news judgements provided in the previous chapter, it is evident that on some nights there is near-unanimity. A common perception is most likely when there is 'hard' news, particularly in the political and economic fields. It is evident also that within a single organisation – ITN or BBC – there can be diversity of treatment. The pluralism of Channel Four News in reporting the Greenham women's protest week, contrasted with the sociocentralist approach of News at Ten, is one such example.

In this chapter we look more closely at one week's activity in ITN's News at Ten and in the BBC's Nine o'clock News. Judgements are compared on four nights; but to provide a better understanding of the influences at work we have described first ITN's procedures and then BBC television news.

The week of our fieldwork – 31 October to 3 November 1983 – was a busy one. US forces were fighting in the island of Grenada, a Caribbean member of the British Commonwealth, having invaded it the previous week to dislodge a Marxist government. In the Lebanon, Beirut was another battle-ground, with rival groups fighting for control and with US warships standing offshore. At home the Commons debated the arrival of Cruise missiles, expected any day soon, and the Defence Minister gave warning that intruders at the Greenham Common base could be shot. The Old Bailey trial of the mass murderer, Denis Nilsen, was drawing to its end. The government ordered an inquiry into the release of radioactive waste from the Windscale nuclear plant; and, for a change, unemployment figures were down.

We begin with decision-making at ITN.

NEWS AT TEN: THE PROGRAMME EDITOR

The key decision-maker for News at Ten is the programme editor, counterpart of the BBC's 'editor of the day'. The two regulars at that time were highly experienced – Sue Tinson, with nearly 20 years at ITN, having started there as a trainee straight from Hull University; and Jill Chisholm, previously political correspondent of the *Rand Daily Mail* in South Africa but with ITN for the past 12 years, first as a scriptwriter and latterly as a programme editor. They are the journalists who finally decide what goes into the programme and what is dropped; they decide also about emphasis and treatment, and about last-minute changes.

They in turn are influenced by various factors, as noted in Chapters 1 to 3: (a) by whether the audience are familiar with a topic; (b) by guidance and advice from David Nicholas as editor and chief executive of ITN, and from his deputies; (c) by the comments and asides from other participants at the conferences and at the less formal gatherings at 3 p.m. and 7 p.m.; (d) by informal conversations and consultations during the day; (e) by the views and advice, especially on pictures and visuals, of the programme director and the chief sub video; (f) by the programme editor's own background, experience and interests.

The process of informal consultation is continuous throughout the day. Examples will be found in the account below of the programme editor's last hour before going on air on Monday 31 October – hectic, but no more so than normally – and in the sequence of discussions with the political staff, and later with David Chater on the bone marrow transplants. It is a two-way process. Much of the talk is in a form of light-hearted verbal shorthand. The news desks are also much preoccupied with getting the pictures and soundtrack back – with the satellite bookings and with line bookings, all of which are costly.

In a typical 20-second exchange at the 7 p.m. meeting on Tuesday 1 November, Sue Tinson says she will end the Grenada item with Jon Snow from Washington, dropping Nick Gowing from Cuba.

She notes the foreign news editor's expression and asks:

'You're looking miserable! Have I said something?'

Alastair Burnet: 'What does it cost if we drop it?'

Tinson: 'Nothing at all! It's all a Channel Four extravaganza.' [She meant the satellite cost and the length of the item.] And turning to foreign man: 'Sorry love, did you want to say something?' Foreign news editor: 'No, no, nothing at all. I'm just looking miserable. I'll do a dance for you if you like.'

In the end, though, the programme editor must make up his or her mind quickly.

On visuals, the ITN programme editor appears to delegate more to the director and scriptwriter than at the BBC. Thus, at the Tuesday 7 p.m. meeting, the programme editor left it to them to arrange a sketch map of Greenham Common, to illustrate the four lines of perimeter fencing through which protestors would have to penetrate before firearms might be used against them. The programme editors deny, however, that the pictures ever dictate news priorities. Good action pictures are regarded as an excellent bonus, but the final judgement, it is said, must be based on the value of the story – its significance in social or political or human terms, its likely interest to the audience, and only then its pictorial appeal.

On personal background, programme editors at ITN and duty editors at the BBC generally tend to believe that their years of experience as journalists and their years within ITN or the BBC count for more than their own social, educational and family roots. That may be justified, and Don Horobin (then deputy editor, now retired) insisted that staff were appointed for their professional competence not their personal or political views. Common sense nevertheless suggests that nobody with a visibly Marxist or Fascist background is ever likely to get far in ITN – still less in BBC news and current affairs, where security clearance is an absolute requirement (though unacknowledged) in the more responsible appointments, from reporters upwards. And it is impossible to discount entirely the fact that a majority of broadcasting journalists come from fairly prosperous, educated (to sixth form or higher), middle-class backgrounds.

An exception to the tendency to dismiss personal background as an influence is Jill Chisholm's comment that working for the *Rand Daily Mail* in South Africa, with so many restrictions on what could be published, taught her to 'constantly fight against the limits, to get information across'. As to whether women as programme editors may make decisions different from men, Tinson said 'no' and Chisholm 'probably yes', the latter indicating particular areas of difference such as the coverage of medical stories. This tends to confirm that individual attitudes are significant in news decision-making.

DAVID NICHOLAS: THE EDITOR'S GUIDANCE

As to individuals, the editor is influential. David Nicholas – a cheery enthusiast, if sometimes with a furrowed brow – presides over his morning and early evening conferences in a friendly fashion. From time to time during the day he is to be seen around the main newsroom, apparently preferring to talk to people about the day's events or problems there rather than summoning them to his room. Except when prevented by meetings at the IBA or outside negotiations or his own board commitments, he keeps in close touch with the news editors and programme editors. He speaks still with a mildly Welsh intonation, reflecting his Neath and Aberystwyth antecedents; and as a journalist he worked successively for the *Yorkshire Post, Daily Telegraph* and *Observer* before joining ITN in 1960. He became deputy editor in 1963 and editor in 1977 (at the age of 46).

At the morning conference, Nicholas's comments are not for mandatory action. On the Tuesday at 10.30, for example, apart from asking a few questions, he indicated a view on only three items as they came up on the newslists – on the Nilsen mass murder trial, that if it were to end they would have to ask the network for extra time, because of the ten-minute 'backgrounder' already prepared; on the YTV documentary about leukemia around Windscale/Sellafield, that he would be reluctant to see anything tonight, because it should have been done on Sunday; and on Jon Snow's prediction of the Americans having to come to the British Government for help over Grenada, that from what Nicholas had heard of its sources, it could be a cracking story and an obvious lead if it came up all right.

At 5.15 that night, after the arrival of the first Galaxy transport aircraft at Greenham Common and the Commons exchanges on the possibility that demonstrators inside the inner perimeter might be 'shot', Nicholas commented that it was 'lively stuff'. He thought it might make the lead, the more because Jon Snow's report from Washington now looked like being less strong than foreseen in the morning. While happy with the prospects for the first half of the programme, he thought the second half 'weak'. In practice Greenham and the Cruise complex became the lead at 10 p.m., and the second half was drastically curtailed because of extra time given to the three top items.

The 10.30 meeting next morning provided a sequel and the one forceful directive of the week from the editor. While he warmly commended the way the Cruise item had been handled the previous night by David Rose at 5.45 and 10 and by Peter Sissons in the Channel Four News, he noted that as the night wore on there had been an 'elision'. BBC radio and *Newsnight* in their discussions had virtually accepted that shooting was possible at any time. It was as if 'they'll open fire on the sidewalks'. ITN must take care that the CND and others were not allowed to get away with that. He said that John Timpson on *Today* (BBC radio) that morning had handled it properly. The impression must not be given that there was an 'open season' to open fire.

On a quite different topic Wednesday's 5.15 conference provided a significant little debate on news priorities. Graham Forrester, the programme editor, said that as things stood he intended to make shipbuilders the lead – the possible deal in Newcastle between the unions and British Shipbuilders. It was 'back from the brink'. Horobin (deputy editor), sitting on a sofa opposite Forrester, looked as if he has been asked to swallow a slice of sour lemon. Nicholas knitted his brows in doubt. Discussion of the rest of the running order followed, and at the end Nicholas said that the top of the programme was 'the worry'. Forrester, while not backing away from ship-builders, said that if necessary he could still lead with the Queen dedicating the memorial near the Admiralty to her uncle, Lord Mountbatten. Alastair Burnet questioned whether they should be so pessimistic about the shipbuilders' story – 'Why turn it down when it's good news?' He compared it with a week ago when they were heading for a confrontation between the unions and British Shipbuilders. Then it had been a classic British trade union story; now it was looking much better. Forrester said that the shipbuilders had indeed been on the verge of disaster and might now be pulling back from that, so why not lead with it? Nicholas did not dissent.

In the end, shipbuilders stood as the lead in the running order, though just before transmission it had to be switched to second place in a 'hair-raising' last two minutes because of last-minute developments in Newcastle, delaying arrival of the report until the programme was on air.

The influence of David Nicholas is atmospheric and personal rather than by formal directive. Next to nothing is put in writing, unlike the massive minutes and memoranda that flow through the BBC. Because ITN is compact, he can talk to programme editors, reporters and occasionally scriptwriters, and he can look at sensitive items on videotape or monitor in his own room, unobserved.

IN THE NEWSROOM: CONSULTATION, CONVERSATION

Of the presenters, Burnet is the most senior and the most interventionist. He also carries the extra weight of being a director of ITN as well as being a former editor of the *Economist* and then the *Daily Express*. He is careful, nevertheless, not to exert his weight. His style in the general gatherings is frequently puckish and joking rather than stating an explicit opinion. He is most outspoken when Tinson is programme editor because, as he himself says, 'We've known each other for twenty years and done programmes from New York live and from Salisbury or Harare as it's now called, and if we're not allowed to be argumentative with each other, who is?' Between Chisholm and Burnet there is almost as much verbal give and take, for they too have worked a long time together. With other programme editors, he is more restrained.

A typical interchange between Burnet and Tinson ran recurrently on the evening of Monday 31 October. The Commons debate to approve deployment of Cruise missiles took place that afternoon, and both had listened to it on the audio link from Westminster for much of the time between 3.30 and 5 p.m. Just before the 5.15 conference they went into a private huddle outside Nicholas's door, and at the conference there was some bantering repartee. Tinson thought Healey very effective, particularly in pointing to the parallels between Grenada and Cruise: how likely was it that the Americans would consult us over use of Cruise (they had not done so over Grenada)? Whose finger would be on the trigger? She also liked Healey's comparison of the distance between Grenada and Washington with the distance from London to Moscow: if an island 1400 miles away was a threat to the US, she said, so is the UK to the Soviet Union! Burnet was sceptical. Ian Gilmour had 'demolished' Healey, he said. He admitted that the Defence Secretary was poor in opening the debate but his indication of the dates and timetable for Cruise was 'quite good stuff', even if no missiles had yet arrived. They were to be active by the end of the year. Nicholas expressed no view.

The exchange was renewed round Tinson's desk in the newsroom just after 6 and again at 7. This time, however, Tinson set out what she wanted. She had talked to Glyn Mathias at the Commons; Healey was to be given some attention, but Heseltine on deployment would be the lead. That in the end was what happened.

During the fieldwork, both in December 1981 and in November 1983, there were occasional criticisms from the middle ranks. The main one in 1981 was of an 'establishment orientation' at the top of ITN, which tended to be unsympathetic to the reporting of radical movements or views. Similarly in 1983, one critic in the newsroom said that some people at the top believed that 'nothing' from Cuba ought to be carried unless it was derogatory of Castro – a complaint not wholly borne out by the time given on air to Nick Gowing's reports from Havana, which were not anti-Castro. Another, on the style of handling major items, suggested that there was reluctance or even hostility to exploring the more subtle aspects of an event. Neither point, however, was necessarily directed at the topmost tier. The critics were not specific.

THE LAST HOUR – AND AFTER

Shadowing the programme editor for three or four nights is a stimulating experience. How does he or she keep contact with so many uncompleted stories? How decide whether to suggest a change of wording here, a different choice of pictures there, or a last-minute revision of the running order? How keep calm and clear-headed when, with less than half an hour before going on air, three of the five top stories are still not at hand?

Consider the last hour on the evening of Monday 31 October. While keeping open the possibility that she might lead with the miners just saved in a Yorkshire pit (first news having come from YTV at 7), Tinson had decided to put Grenada first and the Commons debate on Cruise second. She also decided to sandwich between the two a report from Gowing in Havana about Cubans missing in Grenada, and to tack on to the Commons a brief report of demonstrations inside and outside the House. That left the miners in fifth place.

Of those five stories, at 9 p.m. only the Havana report and the one on 'demos' at the Commons were available. None of the three major items had come in. (That is usual enough.)

9.00. Sandy Gall (co-presenter with Burnet) tells Sue Tinson that *Panorama's* interview with the Governor-General in Grenada, just transmitted, was quite good. Sir Paul Scoon had given his reasons for calling on the Americans to come to the rescue rather than the British. Was there no chance of getting a bit of it from the BBC? (Gall is sitting opposite Tinson; each desk has its own monitor and earpiece, so that anyone can tune to BBC or ITV channels or incoming news links.)

Answer: No. That's been investigated already. Because the Panorama interview resulted from an initiative by a BBC News crew in Grenada, no clips are being released. (If it had been a *Panorama* crew, probably they would have been.) But ITN's Brent Sadler may still send something before 10.00. Earlier in the day he signalled that he expected to see Sir Paul Scoon, but Sadler has apparently not yet arrived back in Barbados, from which he would have to transmit by satellite.

9.05. Sue Tinson tunes to channel incoming from Westminster. Glyn Mathias is in the ITN studio there, preparing to sum up the Cruise debate.

9.08. Foreign desk says still no sign of Brent Sadler. Maybe he has decided to stay overnight in Grenada. Maybe he's on to a better story. CBS pictures will be coming soon from Barbados, via satellite booking shared by CBS, ITN and some others.

(Later it turned out that Sadler had been detained by US marines for two hours because his taxi driver had a name like one of 'General' Hudson Austen's men; he was released only when a US intelligence officer recognised Sadler, having seen on CBS cable news some of his reports from Beirut. By then it was too late to get back to Barbados.)

9.10. Sue Tinson watches Mathias record from Westminster. If necessary, he will revise his script just before 10 p.m. and go live into the programme. Mathias reports that Heseltine told the House the launchers for Cruise missiles would be arriving at Greenham Common soon and he will make a further statement when the missiles come.

Sue Tinson's marginal comment: 'Glyn is extremely competent to get on with his own thing. He and the scriptwriter, a most senior scriptwriter, had agreed on what to say.'

9.15. Nicholas on phone to Sue Tinson briefly.

9.17. Foreign desk confirm that Snow in Washington is expected by satellite soon after 9.30. Since nothing from Sadler seems likely, Snow may make the lead. Katy, scriptwriter dealing with Grenada and Cuba, says there's less development than expected. The American admission that they bombed a hospital by mistake on the first day appears the strongest element. She is scripting accordingly for Burnet's opening.

Burnet's marginal comment: 'If it was the night Grenada was invaded, I'd do it myself. On a more restful night, let the scriptwriter do it. Yes, in racing parlance it's "training on the course". But I do see the script and change it if necessary.'

9.23. Sue Tinson watches closing headlines on BBC Nine o'clock News. Nothing there to suggest a change of plan; but she had earlier caught a moment of their report on the threat to the Scott-Lithgow shipyard over late completion of a platform for Britoil. That's not in ITN running order. Chief sub doubts whether it's worth while – there have been so many such items before. After brief talk they agree that the Britoil statement sounds nearer finality, so chief sub gets a scriptwriter to ring industrial correspondent, check facts and write brief extra item, to go in second half of programme.

9.28. Sub scripting for introduction to Mathias on Commons debate is bothered that no date is given in ITN's report for arrival of the missiles. The BBC has said that they are expected in about three weeks. Someone suggests ringing the *Guardian*, since they had an 'exclusive' this morning reporting Heseltine's confidential memorandum to the Prime Minister on how to handle public relations when the missiles come (the Tisdall document, as was learned weeks later). Consultation with Glyn is proposed, if he can be reached, but at that point he comes on the phone. A Defence Ministry man, who had stalled when questioned earlier in the day, now confirms that the missiles will come in about three weeks. A little later the sub goes to the studio to insert a new sentence in Burnet's introduction.

9.30. The director is off to the control gallery with the floor manager, vision mixer and assistant. They have been sitting on Sue Tinson's right, in the newsroom. Camera rehearsals will start in a few minutes. One is clutching stills, graphics and slides. Burnet and Gall ought to be in their places in the studio almost at once, though Gall reappears in the news room about ten minutes later to check a point. Sue Tinson is still holding to her running order.

9.35. Sue Tinson is using her desk monitor to check all incoming channels for Jon Snow from Washington. Foreign desk says it ought to be just coming up, via satellite. Snow will probably have to be the first component in the Grenada package, though there is an early Sadler, recorded Sunday and transmitted this morning, on the island returning to normal, the preparations for a return to civil government and US soldiers trying to 'purge' the remaining Marxists.

9.43. Sue Tinson says still no sign of Washington, nor of York-shire miners' report.

9.45. Sue Tinson disappears. It turns out that Snow from Washington has just come in, but because of reequipping in technical area it was not on the monitor. Katy has heard the words, and says it's OK, but hasn't seen the pictures. Sue Tinson wishes to see and hear both. She's gone to vt area.

> Comment afterwards: 'I could still have switched back to Cruise at a very late stage, but there wasn't much to choose between Cruise and Grenada. It was a very good piece from Jon Snow, as usual, and there were new pictures coming in all the time from Barbados. Visually, it made a good top to the programme. It was a strong story, so I stuck to it.'

9.52. Sue Tinson reappears. Yorkshire story still not coming in.

9.54. Latest US casualty figures in Grenada on Reuter from Washington – 18 dead, 1 missing, 86 wounded. Writer takes off for studio, to write these into Burnet's opening script. Also writes a note for the caption generator, so that the figures can be put on screen.

9.58. Yorkshire package begins to come in from YTV (it's checked by sub and cue prepared for transmission as requested at 10.11).

9.58½. Sue Tinson off to control gallery.

10.00. Programme on air.

While on air, two stories were dropped from the running order after the commercial break, because the aggregate length of the Grenada, Cruise and Lebanon packages was greater than at first expected. At 10.16 the first Commons voting figures come by phone, and at 10.20 the sub takes a script for Gall to the studio for the final 'recap' on the main news. A second vote is expected, but unlikely to be in time. At 10.23 an amendment to the Scott-Lithgow story is dictated to Burnet on the 'talk back' (through the button in his ear); he will be coming to that item in a minute or so.

The late arrival of three out of the top five stories is not unusual. On Tuesday night none of the top three stories was in at 9.30 – the last starting to run only at 9.58, but on air at 10.06. On the Wednesday night for Graham Forrester the last few minutes were 'extremely hair-raising'. Because the shipyards report from Newcastle was late, as already noted, at 9.55 he switched the lead to the Cuban wounded being flown home from Grenada, which meant changing the 'bongs' (or headlines) and their pictures as well as the running order.

At 10.35 on Monday, after coming off air, Tinson returned to the newsroom. She was rather dissatisfied with the programme. 'It didn't flow', she said. The lead was not strong enough, and the programme was weighed down by three big packages – Grenada, Cruise and the Lebanon. Most of the audience probably 'didn't give a . . . for the Beirut piece', though it was important and ITN had a duty to give it. There were no light or cheerful items in the programme, and she had had to drop a women's hospital story which would have helped.

Next morning she was more cheerful about the previous night. No, it had not been as good as the ones she'd done in the previous week; but, yes, it hadn't been too bad. She'd agonised for half an hour afterwards about whether she had chosen the right lead. Just after 11 p.m. she'd spoken to Jon Snow at his hotel in Washington, mainly about what he was going to do today, and then she'd felt better.

POLITICAL NEWS JUDGEMENTS: THREE CASES

Intruders may be 'Shot', Tuesday

David Rose covered the story from the House of Commons, and Phil Roman from Greenham Common. Which aspect should come first? The warning from the Defence Secretary, the reaction in the Commons, the reaction of the women at Greenham and CND, or the fact of the first Galaxy landing with equipment for the missiles?

ITN's lead-in started with the warning, then mentioned Monsignor Bruce Kent's CND counter-warning that troops who cooperated in the arrival of the missiles could be considered 'war criminals' if the missiles were ever fired, and next reported the arrival of the first Galaxy (with pictures of the huge aircraft taxiing up the runway). David Rose in his first sentence combined both the minister's warning and the shock among MPs – but the core of his report was an explanation of the four protective belts through which a protester must penetrate before he or she risked being shot. The BBC began with the Galaxy landing, then the arrest of demonstrators, and next Mr Heseltine's warning. It, too, went on to explain the four layers of defence – with a filmed report which must have been prepared before Mr Heseltine replied to questions in the House. It also included Mgr Bruce Kent. David Rose wrote and recorded three versions of his report: a short one for the 5.45 bulletin, a longer one for News at Ten designed to go with a diagram showing the four protective lines, and finally an intermediate revision when the second version was found to be too long. The BBC and ITN reports both quoted the condemnation by Mr John Silkin, Shadow Defence Secretary, of Mr Heseltine's warning, as well as Mr Heseltine's own comment that in the dark it might be difficult for a soldier to distinguish between a peace protestor and a terrorist.

For those who subscribe to Tony Benn's view (*Guardian*, 12 December 1983) that both BBC and ITN bulletins 'are little more than a rehash of the same right-wing attitudes', particularly in their reporting of nuclear controversies, the effort of reporters to provide a fair and accurate account of proceedings in the Commons may appear irrelevant. For others who wish to hear a summary of the arguments and then make up their own minds, such reporting is invaluable. It is again true that the government stand and official briefings received more air time than the Opposition or the CND, but Bruce Kent received prominence from both channels.

Phil Roman returned from Greenham Common to ITN House about 7.30, to recut his report. He had been at Greenham for four days and three nights, with little sleep. At first, he said, he had had difficulty in interviewing the women because he was wearing standard ITN blue protective clothing, and with his short hair he had been mistaken for a policeman. Latterly he had been accepted. Even so, it was not easy to find women who were both willing to be interviewed – many preferred not to be – and 'ones who would not portray the Greenham women, as they did not wish to be portrayed, as fanatics'. He had found the reaction to Heseltine less strong than the reaction to the first Galaxy arriving. Heseltine's warning had come as no great surprise to those with whom he had talked, whereas some had been distressed by the arrival of the Galaxy.

Had he received any advice or direction about coverage? 'None: I was left to my own devices.'

Americans in Grenada, Wednesday

Reporters working in a turbulent location such as Grenada have a hard time deciding whose information to accept. Programme editors back at base also have a hard time deciding, often with only minutes to go, whether to accept a report intact or edit it or drop it. There was, in this week, a perceptible difference of approach between the BBC's Brian Barron and ITN's Brent Sadler; and it was most marked on Wednesday.

Barron early in the week seemed readier than Sadler to accept American information uncritically. On Monday he said that the American commanders were sensibly keeping most of their troops out of the capital, St George's, though the pictures with his report showed soldiers searching in the streets. On Tuesday he showed American paratroops rounding up Cubans, frisking them and tying their hands behind their backs – though he added that the men said they had never been armed, and he also interviewed a British engineer who said he had never seen any of the Cuban workers carrying arms. On these two days Sadler was careful to attribute claims to the American forces and to say that, while many Grenadians seemed thankful for the invasion, it was impossible to guess what everyone was thinking. He also noted that 'some leftists' thought the invasion was a curtain-raiser for intervention elsewhere in the Caribbean.

On Wednesday Barron began his report with the departure of the Cuban wounded:

> They left in defeat from the airport they had struggled for two years to complete. Some were carried, some walked or limped away from their most humiliating international reverse in a decade . . . As the vanquished left without ceremony,

American paratroops too were gathering for a massive airlift back to Fort Bragg, 'mission accomplished' . . .

The tone on ITN was in marked contrast, with a simple statement that the wounded were on their way home, while some 600 Cubans still remained as prisoners of the Americans in Grenada. Barron's use of 'humiliating' was evocative – indeed possibly offensive to some of his audience, since wounded men may deserve sympathy and it was doubtful whether many of them had even been armed. It is perhaps a point in Barron's defence, however, that the colonel in charge of the Cuban part-time soldiers in Grenada was reduced to the rank of private on his return home.

While Sadler was reporting the gradual return to normal life for civilians, Brian Barron that Wednesday sent a second report with a rather different tone. It was used later in the BBC's bulletin. It said that while generally the American troops had 'behaved impeccably', Barron had received 'a detailed and authenticated report' of the rough treatment and intimidation of some top-level political prisoners. They included the Deputy Prime Minister, his wife, and at least three other ministers. 'With hands lashed behind their backs, feet splayed, they were propped against a wall only supported by their heads, and a US NCO brandished a knife in their faces.' Their whereabouts was now unknown, Barron said.

Bone Marrow: a Tragic Story, Thursday

This brought the most immediate public response of the week, with 20 calls to ITN while the programme was on air. The reporter, David Chater, had started work on it the previous day – and in the context of the government's economies in the NHS it had a political as well as a human dimension. As broadcast in the News at Ten it came after two other NHS items, one in the Commons and the other the closing of the South London Hospital for Women. The bone marrow report began with the government's decision to provide an extra £650 000 over 14 months for transplants and went on to Chater's interview with the parents of a six-year-old boy who had not been selected for treatment and was bound to die. The boy himself was seen playing in front of his parents as they talked.

On Wednesday David Chater had talked to the specialist at Westminster Hospital in charge of bone marrow transplants. He had a waiting list of 43 – one year's work. Although in Britain more operations of this type were carried out than anywhere else in the world, the professor said, six patients had to be turned away for every one accepted. It was partly a matter of resources and partly of how far the illness had gone. Chater felt that the item would have greater effect if a disappointed patient could be seen. Westminster Hospital telephoned to three on their list, but they preferred not to be interviewed; the fourth, Mr and Mrs Twiggar, agreed to be.

Chater travelled to Yorkshire at 7 next morning (Thursday), met a film crew there, recorded the interview between 10.30 and 12.00, and then returned to London. The parents said that for them the failure to obtain treatment had been 'devastating'; now they could only watch Adrian gradually go blind and die, which might take six years. After returning to London, Chater went to the DHSS, by previous arrangement, to interview the Health Minister Kenneth Clarke about the South London Women's Hospital, but while there he added some questions about bone marrow transplants. Eventually News at Ten dropped the South London section of the interview but used part of the bone marrow exchange. In it Kenneth Clarke said that no death is ever acceptable, that doctors had difficult judgements to make about which patients to give priority to, that the DHSS had to direct money to the areas of greatest need and that 'one must not be misled by overdramatic campaigns or by overenthusiastic consultants'.

Jill Chisholm viewed the item with Chater in a vt cubicle between 9.28 and 9.35, and subjected him to a rigorous cross-examination. Was it absolutely certain that the child could not now be saved? How far was the year's delay responsible? How much had the mother been told, and when? Was it completely clear to the minister that they were talking about a particular case, involving a child? Were they not making him appear callous? Were they misrepresenting him in any way? David Chater said that the minister knew they were talking about a child. The question had been put to him three times, and the extract was his most concise answer. It began with the reply that 'no death is ever acceptable'. Chisholm asked for one change in Chater's commentary, which he then had to record. The vt editor commented: 'That was nothing – she's a tigress.' The item was ready at 9.50.

UNANIMITY OR NOT? A STRAW POLL

On the Wednesday a form headed 'News values' was distributed to people at the 3 p.m. meeting and at the 5.15 conference. They were asked to reply anonymously – with 'no collusion' – on their personal estimate of news values the previous night. They were to award points from 0 to 10, both for the overall value of an item and for aspects within it. Respondents were asked to assume, for the purposes of the exercise, that pictures of equal value were available on each item. About 20 forms were distributed; 12 came back. Nicholas agreed that while other replies might be anonymous his need not. The results are shown in Table 5.1.

The results show, overall, a high level of unanimity among the ITN staff – though with some wide variations of judgement about individual items. Perhaps not surprisingly, the returns also show general agreement with the decisions taken by the programme editor. The Armitage report on social security pay is the exception: when including it in the questionnaire, I knew it had not been carried by ITN but did not realise that it was second in the BBC's running order. I had simply read the reports in the *Guardian* and *The Times* that morning. In fact, the item had never been offered to the programme editor: the copy appears to have been lost or mislaid on the news desk, most unusually. Andrew's new girlfriend also was not offered – it was a *Sun* and *Daily Express* feature.

Nicholas also provided a running commentary as he filled up the form. Cruise: 'freshness, an outstanding story'. He also wrote in an extra sub-item 'Mgr Kent's warning of war crimes' and gave it nine points. On social security, he said it was a bad omission. 'I look to News at Ten to mop up everything, even if in half a phrase.' On the kidney failure story (not to be confused with Thursday's bone marrow report), he said it was 'an ideal top of part two'. He greatly liked the headline in the 'bongs', on Sicily having better facilities than Britain. Grenada

TABLE 5.1　*Straw poll: the results*

	Total score	Highest	Lowest	Nicholas
Cruise				
Overall	*106*	10	7	10
Troops reinforce Greenham	62	8	1	5
Galaxy arrives	85	10	3	8
Intruders could be shot	100	10	6	10
Social Security				
Armitage committee recommends £11 a week extra	57	8	0	8
Kidney Failure				
Overall	77	8	5	8
Doctors say they don't tell patients	65	7	2	5
Doctors say resources inadequate	69	8	4	8
Goverment promises Kidney Appeal in January	48	8	1	8
Grenada				
Overall	87	10	4	9
Lady Young says UK will train police	56	10	0	9
US navy shows strength off Cuba	80	10	5	9
Scoon to have commonwealth advisers	58	10	1	8
US admits many casualties from 'friendly fire'	72	10	2	10
Prince Andrew				
Meets new girlfriend at picture gallery	*41*	8	0	8

he thought was rightly placed as the second lead, but he would
have begun with the Americans admitting that many of their
casualties were from 'friendly fire'. The point had been well
developed on Channel Four News. As for Andrew, if ITN had
known about his new girlfriend that would have done well as
the 'tailpiece'.

THE BBC'S NINE O'CLOCK NEWS: DECISION-MAKERS

For reasons already outlined in Chapters 2 and 3, the 'editors of the day' at the BBC tend mostly to be left to themselves to decide what will go into their programmes. While Peter Woon was editor, television news (1980 to early 1985, when he was promoted to the senior BBC post in the United States), he delegated responsibility. He was heavily committed to management and other meetings, taking up much of his time on midweek mornings, and he believed in letting his programme editors get on with their jobs with minimum interference. His deputy, Robin Walsh, was to be seen in the newsroom more frequently than Woon. Previously an assistant editor and an 'editor of the day' on the Nine o'clock News, he was readily available for consultation.

Woon's successor, Ron Neil, took over just as this book was being completed. Neil had been in charge of *Breakfast Time* during its first two years – a programme that was initially a triumphant success for the BBC, beating the rival TV-am in audience figures largely because of its friendly and informal manner and because it offered a greatly superior news service and weather forecasting. It had behind it the resources of BBC television news, with the most extensive network in Britain, adequate staff and strong regional representation. That *Breakfast Time* produced the most thorough and dramatic account of the Brighton bombing in October 1984, with pictures of Mr Tebbit being dug out of the hotel rubble and an interview with the Prime Minister recorded at 4 a.m., was no coincidence; TV-am had no live pictures and no interviews from Brighton.

For the last nine months before becoming editor, Neil was responsible for the new format *Six O'clock News*. With a full half hour available to it, with computerised graphics that were the envy of other BBC news programmes and with a fresh team it quickly proved to be more serious and informative than *Sixty Minutes*, which had been killed off to make way for it. Apart from its ponderous opening titles, Six O'clock News was well received. With two such successes behind him, Neil was one of the obvious candidates for the post of editor, television news.

Both Woon and Neil – and the deputy, Robin Walsh – had backgrounds in print journalism. Woon was a Bristol man who started work with the *Bristol Evening Post,* moving later to Fleet Street (air correspondent of the *Express*) and to the BBC in 1961. Neil was a Glaswegian, joining the Scottish office of the *Express* at 18 and staying with that paper for eight years;

from the *Express* in Aberdeen he moved to the BBC there as a reporter, and then to *Nationwide* in London in 1969. He was the first deputy editor of *Newsnight* when it started in 1981. As already noted, he is a more active interventionist than Woon and likely to change the style of BBC television editing.

Robin Walsh, continuing as deputy and hitherto more readily available to the 'editors of the day', is a Northern Irishman who started work with the *Belfast Telegraph*. Later he moved to Ulster Television as news editor, was then the BBC's news editor in Northern Ireland from 1974 and in 1981 came to the Nine o'clock News in London. Among the senior assistant editors, John Anderson has a similar Belfast background, though he graduated at Cambridge before joining the *Belfast Newsletter*; Rick Thompson went straight from Oxford to the BBC as a news trainee.

Also influential in decision-making are the principal presenters – John Humphrys and Sue Lawley in 1983–4; Humphrys and Julia Somerville in 1985 (Lawley having moved to Six o'clock News). Humphrys's long experience as a foreign correspondent, from Watergate to the birth of Zimbabwe, gives him added authority and he rewrites scripts more often than the other presenters. And at Westminster, though frequently visiting the Television Centre, is the BBC's political editor, John Cole. His background also is in print journalism and in Northern Ireland; for six years he was news editor of the *Guardian*, for six its deputy editor and for six more (1975–81) deputy editor of the *Observer*. His view on the treatment of political events carries weight.

BBC CONFERENCES AND CONSEQUENCES

As a sample of conference talk and its consequences, consider the days of our fieldwork. On Monday 31 October, Walsh was in charge at the 9.30 meeting. Having seen the preliminary news lists, he suggested that the Commons debate on the arrival of Cruise missiles looked the strongest prospect. He noted that an interview had been arranged with the Defence Secretary, Mr Heseltine, and said jokingly to John Anderson 'You will take that, won't you John?' He also noted that that morning's *Daily Telegraph* carried a report suggesting that Mr

Cecil Parkinson, who had resigned office only a month earlier, might be brought back to the Cabinet if there was a mid-term reshuffle. He asked that that be pursued. (The BBC's political staff, however, were unable to secure any confirmation reliable enough to justify a report; and although Mrs Thatcher was known to think well of Mr Parkinson, mid-term was still a long way off.)

At John Anderson's 3.05 informal meeting with his team, the priorities within the Cruise complex were discussed further – whether to lead with the Commons debate or a report from Greenham Common or the Heseltine interview – but both then and at the 3.50 meeting in Woon's office, Cruise was still seen as a stronger story than Grenada. Woon himself expressed no preference. At Anderson's 6 p.m. meeting in the newsroom he stated his intentions, much as Sue Tinson did (see above) at the 7 p.m. gathering at ITN. He wanted a lengthy introduction drawing the main points together, then pictures of the Greenham women – either the demonstration outside Parliament or at Greenham, depending which was best – then the main report on the Commons debate.

That was what happened. The long introduction by Humphrys included pictures of the demonstrators outside the House of Commons; Mr Heseltine's statement that no missiles had yet arrived, though the launchers were expected in the next few days; Mr Healey's demand for a British veto on firing of the missiles, especially after the way that the US had 'brushed aside' British advice on Grenada, and Mr Heseltine's rejection of that demand. The main Commons report relied on voice recordings from the House, with still pictures of the speakers superimposed on a view of Westminster from across the river. It included the Defence Minister's admission that the invasion of Grenada had been a 'damaging disagreement' with the US. The text is quoted below.

Next morning at 9.30 Woon was again taken up with management meetings. At 3.50 he offered a number of comments. On the Armitage report to the DHSS recommending increased social security payments – the story that ITN's news desk somehow lost – Woon thought it important and asked whether European comparisons were possible. (Later they proved too difficult to state concisely.) On Grenada, he was concerned that ITN was carrying reports from

Cuba while the BBC had none: the Cuban dimension mattered. His third comment was on the story of an attack in prison on the 'Yorkshire Ripper', Sutcliffe, which ITN had carried the previous night while BBC news had not. He suggested that interest in the court case against the attacker had been underestimated. (A brief report was included in the Nine o'clock News that night, though News at Ten dropped it.)

On Wednesday at 3.50 he questioned the way Brian Barron was covering the events in Grenada. Barron tended to say that the only resistance to the American forces was from the Cubans. Was this true? The foreign editor thought that Barron was saying rather more than that; but Woon asked for a check. Barron's report that night on the 'humiliation' of the departing Cubans contained the controversial phrasing mentioned above; but from the next day onwards there appeared to be more vigilance over his phrasing and his 'sourcing' of his information.

The following day at 3.50 Woon asked about the unemployment figures, which were slightly down. Was it a turnround? Would it be in the headlines? The advice from his staff was 'no' on both points. Woon persisted: was it not possible at least to say 'Our industrial correspondent says it is a turnround'? The advice was still 'no': the item stayed at sixth place in the bulletin, though ITN at 10 placed it fourth.

THE EDITOR OF THE DAY, 31 OCTOBER

From early morning Anderson expected a 'heavy' day. The defence debate was bound to need assessment. Events continued in Grenada. Talks were to open in Geneva between the warring factions from the Lebanon, though they might not go far on their first day. A long piece from Michael Buerk (3 min 20 secs) previewing the South African referendum had been waiting for some days and must go that night because the voting was next day. The Windscale story – Yorkshire Television's documentary on radioactive waste – was running, though Anderson had reservations about it because it was being given publicity before anyone had seen it. A press conference was due that morning.

Between 10.15 and 11 Anderson took a number of telephone

calls, including one from Keith Graves in Geneva and one from the science correspondent, James Wilkinson, who was working on a story that might or might not be ready that night. On Geneva the foreign editor mentioned that, if the material was not strong, it would be cheaper to take pictures from Eurovision (a shared service among European networks) rather than book a circuit even though Graves had his own crew there. Through Eurovision pictures were coming also from Grenada, from the Argentine election and from the Turkish earthquake.

In the early afternoon the foreign desk told Anderson that the Americans had admitted to bombing a mental hospital in Grenada by mistake and that Barron was expected to have an interview with the Governor of Grenada, Sir Paul Scoon. The home desk said that John Cole would be covering the Cruise debate, that the Windscale story seemed promising, but that a report from Wales about deaths in a Merthyr hospital now looked less strong. At 3.05 and 3.50, as noted above, Anderson held to his preference for Cruise over Grenada.

Soon after 5 he discussed headlines with John Humphrys. They went over them again at 6.45 with the director. After that he talked to Christopher Wain, who had recorded the interview with the Defence Secretary; Anderson was still trying to secure an orderly presentation of all the elements in the Cruise story. He had already at 6 given directions on how he wanted the lead prepared. At 7 he gave exact timings for each item in the programme to the 'shift leader', who must make sure that all scripts are ready and of the right length. Soon after that he was told that there was a new story about the Scott-Lithgow shipyard on the Clyde being at risk, and later he saw a report by Martin Adeney (industrial editor) on that. It meant adjustments to the running order.

Barron's interview with Sir Paul Scoon came late, by satellite from Barbados, after the tape had been flown there from Grenada. It was in the form of 'rushes', or unedited tape, requiring fast work by the video and sound engineers to have it ready to run as third item in the programme. (The envious comment on that interview by Sandy Gall at ITN has been noted above.) At 8.50 Anderson asked the 'presentation' coordinator for BBC1 whether he could have an extra minute for the bulletin, but that night it was difficult; he was anyway going to have to drop at least five items that had been prepared. At 9 the programme was on air.

Afterwards, much like Sue Tinson at ITN that night, Anderson was less than satisfied with the programme. He was not too distressed about the items he had had to drop, apart from the casualty figures from the Turkish earthquake (1200 now believed dead). The grouping of items towards the end had been awkward, because of the long report on the South African referendum. Looking back he thought it would have been more effective to have closed the programme with that, long though it was, rather than with a short item – which had been attractive because it was 'good' news about industrial achievement.

His real disappointment was that the Commons debate, though 'enormously significant' had 'just seemed to fade'. He thought Cole had handled it well, with balance between the sides on issues such as 'dual key', but after the opening speeches there had been little more. He still judged it to have been stronger than Grenada. But, he said, 'perhaps there is too much mystique about leads'. It counted for more to feed people with the information that was important to them, whatever the position in the running order. People could make their own choice about what mattered to them, as he was sure they did.

CRUISE: THE CHOICE OF WORDS

Both BBC news and ITN were striving to report accurately and without bias. Both are, inevitably, to some extent prisoners of their own preconceptions and past coverage. But since they are frequently criticised by right and left on grounds of prejudice in favour of the other side, it is worth examining the headlines and opening words of each on the Cruise complex of 31 October.

BBC Nine o'clock. John Humphrys to camera (with picture of Cruise missile behind and caption 'Countdown to Cruise').

> Countdown to Cruise: the missiles are coming to Britain in three weeks, and Mr Heseltine speaks of a categorical agreement with the Americans.

[After other headlines] Good evening. MPs were told today that Cruise missiles have not yet arrived in Britain, and it's believed that they are not likely to be here for another three weeks. And when they come, said the Defence Secretary Mr Heseltine, the Americans won't be able to fire them unless Britain agrees. Mr Heseltine said that the launchers for the weapons will be here shortly. He promised there would be a full statement to MPs when the missiles themselves were on British soil.

As the Commons debate on Cruise goes on tonight [picture of torch-carrying crowds in Trafalgar Square] there's a demonstration in London organised by CND. Earlier women outside Greenham Common where the missiles will be based had said [sound of singing in background] they were prepared to 'put their bodies between the missiles and the people we love' to stop them coming here.

In the debate Denis Healey, the shadow Foreign Secretary, had said that the deployment of Cruise was the most important decision that Parliament would be asked to approve under this government. And he raised the question of whose finger would be on the trigger. He said that there was an unanswerable case for Britain to have a veto over the firing of Cruise.

[Into Healey's voice, with still picture] Last week the United States brushed the United Kingdom aside when the threat was vague and distant . . .

ITN News at Ten. Alastair Burnet after the second 'bong' (over picture of Cruise missile).

Mr Heseltine says Cruise must come, though it's not here yet. (And after fourth 'bong', into Grenada report.)

[At end of Grenada item] . . . What's happened in Grenada has overshadowed the Commons debate on Cruise and Pershing missiles today. The Cruise missiles are expected at Greenham probably in about three weeks' time. They're voting on that in the Commons now.

The Defence Secretary, Mr Heseltine, said the invasion of Grenada was 'a sincere and damaging disagreement between two close allies'. But he said that in the last resort the

Western alliance was faced with a common threat. The government would still go ahead with the deployment of American missiles, even without any dual key control.

[Glyn Mathias, to camera from Westminster studio] Mr Heseltine didn't tell the Commons when the first missiles would be arriving . . .

It may be argued that the BBC version gives undue credence to the view that 'the Americans won't be able to fire them [the missiles] unless Britain agrees'. It clearly says, however, that this is Mr Heseltine's case and it goes on to Mr Healey's contesting of it. It might also be argued that both versions add authority to the government's insistence that the missiles will come to Britain. But the government was here making its determination plain, and as the government it was in a position to make sure that its decision was carried into action. No report of the event could escape that fact.

Conversely, it may be argued that ITN's version makes too much of the damage done by disagreement over Grenada. Yet the words about a 'damaging disagreement' were the Defence Secretary's, and they were relevant to the tension that could be repeated in a European crisis.

Altogether it is hard to see how either BBC or ITN could have been more careful or more detached in their reporting.

CONCLUSIONS

News values. The judgements reported above are consistent with the seven categories of news values stated midway through Chapter 1 – starting with the social, economic, political and human significance that an event is believed to have; going on to the dramatic elements and action within it, then to the elements of surprise, the personalities and so on. Again, 'significance' is not precisely defined. Programme editors appear to share something close to a common view of what is significant for their audiences, and the straw poll at ITN bears this out.

Their unstated assumption – unstated because journalists generally regard such assumptions as self-evident – is that events such as the American invasion of Grenada mark a development in US international policy (armed intervention in an independent country because its government is unfriendly) that is potentially threatening to world peace. Equally, on any scale of human values the accidental bombing of a mental hospital and killing of some 50 people is an event to be recorded. On a possibly lower scale of significance, but relevant to the prosperity of British shipyard workers and others, the Newcastle negotiations were deemed worth prominence in both BBC and ITN main evening bulletins. As usual, it can be argued that the settlement of a dispute was 'bad' news rather than 'good' news because the trade unions did not win everything that they wanted – or because a revolutionary confrontation had been avoided. Whether bad or good, however, the programme editor was surely justified in seeing the news as significant.

Sociocentralism and pluralism. As noted in the previous chapter, within a single organisation such as BBC television news and ITN, programmes or items within programmes can be sociocentralist or pluralist. The overall effect of the BBC's Nine o'clock News and ITN's News at Ten is most probably to buttress the established order, though that cannot be proved with any precision. Because journalists are working within their concept of the existing knowledge and interests of their audience – knowledge and interests which, incidentally, their own past programmes have helped to shape – they inevitably tend to reinforce the status quo. But sociocentralism is not the same as consensus or conformity. It implies a concern with maintaining the continuity and harmony of the established society – and so is against those who want sudden or violent change – but within that broad 'centralism' there is room for reporting argument, debate, minority views and reform. The assumptions in both newsrooms that they must report the reactions of CND and of the Greenham women to the imminent arrival of Cruise is one example, just as, in the previous chapter, Channel Four News adopted a pluralist approach to the Greenham week of protest and gave the women the opportunity to speak for themselves. That is easier, of course, in a long bulletin or in a current affairs programme.

Accuracy and fairness. Both Nicholas and Woon – and the programme editors of BBC and ITN – were seen to be intent on securing accuracy and fair reporting.

Competitive stimulus. The monitoring by each of the other's output is a stimulus to both. It is a reminder to each of topics and perspectives that may have been neglected. It is more likely, in the long run, to broaden than to narrow the journalists' agenda – though the introduction of new topics and new dimensions is more readily achieved through the 'heavy' newspapers or through feature programmes (as over the Windscale pollution) than through compressed news bulletins.

A 'refracted' image? Schlesinger, as quoted earlier, suggests that the image of events presented by television news is 'refracted' and not a mirror of reality. There is no way of proving or disproving that. Events are so numerous and varied that any selection may distort, but without selection there can be no reporting. What emerges from this case study is that television news desks, reporters, cameramen and programme editors are trying to present as complete and relevant an account as limited time and limited resources will permit.

NEWS LISTS AND NEWS PRIORITIES, TELEVISION

Table 5.2 is an analysis of the number of items included in the noon news list (or 'prospects' list) for ITN's News at Ten on

TABLE 5.2 *News lists*

	Tuesday	Wednesday	Thursday
Home items listed	13	10	13
Number used	7	7	6
Foreign items listed	7	8	8
Number used	5[a]	6	8
Total items in bulletin (not including break)	13	26	16

[a] Merged into three items on air.

NB: From the fact that an item was listed, it does not follow that the outcome was predictable – often the outcome was entirely uncertain, whether it was the Nilsen jury retiring or the meeting of British Shipbuilders with their unions. In the foreign lists, the high correlation of numbers listed and numbers used is partly because the list reflects locations abroad where ITN staff are at work, and whenever possible they will send reports every evening.

three days, together with the number of home and foreign items ultimately broadcast.

As can be seen from Table 5.3, the programme running order for News at Ten as planned at 7.30 or 8 p.m. may have to be altered when the programme goes on air – often to a greater extent than in the example shown, for Monday, 31 October.

To illustrate the comparative priorities at the BBC's Nine o'clock News, its running orders and durations (in minutes and seconds) are also shown.

TABLE 5.3 *Programme running order, News at Ten, Monday, 31 October*

As planned (pre-transmission)	Actual–final place and duration	BBC 9 o'clock place and duration
1. GRENADA: hospital bombed; US casualties; plus Washington roundup	1/4.27	3/2.45
2. CUBA: men missing in Grenada	2/1.38	—
3. CRUISE: Commons debate	3/3.08	1+2/3.43
4. DEMO: outside Commons, and inside	4/0.28	1+2/(0.18)
5. MINERS: six saved in Yorks.	5/1.35	4/1.22
6. SHADOW CABINET: Kinnock's choice	6/2.02	8/0.38
7. NILSEN trial near end	Dropped	7/1.24
8. SHEFFIELD MURDERS: police warning	7/1.04	—
(9. Commercial break)	—	—
10. LEBANON: Geneva talks, Beirut fighting	9/3.13	10/1.34
11. ARGENTINA: election result	10/2.04	9/3.28
12. TURKEY: 1200 dead in earthquake	11/0.21	—
13. TOYS: Corgi liquidates plus Scott-Lithgow at risk	12/0.10 13/0.12	6/0.20
14. RIPPER: trial of prison attacker	14/1.48	—
15. HOSPITAL: Merthyr deaths inquiry	Dropped	—
16. WALKER: fuel-saving campaign	17/0.52	—
17. SOCCER results	15/0.10	12/0.11
18. TAILPIECE: bolting horse	Dropped	—
Commons vote (late extra)	16/0.20	—
Windscale	—	5/3.00
South African referendum, Wedny.	—	11/3.50
Rolls-Royce seek aid for engine	—	13/1.20

6 Decisions (3): the *Mail* and *Mirror*

CHART 6.1 *Newspaper sales, 1948–84*

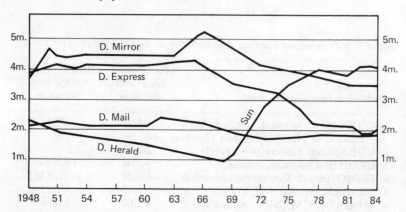

The sales graph shown in Chart 6.1 tells the story of popular newspaper competition. For more than 25 years the *Daily Mirror* was unchallenged 'top of the pops', selling over four million copies daily. After Rupert Murdoch bought the *Sun* in 1969, his war of attrition – with page 3 nudes as a primary weapon – hit both the *Mirror* and the *Express* hard. Because of changes of management and editorial control, both had already become uncertain of their roles. For most of its peak years, the *Mirror* was under the editorial direction of Hugh Cudlipp (now Lord Cudlipp), an exuberant risk-taker and author of *Publish and be Damned* in 1968; he moved up to be group chairman after the removal of Cecil King (see Chapter 2). After that, the paper never again seemed as sure of itself. At the *Express* group, Lord Beaverbrook had died in 1964; and in 1977, after years of declining fortunes, his son sold out to the Trafalgar House conglomerate.

116

The *Mirror* always competed at the most popular end of the market, though always since 1945 with political loyalty to Labour and with a social consciousness which restrained its competitive tactics. The *Mail*, by contrast, never aimed at such a mass circulation. It placed itself in the middle ground, half way towards the 'heavies', aiming at the Conservative middle and lower-middle classes. Having been in a long gradual decline in the 1960s, it began to recover in the 1970s after its merger with the *Daily Sketch* and the appointment of David English as editor.

For both *Mail* and *Mirror* the editorial implications of these changes will be seen, in part, in this chapter. The *Mirror*'s uncertainty of purpose continued in 1984–5, not altogether helped by the turbulent transfer of ownership to Robert Maxwell in the summer of 1984. The period of our main field-work, however, was some months earlier – in mid-January 1984. The *Mail* remained fairly steadily on course, with a small improvement in sales and no marked changes of character.

As noted at the beginning of this book, neither the *Sun* nor the *Express* would allow us to observe its newsroom at work. Consequently the most uninhibited and extreme forms of popular journalism are not covered here. Competitively, however, both the *Mail* and the *Mirror* regard themselves as vigorous and tough. They provide at least some insight into editorial decisions among popular newspapers.

THE MAIL: DAVID ENGLISH IN ACTION

The editor of the *Daily Mail* is a dominant leader. 'Tune in to David – you pick it up that way' was the concise reply of one senior *Mail* man to my questions about news values. And another: 'He's on the back bench, talking all the time. You learn what he's after, and you learn a lot quickly. If you don't, you'll hear about it. It's his paper, and his instincts count.' To a young reporter who has done something that earns the editor's approval, a conversation with English in the newsroom is an accolade – and some of the higher executives will come round discreetly afterwards to find out what he has said. They want to keep in touch, too.

English, interviewed in the spring of 1984, said that he had consciously put into practice his belief that to survive and succeed a newspaper must have a personality, and that that personality 'stems from the editor and the people around him'. In setting out to appeal to middle-class Conservatives, the *Mail* reflects English's own Bournemouth background (though he claims that it also has many readers with a Labour or Alliance outlook). His four years in the United States, as Washington correspondent and then in New York for the *Express,* gave him a taste and liking for the American style of free enterprise. He would cheer if British papers were to treat the Press Council with the robust disdain that major American newspapers show to anyone who tries to probe into their affairs. (There should be no regulatory body, he said, though 'because the Press Council is there, to some extent one's got to cooperate with it'.)

For more than half a century the *Mail*'s journalism has been politically partisan. English, when interviewed, approved of that within limits. 'Being human beings', he said, 'we start from a subjective point of view in almost everything we do.' Without its political personality, he argued, the paper would be 'immensely boring' and would not sell. But professional standards and commercial commonsense must also apply. 'Professional standards say that you must not deliberately distort or invent or twist events to give a completely unfair or untruthful version.' Commercial common sense meant that you must not be so partisan as to provoke a hostile reaction from a significant number of readers.

That comment must be weighed against two or three notorious occasions when a hostile reaction was provoked – particularly its revelation in 1977, false as it turned out, of a 'slush fund' supposedly operated by British Leyland to secure contracts corruptly. That led to a costly libel action. It had a political element, since BL was then largely sustained by subsidies from the Labour government. English acknowledged afterwards that the *Mail* had not taken sufficient care in verifying the facts. As an aside, during an interview, English said that the biggest reaction from readers came after publication of a front-page picture of Lord George Brown (former Labour Cabinet minister) stumbling as he left the House of Lords one evening: that brought 'hundreds and hundreds' of letters from readers who thought it was unfair.

English 'reflects the readers' interests', one of his deputies said. He is alert to their hopes and fears, their social values and their prejudices. His power as editor is built on his grasp of what 'a struggling middle class or lower middle class want' – and from that grasp derives the *Mail*'s belief in private education, private housing and freedom from union pressure.

In 1981, on Mrs Thatcher's recommendation, a knighthood was conferred on David English.

He was away on his annual skiing holiday during the period of our fieldwork in January 1984. I therefore went back for a night in March, to watch English in action. The 5 p.m. conference was low key compared with others where I have seen him in action. What followed was of a higher intensity, giving shape and direction to that night's paper. A new centre spread, a new feature page, a special drawing of Prince William, and a new front-page political 'splash' were some of the results. As a cadenza the editor took a series of private telephone calls from South Africa, masterminding secret negotiations for what turned out to be the *Mail*'s sponsoring of the move to England by the young Olympic athlete, Zola Budd.

Conference and After

At the conference Ron Birch, deputy news editor, put forward as top story the 'Raffles escape' from police custody of a 'ruthless cat burglar', and as second story the NUM executive considering (8 March) whether or not to go for a national strike. English neither assented nor dissented. He showed rather greater interest in the top foreign item – the release in Saudi Arabia of a British businessman 'incarcerated in medieval dungeons' for more than two years, never charged with an offence, but with serious injury to his spine while in detention. He also asked for a more persuasive effort ('have we made an offer?') for the full story from the policewoman in New Zealand, now being asked to resign after taking part in the cricketer Botham's 'smashing night out' in which a picture window was broken during a mock cricket match in a hotel bedroom.

At 5.30, just after the conference, English moved out to the back bench in the newsroom. The next 20 minutes were an intensive reshaping of pages 12 and 13, previously planned for 'Femail', and of the centre spread (pages 20–1). He scrapped the existing centre spread and substituted fashion pictures modelled that morning by a girl said to be Prince Edward's close friend. The modelling session had been arranged exclusively for the *Mail* – 'a stunning girl', English said, making brother Andrew's current companion 'very ordinary' – and the clothes had been chosen by the paper's fashion editor as a preview to London Fashion Week.

English had a vigorous but friendly argument with the fashion editor, Jean Dobson, about headlines and layout. English eventually capitulated on the first, and a compromise was reached on the second. Two hours later, in the composing room, the centre spread was the first thing David English wanted to inspect. He was pleased with it but still asked for two small adjustments.

Anwar's Widow

Having ripped out the old centre spread and devised a new one, English dealt with the old pages 12 and 13. These were to have been 'Femail', but their contents were deferred. One became a news page – pressure being heavy – and one a feature page. The latter was an exclusive interview with the widow of Anwar Sadat (the assassinated president of Egypt) who was about to come to Oxford for PhD studies in English and Arab poetry. Could it be ready in time? English took off for the features department. The features editor went into a ritual of mock despair: it was impossible, at such short notice, but 'yes' it would be done. And it was: 'the big interview – why I never cried when they shot down my husband.'

Other feature pages were also overhauled, and the drawing of Prince William's 'mini-Jag' – a birthday present from apprentices at Jaguar in Coventry – was commissioned. A sceptical onlooker said 'It will never get into the paper', but it did.

Maggie Mauls the Market

The highlight of the evening was the choice and treatment of the 'splash'. Between 6.30 and 6.50, in discussion with night editor Ted Jeffery, English had agreed that the Briton released in Saudi Arabia should become the foreign-page lead and that the NUM decision to let each area determine whether or not to strike would probably be the page 2 lead. That left as contenders for the splash the 'Raffles escape' and a new story about the wrong episode of *Crossroads* being transmitted on ITV. Neither was a strong enough prospect, and the *Crossroads* story dropped out when the wrong transmission proved to be in the TV South area only. At about 7 p.m., while alternative ways to illustrate Raffles were being debated, the news desk reported word from the *Mail*'s Gordon Greig at the House of Commons and from the Press Association (PA) of a strong speech by the Prime Minister on 'running out of patience' with the Common Market. English said it was a possibility but they'd have to see the copy. Jeffery a few minutes later produced the first pages from PA, saying that there were some powerful phrases. The editor remained sceptical, suggesting that it was a tactical ploy before the European summit, but when Gordon Greig's copy began to run his enthusiasm grew. On his second page, received at 7.40, Greig said that Mrs Thatcher was 'ready to risk divorce' from Europe, a phrase that David English underlined as he read it. That seemed to tip the decision. Although in the end that phrase was deleted from the copy after consultation with the *Mail*'s diplomatic correspondent and with Greig, it was decisive. The splash must be on Maggie, with Raffles as the second story.

Reinforcing the choice, Jeffery recalled that earlier in the week Jacques Chirac, the Gaullist leader and mayor of Paris, had said that Britain ought to be temporarily excluded from the Market. A foreign sub was despatched to find his exact words so that they could be incorporated in the story, and the diplomatic correspondent was asked to write a brief interpretative piece as soon as he had completed the Saudi story.

At 7.50 English started to rough out front page designs, some with Raffles on the right of the page and some with Raffles lower down. He decided at once that there must be 'boxes' with some of Maggie's key words, the first being:

They must stop behaving like ostriches	later changed to	'My message is: Stop behaving like ostriches'

For the main headlines his first thought was:

MAGGIE MAULS THE MARKET	or	MAGGIE'S SCORN FOR EUROPE

Jeffery preferred the wording of the first: it had a 'tigress' feeling. English tried variations with the main headline across the top of the whole page or down the left side, and very quickly chose the left-side layout – though still with variations:

CHART 6.2 Mail *'splash'* layouts

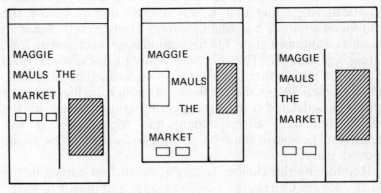

Yet other designs were sketched and discarded: the simple plan in Chart 6.2 won. The staff draughtsmen then went to work on the detail.

As an afterthought, English asked for the report of Mrs Thatcher's implied criticism of Prince Charles to be placed below the continuation of Greig's story on page 2. His headline:

PS to Charles:
I'm not too pleased with you, either

For most of the run, the page 1 plan stood as drafted. In the final editions, however, the splash was changed. About 1 a.m. word came that a Cruise missile-launcher and escort had moved out of the Greenham Common air base. That became the lead, with Maggie's mauling of the market below. London distribution being somewhat unpredictable, both front pages were on sale at King's Cross station in the morning.

Among other activities were a discussion with the diplomatic correspondent about how far Maggie was likely to take her assault on the Market; another with Jeffery and the duty lawyer about contempt of court risks on the Raffles story (the lawyer being nervous about listing crimes for which the man had not been convicted); and with Jeffery again on the inside-page leads.

When the first edition of the *Sun* arrived, he admired its centre spread on how Andrew and Edward acquired their girls: there was no substance in it, he said, but it was very well done. He laughed over some other bits of the *Sun*. 'They're shameless. They can't lose.'

At 9 he watched the first few minutes of the BBC's Nine o'clock News; then departed, leaving Jeffery in charge on the back bench. A satisfactory evening, he said as he left.

COLLECTIVE DECISIONS, NIGHT AND DAY

Peter Grover deputises when English is away – an aquiline man, of quieter manner, but with a sharp interest in all that is going on. Although he could easily be mistaken for a classic Eton and Trinity type, he left school at 16 and took the no less classic route into journalism. Starting in the Exeter office of the *Western Morning News,* he moved to a Bristol evening paper, then the *Evening Standard* in London, and then the *Daily Sketch*. There he worked closely with English, and before the merger of *Mail* and *Sketch* in 1971 he planned the new tabloid layout for the *Mail* – and then moved to the merged paper when David English became editor.

Third in the top tier is Chris Rees, associate editor. He too is directly involved in the hour-by-hour decisions. Like English, he went to grammar school in Bournemouth – though later – and then into journalism through local paper and news agency work. After a short spell in Fleet Street, he went to Australia for eight years and then returned to the *Daily Mail* in 1973.

In the editor's absence, both Grover and Rees are likely to be on the back bench intermittently in the late afternoon and mid-evening. When English is there, one or other of Grover or Rees will commonly sit with him. All three enjoy sketching out page plans for the 'splash', which are discussed with Jeffery before going to one of the night make-up draughtsmen for precise layout. (Unlike the simple sketches put forward by the production editor at *The Times* or *Guardian*, even the preliminary drafts at the popular papers are prepared full size, and the draughtsmens' final version is exactly to scale with complete headlines.)

Two others count – Ted Jeffery, the assistant editor in charge of night production; and Arthur Firth, his deputy, previously editor of the *Daily Express* but one of the casualties in the many recent changes there. Jeffery is a Devon man who went straight from Dartmouth Grammar School to the *Dartmouth Weekly*; then six years of war service, then three in local papers in the Midlands and Lancashire. From 1949 to 1953 he worked in the northern office of the *Express*; then to London, to the *Mail* for one year and the old *Daily Herald* for three; then back to the *Mail* where he has stayed ever since. He has been on the back bench in one or other post since 1959 and was put in charge of night production by English in 1971. He is an undemonstrative man, generally genial, though with the occasional acerbic comment. He is not overtly political, though in common with his paper's character he is interested in political affairs and not slow to take a dig at the Opposition or the Tory 'wets'.

Sitting as an observer on the back bench, it is often difficult to say at exactly what point a decision emerges. Between 3 and 4 p.m. Jeffery will have talked to the news editor, run through the pictures, discussed the inside news pages with Arthur Firth, and agreed on a number of probabilities for placing on pages 9, 11, 13 and others; pages 2 and 3 will be deferred until later. English, Grover or Rees may well eavesdrop or take part in the discussion. Page 4 is foreign. Soon after 6 p.m. first thoughts for page 1 will be sketched on the back bench, and Jeffery will be planning page 3. Most probably three stories will have been marked for the front page, but discussion will continue as pictures and copy come in. If English is there and indicates a preference, that is decisive; similarly, in his absence, Grover is the final arbiter. But after about 8 p.m. Jeffery is normally in full charge. There is a good deal of dialogue on the back bench and with the news desk and picture desk, which are conveniently close. Jeffery is quick to make up his mind, but not dictatorial.

On two of the first three nights of our fieldwork, the *Mail*'s eventual page 1 'splash' was not listed either at the morning conference or at 5 p.m. On the first night (Monday 16 January), just as the 5 p.m. conference was starting, the *Mail*'s 'Showbiz' department reported that the pop star Paul McCartney and his wife had been charged in the Bahamas with drugs offences; that eventually became the lead. On the second night Mr Heath's expected rebellion against the government's 'rate-capping' Bill topped the news editor's list both at 11 a.m. and at 5 p.m. – though in the end it was an even stronger story than foreseen. On the third night 'hard' news was scarce, and in the end the paper led with an exclusive which the news editor had been keeping concealed until it was needed. It was about proposals on penal reform in a Howard League report – a strong story, followed up next day in the 'heavy' newspapers.

WHY WERE THE DECISIONS MADE?

When questioned next day about their choice of topics for the front page and relegation of others, Peter Grover and Ted Jeffery not surprisingly gave similar replies. These nevertheless give insight on their judgements.

Monday Night, 16 January (Tuesday's Paper)

Grover said that the McCartneys on a drugs charge in Barbados was 'the only story of the day that came as a complete surprise – everything else was predictable'. The Ford decision to close its Dagenham foundry had been previewed the previous week. So had the Royal pay rise – the likely 4 per cent increase for the Queen. 'We knew that they were not reducing it to a "bicycling monarchy".'

Jeffery likewise said that the McCartney story had great

appeal for 'a paper that covers the full spectrum of news from the popular to the quality'. It was completely new – not on the agency tapes, not on the radio or television news, and for early editions might be in only one other paper. The *Mail* hoped for an exclusive picture, too.

People want to know about Paul McCartney [Ted Jeffery said]. He's a very well-known and popular figure not only for the younger generation but for 40 year olds and older. He's a millionaire. He's the best example of the pop revolution, almost a father figure. And he's had a pleasant image, only slightly marred by this.

[How did Jeffery know that McCartney was of such interest?]

Conversation, I suppose. You discuss it with your own family, your children. You hear what they're talking about to others in that age group. And telephone calls to the paper. These do seem to indicate a considerable and continuing interest in the McCartneys.

For both Grover and Jeffery there was a bonus factor. Peter Grover had some recollection, in the back of his mind, of a pledge by Paul McCartney three or four years earlier never to take drugs again. Going through the files, they found a *Mail* front-page story from Anchorage, Alaska in 1980 – an interview while McCartney was flying home after a minor conviction in Japan – in which he said 'Never again.' A small reproduction of that headline was built into the front-page splash headline, giving it added effect.

On other possibilities, Grover dismissed a speech by President Reagan, more conciliatory than before to the Soviet Union. 'We knew the *Guardian* and *The Times* would splash that. It's a story that largely rests on its interpretation . . . It's not a political splash for us.'

Tuesday Night, January 17

The splash was on the former Prime Minister, Mr Heath, leading a Tory revolt against the government. Neither Grover nor Jeffery had the slightest doubt about the choice – although

all the other popular papers were leading on the charge against
Linda McCartney at Heathrow of possessing cannabis on her
arrival from the Bahamas.

> Heath was a major political story [Grover said], and our
> readers expect us to react to the big political story of the day.
> The previous day there wasn't a big one. Not only did Heath
> vote against the government, but he coupled it with his
> Guildhall speech [on the economy, the same day] as well. It
> was a major outburst by a former Prime Minister against his
> party. I think it's absolutely the right balance for us, having
> done the McCartneys the previous day . . .

> [And Jeffery] It wasn't a normal rebellion, abstaining. He
> actually went into the lobby, voting against his own party.
> Although he now says that it happened quite frequently in
> the nineteenth century, it's the first occasion in the
> twentieth – an ex-Prime Minister and ex-Chief Whip, adept
> in the past at getting people into his lobby. It marks a
> watershed.

On the choice by the other popular papers to lead with
Linda, there was unanimity again. Jeffery said that the others
had 'missed the bus' the day before, and so were jumping in.
Peter Grover called it 'a desperate attempt to catch up',
especially by the *Express* which had much underplayed it the
previous day.

Without Heath's revolt they thought the *Mail* would probably have led on the crash of a Jaguar aircraft close to the
Porton Down chemical warfare research centre.

Wednesday Night, 18 January

Wednesday night was entirely different, because no obvious
lead stood out – and indeed there were seven different splash
stories among the nine Fleet Street papers. In the end the *Mail*
went for the special on sentencing policy which its news editor
pulled out of his private reserve. It had to be used before long
anyway, and it was followed next day both by other papers and
by radio and television. Jeffery described the proposal to make

criminals pay for the damage they did as not only 'a good talking point' but significant because it could bring shorter sentences and relieve the overcrowding in prisons. Since *Mail* readers were always interested in crime, he had no doubt of its value.

THE POLITICAL DIMENSION

Politically, the high point of the week was Heath's 'treachery'. On Radio Four next day the former Prime Minister was angry with the *Mail*. He called it 'a gross abuse of the freedom of the press, and extremely dangerous'. He thought the paper was getting 'close to the end of democracy'. It had resorted to 'abuse of the grossest kind'. Only the *Mail*, he said, had such a narrow and bigoted approach.

In fairness to Mr Heath, it must be noted that this was a brief passage at the beginning of a long interview with Sir Robin Day, who then drew out of him an exposition of his reasons for launching his attack on the government at this juncture – that he believed the Conservatives were reversing their own fundamental philosophy, that they were destroying the character of local government and putting nothing in its place, and that the rate-capping Bill contained none of the safeguards of his own prices and incomes legislation.

Here is a comparison of late edition headlines and opening texts.

Daily Expresss Ted leads
page 3 top 33 rebels

Former Prime Minister Ted Heath led a Dad's Army meeting of Tory troops in the Commons last night. In an old-stagers' revolt, they voted with Labour against the Government's rate-capping Bill. The dozen Tories who followed Mr Heath through the Opposition lobby were mostly sacked Ministers and has-beens . . .

Guardian Heath heads 40 Tory
page 1 top rate rebels

The former Conservative Prime Minister, Mr Edward

Heath, last night led a revolt of at least 40 Tories in the Commons against the Government's attempt to curb local authority expenditure. At least that number of MPs joined him in opposing or abstaining in the vote . . .

Daily Mail   HEATH'S 'TREACHERY'
page 1 splash

Edward Heath finally and openly walked the plank of party disloyalty last night when he led a Tory revolt against Mrs Thatcher over plans to curb high rates. After years of sniping and back-biting since he was overthrown, the former party leader kicked over all the rules and conventions to vote against his own Prime Minister in the Commons . . .

Daily Mirror   Heath leads a
page 2 top   rates revolt

Former Tory Premier Edward Heath led a major revolt against Mrs Thatcher's Government last night. He was joined by 12 other rebel Tory MPs, including former Cabinet Ministers, in voting against the controversial Rates Bill in the Commons. It was an unprecedented move for Mr Heath . . .

Sun   Heath leads 34
page 1 column 1   in revolt

Former Premier Ted Heath last night led a major Tory rebellion against Margaret Thatcher's 'curb the rates-Bill'. Mr Heath was among 14 Tory MPs who voted against plans to clamp down on big-spending councils . . .

Daily Telegraph   TORY MPs REVOLT ON RATES
page 1 lead   Attack on Bill led by Heath

The Government's controversial Rates Bill was given its expected second reading in the Commons despite a rebellion by Mr Heath and other Conservative MPs . . . [Mr Heath was not mentioned again until the fourth paragraph.]

The Times   Heath leads Tory
page 1 lead   rebellion
                                                  over rate capping

Mr Edward Heath last night led a Conservative rebellion against the Government's rate-capping legislation, voting with the Opposition against a three-line whip for the first time since the Conservatives were returned to power under his successor, Mrs Margaret Thatcher, in 1979 . . .

Of the opening paragraphs quoted above, the *Mail*'s is the most colourful. The other popular papers, of course, were preoccupied with Linda McCartney – and only the *Sun* found space for Heath on its front page. If any others had been choosing the Commons for its splash, more vigorous opening paragraphs would have been highly probable. For the *Mail* what Gordon Greig dictated by telephone from the House was used virtually unchanged (only two small tidyings – 'on plans' instead of 'on the new plan' in the first sentence and transfer of the words 'in the Commons' from the first to the second sentence).

It was Greig's fourth paragraph – 'Thatcher loyalists immediately accused Mr Heath of "treachery" ' – that at 10.45 sparked a revision by Ted Jeffery of the headline, which for the first edition was 'Heath's rebellion'. Asked about the change next day, Jeffery replied:

It's what some of the Tory loyalists were saying. It's not my opinion on Mr Heath. We're describing what loyalists were saying. It may not be acceptable to a number of people up and down the country, nevertheless it's what some Tories were saying after the vote . . .

To be frank, I wanted a better word than 'rebellion', which we had used and other papers were using. And this was more than an ordinary rebellion. We've had rebellions by top Tories before, but this was a former Prime Minister going into the Labour lobby to vote against his own party – and with other ex-ministers – and after an exceptionally strong speech in the Commons and another in the City. He was certainly going public, in a very public way.

Part of Mr Heath's case against the *Mail* was that, in his own words, 'a newspaper can say "all these members are calling him a traitor" but they don't have to give names or numbers to prove anything'. True: though there is a certain irony in the fact that while he was speaking on the *World at One* radio programme the parliamentary Lobby – the group of privileged journalists who are accorded special status in the Commons – were celebrating their centenary with a lunch at the Savoy Hotel with the Prime Minister as principal guest. One of the Lobby's rules is that MPs who talk to journalists informally in the precincts of Parliament may not be named. Mr Heath may now feel that the rule is reprehensible, but while he was Prime Minister he and his colleagues made extensive use of it – as his predecessors and successors have done and still do.

From early in the evening Gordon Greig at the Commons knew that his report was virtually certain to be the splash. Just after 6.00 p.m. he talked by phone to the news editor, Paul Dacre, and again at 6.20. Dacre had picked up from ITN the fact that Heath, in an interview for Channel Four News, had said that he was going to vote against the government. Greig said, even then, that he simply could not believe it. (My evidence for this is that Dacre was relaying bits of the conversation over his shoulder to Jeffery, and at the time I was sitting between the two.) Dacre said there was no doubt that it was in the interview for ITN and asked Greig to 'talk me through the significance'. He relayed to Jeffery that, if it happened, it would be without precedent so far as Greig knew: 'it's either the end of Heath or the beginning of something bigger.'

From about 10.07 Greig was on an open line from the Commons to Jeffery, counting the Tory rebels through: '. . . eight, nine, ten – play safe, about ten'. Although the front page had already gone to the foundry in the composing room, it was pulled back for an extra sentence. At 10.15 Greig called again – 10 Tories voting against, 20 to 30 abstaining. At 10.20 the sub went up to the composing room to make a further change, for a 'slip page'. At 10.30 further changes were made, with the rebel vote corrected to 13: that copy stood for the second edition, off stone 15 minutes later. At 10.40 Greig's new introduction began to come in – and at 10.45, as already described, Ted Jeffery revised 'rebellion' to 'treachery'.

Whether the boundaries of fairness and accuracy were transgressed is a matter of individual judgement. As so often in dealing with political events, interpretation must be an integral part of reporting. David English believes in partisan journalism, and his staff readily follow his lead. My guess was that, when the paper reached him in Switzerland, he was delighted with it; that proved to be correct.

INITIATING THE NEWS: THE NEWS EDITOR

Without the news editor's daily disposition of the reporters, his coordination of the specialists and chivvying all round, the paper would be lost. From 8 a.m., by Paul Dacre's own account, he is thinking continuously about what will make next day's front page – 'the story of significance' – what will brighten page 3, with a prominent personality or a topic to get people talking in the pub or whatever, and what is needed for other news pages. The splash and page 3 are the prime targets, and of his morning news list he says 'by and large it's a good hit ratio'.

Believing that English's strength as editor stems from his ability to reflect *Mail* readers' interests, Paul Dacre also thinks in those terms – the hopes, fears and preoccupations of a struggling middle class. His own background is public school (London, dayboy) and Leeds University, graduating in English. His father was and is a journalist with the *Sunday Express*. Dacre edited a student newspaper which won awards, and was then 'lucky' in getting a job with the *Express* in Manchester. After two years there he moved to a holiday relief post with the *Express* in London, then to being a staff reporter and feature writer. From 1976 to 1979 he was in Washington and New York for the *Express*, until English invited him to join the *Mail* in New York. In 1980 he was brought back to London as deputy news editor, and in late 1982 became news editor.

Asked about readership research or direct contact with readers, he said that it was mainly a matter of 'gut instinct'. He regarded his time with the *Express* as having given him a good grounding, not least his years in New York. The only acid test, however, remained 'does it interest me?' The news desk takes most of the calls from readers, which are a partial indication of response.

During the day, the more contentious stories are the subject of consultation between news desk, back bench and whoever is in charge (English, Grover or Rees). On Monday and again on Tuesday there were three or four consultations, each lasting some minutes; they were about the reliability of stories, the angles to be pursued, and once (in the context of the abortion debate) about how to find healthy babies born after only 24 to 28 weeks of pregnancy, with parents willing to have them photographed. The last in the end produced a cheerful picture for page 3, with a report by the *Mail*'s medical correspondent.

On Wednesday the longest consultations were legal. A *Mail* inquiry into the illicit sale of heroin and other hard drugs had taken place; its use that night was planned for part of page 1 and the whole centre spread, which had been cleared of advertisements to give it maximum space. It was the work of Tim Miles, a general reporter in his early thirties. He had been present at the delivery and sale of heroin in Kilburn and of cocaine in Battersea, and had inquired more generally into drug trafficking. Crime was his field.

Early that afternoon, after consultations with Grover and Dacre, he was sent off to New Scotland Yard with a dossier on buying hard drugs and with two lawyers, one of the *Mail*'s and one engaged separately (though paid for by the *Mail*) to look after the interests of Miles. An extremely long session took place with the Drugs Squad, which culminated with the police wanting a statement from Miles which his lawyer advised that he ought not to sign, although its terms had been agreed, unless they gave an undertaking that he would not be prosecuted for buying prohibited drugs. The CID officers argued that to give such an undertaking was beyond their authority, and that without a signed statement they could not get the search warrants that they needed. Soon after 5.00 p.m. Peter Grover had to be pulled out of the evening conference, to discuss a way out of the impasse – which in the end was found, to the satisfaction of the *Mail*, Miles and the CID. Altogether it took a lot of executive and news desk time, but it was regarded as well worth the effort.

Miles had already been mentioned by the news desk as someone we ought to interview, as representative of the tougher end of *Mail* reporting. From school he had worked first in an advertising agency, then in the film industry and next as a reporter for a North London local news agency; then he worked in two other Fleet Street agencies specialising in crime, which opened the way to setting up his own agency. But after four years he was 'burned out'; and in 1978 he got a relief job and then a staff post on the *Mail*.

'Freelancing', he said, 'is the hardest training. The foot-in-the-door technique never quite leaves you. Other reporters might find it heavy handed, though I temper it with diplomacy.' His wife was a reporter on the *Sun*. When I asked him whether working for the *Mail* was perhaps more civilised than working for the *Express* or the *Sun*, expecting an emollient answer, he looked quite offended. No, he replied; if I were to ask reporters with experience of the *Express* or *Sun,* he said, they would give the same reply. 'The *Mail* is the toughest newspaper to work for.' At the *Sun*, it was true, they had two hours fewer to their deadlines – but the newsroom atmosphere, he believed, was otherwise more relaxed. There could be little doubt that the *Mail*'s toughness was something of which he thoroughly approved.

Miles seemed representative of a 'machismo' character fostered among some of the *Mail*'s star reporters. Among the reporters generally there is a love–hate relationship with their paper – both a pride in its professionalism, competence and success, and a feeling of being driven and oppressed. The thoroughness and swift reaction of the news desk are acknowledged, but once the desk has made up its mind on the shape a story is to take, often on the basis of no more than the first pages of PA (Press Association), it is extremely difficult to shift. The news desk makes a rapid assessment of the story's character, including the possibility of pictures, and the reporters are briefed accordingly. Especially with the less experienced, the briefing is likely to be detailed. When the reporter rings in from the location, the 'debriefing' by telephone is long and thorough. 'Have you interviewed X and Y? Great! Why is there no comment from Z?' Under pressure from the news desk, a reporter may sometimes invent a 'quote' – though less often, according to those with experience, than on some other Fleet Street papers, 'They [the *Mail*] are very disappointed if you don't stand up the story as they want it.'

The briefing is rarely political. It is about the angle to pursue, the people to talk to and the interests of a *Mail* reader.

If a reporter is sent to a big fire or emergency and finds out that the victims are working class or black, news desk interest diminishes. If the victims or eye witnesses are middle class, news desk interest quickens. This implies no racialism: the *Mail* has two highly competent black reporters and one specialist, all of whom are deployed on a wide range of assignments. It implies only a concentration on what are seen as the aspects of an event that will stir the greatest response among their readers.

On what is seen as a big event, when a 'blitz' is ordered by the news desk with as many as ten reporters on the story, the experience of hunting with the Fleet Street 'pack' can be painful – or nauseating – to anyone who is sensitive. It takes a hardened character not to be revolted by the readiness of the pack to talk or force its way into the houses of those who may have suffered in a tragedy, to ask merciless questions and then to make jokes among themselves about the replies. Again, no *Mail* reporter to whom we talked put primary blame on his own paper; but those who had been involved knew what was expected of them. Competitively, the *Mail* wants its reporters to be the first on the spot and the last to leave.

In its thoroughness, the news desk wants to make sure that a story is factually correct and not based on misinterpretation. One of our fieldwork observations illustrates this. Late on the Wednesday night, after receiving a story from the Nottingham 'stringer', the night news editor put in a call to cross-examine him. The story was of a Catholic priest who had refused marriage to a crippled ex-army sergeant and a nurse, on the grounds that the man could not consummate the marriage. The night news editor put one reporter on to ringing the priest while himself ringing the correspondent. For both, the line of inquiry was the same: what really lay behind the priest's decision? Was there more to it? Was consummation the only reason? Was the woman's divorce a factor? Was there anything to suggest that she had taken advantage of other cripples? And so on. 'It's a marvellous story', the night news editor said, 'but we don't want the priest going on the *World at One* tomorrow and saying we didn't understand what it was all about.'

The priest turned out to be something of an expert on Church law and stood his ground under questioning, explaining at length his interpretation of the requirements for marriage.

The reporter then spoke to the Bishop of Nottingham, with whom the *Sun* had already been in touch. He said that he had heard of the case only that evening, and was asking the priest to reconsider it. The *Mail*'s story was written accordingly. 'It's one that will run for days', the night news editor said prophetically – and he was correct.

THE MIRROR: EDITORIAL MANAGEMENT

The quite frequent tactical changes of course by the *Daily Mirror* are a response either to a national event such as a general election or to 'gut feeling' about the response of readers. A change of proprietor or editor, or the commercial intention to promote 'bingo' are other factors. One obvious change came after the general election of June 1983. According to the editor, Mike Molloy, there had been a lot of 'heavy' coverage in the months leading up to the election and during the campaign; it was decided to give *Mirror* readers a rest and make the paper lighter or more 'downmarket'. The weekly columns by the political editor and the industrial editor were both scrapped, and the staff were told that there must be more happy and smiling faces within the pages of the *Mirror*. Hugh Cudlipp made a similar move after Labour's election defeat in 1959.

This 'lighter' phase of the *Mirror* lasted about six months, until January 1984. Then in one week there was a special 'shock' issue on the National Health Service (17 January); and two days later a front-page leader attacking Mrs Thatcher and profiling a Tory 'Government in Exile', a sequel to the rebellion by Mr Heath and other ex-ministers. The following week there was a series of articles by the Labour leader, Neil Kinnock. When questioned about the reasons for these changes, Molloy emphasised that it was not due to market research but to a reliance on 'gut' feeling. Market research is used, though, for some alterations to style and layout. For example in April 1983 the *Mirror* began giving greater prominence on its front page to a promotional display, with the promise of big bingo prizes as well as trailers for articles on inside pages.

John Parker, associate night editor, said that this was part of the marketing strategy as a result of which the nightly print was increased by 350 000 copies and sales were up by about 250 000. Market research, he said, had shown that this form of promotion paid. Commenting on the different phases Parker said (July 1983, noted in Chapter 4) that in the choice of front-page stories there had been a 'change of pace', moving into a more popular area. Whereas six months earlier the paper might have splashed Chancellor Lawson's thoughts on cutting unemployment benefit, a matter of social significance affecting *Mirror* readers, Wimbledon tennis photographs now came first.

Molloy became editor in 1975, at the age of 35. From art school, at 16 he went straight into Fleet Street and has been there ever since, nearly all the time with the *Mirror* group. He is an acknowledged expert on newspaper layout. His style of editorship relies on informal discussions and private chats. For strategic planning, a discussion with senior executives usually suffices for the policy to reach the rest of the editorial staff. (One of his senior staff described the dissemination of policy as 'subliminal'.) On the day-to-day level Molloy relies on the 'personal touch' to make his views known. 'I don't go for newsroom shouting matches and I don't criticise in conference. It's not good for executives to be criticised in front of others. It undermines their authority.' At the two daily conferences Molloy rarely says much – simply noting the various editors' possible stories. There is little discussion at these conferences anyway.

On the political aspects Molloy said this: 'We are really a Fabian paper not a Labour one, and that's what some Labour politicians do not understand.' By 'Fabian' he implied gradual social change, working through parliamentary democracy, and not through revolutionary direct action. Although loyal to the Labour party in general, the *Mirror* has at times muted its support because of stridency on the party's left. It approved of Michael Foot's endeavour to take action against the militants in 1981–2. It argued that Labour stood no chance of winning the election unless clearly seen as a moderate left-of-centre movement. Of political policy-making within the paper, Molloy said in early 1984 'it boils down to a dictatorship' – though in practice he relied heavily on advice from his political and industrial editors and the chief leader writer. With the arrival of Maxwell as proprietor, the 'dictatorship' took on a new dimension. The 'subliminal' days were over, as Maxwell stalked the building and issued his instructions.

At that point the political editor left. For more than 20 years Terence Lancaster had been in the upper ranks of the *Mirror* group, enjoying close contact with successive Labour leaders – and more widely in the House of Commons. He was close to retirement, anyway. The industrial editor was Geoffrey Goodman, and he stayed. He is a graduate of the London School of Economics and from 1946 was successively with the *Manchester Guardian*, the *Mirror*, the *News Chronicle*, the *Daily Herald*, and back to the *Mirror* from 1969 onwards; he is one of the most senior members of the industrial correspondents' group (see Chapter 9), which, like the Lobby correspondents' group, organises its own private meetings with ministers, trade unionists, industrialists and others. He lists his recreations as 'pottering, poetry, supporting Tottenham Hotspur FC and climbing – but not social'. The third of that inner group was Joe Haines, and he too stayed, becoming political editor. As chief leader writer he had earned a reputation as one of the most pungent in Fleet Street. From 1969 to 1976 he was Harold Wilson's press secretary, working at 10 Downing Street from 1969–70 and 1974–6. Some of that experience is described in his book *The Politics of Power* (1977). He lists his recreations as 'heresy and watching football'.

The *Mirror*'s newsroom, though somewhat barrack-like, is conveniently laid out with news desk, night desk, pictures and sub-editor within talking distance of each other (see Chart 6.3).

The filtering of news begins on the news desk. About 250 or more home news items pass through the desk each day. Generally all Press Association copy is reviewed by one assistant news editor and all staff or specially ordered copy (from local agencies or stringers) by another. The deputy news editor decides which are worth pursuing or at least keeping an eye on, and the news desk copy-taster puts together the staff and agency material on each story so that it can be passed on to the sub-editors. The system provides, of course, for continuous discussion among those round the news desk on the way stories are developing. At the same time, the picture editor is in touch with the way the paper is taking shape and can say what looks like providing the best pictures.

Mirror reporters are not necessarily Labour-inclined, any

CHART 6.3   Daily Mirror: *newsroom layout*

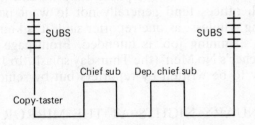

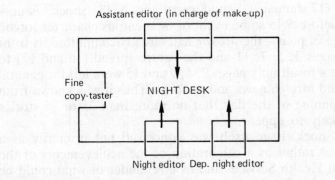

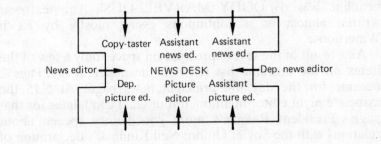

more than *Mail* reporters are Conservative-orientated. Both
groups have absorbed what the paper expects, and the news
desks in both offices tend generally not to want politically
slanted writing – unless, as one reporter said, it is known that
higher up a 'slamming job' is intended. Front-page salvoes
such as 'Thatcher's No Men' (the Thursday splash, 16 January)
are not likely to be written by reporters but by senior staff.

THREE JANUARY NIGHTS AT THE MIRROR

Having decided the previous week that Tuesday morning's
Mirror (17 January) would carry the NHS 'shock' issue –
unless before 5.15 some event of momentous character forced
a change of plan – the *Mirror* had already committed its front
page, pages 3, 5, 7, 11 and the centre spread (16 and 17) to
that. As a result only pages 2, 4, 9 and 15 were left for general
home and foreign news and pictures. Thus it was known from
the beginning of the day that no more than 25 or so stories
were likely to appear.

The 'shock' issue itself was conceived not primarily as a
shock but rather as a celebration of the achievements of the
National Health Service, and as a reminder of what could be
destroyed by the Conservative government's cuts. The splash
headline was 'BLOODY MARVELLOUS'. The text was
written almost as a continuous essay, mostly by Keith
Waterhouse.

As a result of the severe pressure on space, only a few of the
items on the morning list reached the paper at all. Page 2
became for the day the principal news page. At 5.15 the
associate night editor mentioned four chief candidates for that
page – President Reagan's more conciliatory speech about
relations with the Soviet Union; Neil Kinnock's declaration of
support for Tony Benn as Labour candidate in the coming
Chesterfield by-election; more questions to Mrs Thatcher in
the Commons about her son Mark's involvement in Oman; and
the Ford motor company's decision to close its foundry at
Dagenham. Later, having read the copy, John Parker (associate night editor) changed his mind. The Reagan speech, he
remarked, 'really said very little' – though he was prepared to
bet that it would be the lead in *The Times, Guardian* and
Telegraph. It was.

His preference, therefore, was for the Royals' pay rise which 'read well'. But at 7.30 (2½ hours after the first tip at the *Mail*), the news desk told him that Linda and Paul McCartney had been 'busted for drugs' in the Bahamas – a 'much juicier' story, he said. That became the lead, and Parker predicted that it would be the lead also in the *Express, Mail* and *Sun*. In the last two it was the lead, but the *Express* chose to stay with the Ford foundry closing at Dagenham.

At 7.55 Parker went to see the editor in his office, just as the first UPI (United Press International) copy was coming in about the McCartneys being fined for possessing marijuana. With the editor he agreed that that should be the lead, with the Royals dropping to second place. Later, but too late for the first edition, staff copy on the McCartneys came from New York. 'McCartney on drugs – what could be a better lead?' Parker said. He wanted pictures of Linda and Paul to go with the story, which must mention that McCartney was the richest entertainer ever and also mention his latest video.

Altogether, on Monday night, Parker thought the McCartney story of much greater human interest than that morning's splash 'BENN GETS IT'. The news that Benn had been nominated for Chesterfield was 'pretty boring,' he thought – and 'who's going to buy a paper with Tony Benn on the front?' But as a Labour paper, he said, they had to splash it.

For the other news pages, a big mountain rescue of a school expedition in the Cairngorms led page 4; it was on the front page of the *Telegraph* and *The Times,* and a page lead in the *Express* and *Mail* – with material differences in each paper about what had actually happened. Page 9 led with a murder trial which was also prominently placed in other papers; and page 15 with the Walton family's sextuplets, to whom the Merseyside social services were allocating eight nursery helpers, to relieve their parents. When Molloy saw the proof of page 15 he disliked another story on that page, about a drag artist who was imitating Marilyn Monroe. That suited Parker, who killed the Monroe story and its picture, substituting a big and cheerful picture of three of the Walton nannies. 'Great', said the night editor, 'I want everyone to read this. It cannot be bad having six children.'

One other change was to give more space in later editions to the murder trial, because the *Sun* had splashed it for its first edition, going over to the McCartneys later. The *Sun* is the earliest to go to press and is available to rival news desks at about 9 p.m. No doubt partly for that reason, the *Sun* frequently changes its splash after its first edition. The *Mirror* normally has three later editions – the second, with four pages (one sport) available for change, last copy at 9.45; the third, with eight pages available, last copy 11.40; and the fourth, with possibly six pages, last copy 2 a.m.

Tuesday Night, 17 January

With more space, all but three of the 15 items on the morning news list eventually reached the paper, though some in short form. Top of the list was 'McCartneys fly home' and bottom 'Revolt expected over rate-capping Bill'. By the 5.15 conference the McCartney story had grown, for not only had they landed at Heathrow but Linda had been charged there with having cannabis in her bag and Paul had been outspoken about hypocritical British double standards.

In the end this was the splash – 'what could be better than Linda busted a second time at Heathrow?' – but the page carried a picture expected to be exclusive, of the mother who had given birth to a twin months after losing the other baby. Also on the page was a cross-reference to the lead of page 2, with wording devised only after much discussion.

Rates rebel
NO! Heath slams
Thatcher

Late changes were made that night to accommodate extra material from the House of Commons on page 2; and on page 4, at the instigation of the deputy editor (Molloy was out), a Dublin report about the stolen racehorse Shergar was extended. The point of the extension was to make clear not only that the Irish police believed the horse to be dead but that they were now linking it with the kidnapping of the supermarket chief Don Tidey.

The treatment of the top foreign story that night is also of some interest. In the morning it was listed as 'Shultz meets

Gromyko', and little was then known except that a statement was expected from the US Secretary of State. Later in the day the foreign editor, Nick Davies, himself wrote the story from agency copy. He provided seven short paragraphs, which the sub-editors revised and reduced to six for the first edition and then cut to three for later editions. The text and amendments were these:

George Shultz, US Secretary of State, yesterday told the Stockholm peace conference that the West propose to draft a treaty for the global elimination of chemical weapons. He told the 35-nation conference that US negotiators would present the draft treaty within the next few months. He also said the proposals would make provision to stop cheating by any nation.
[Amended to: A worldwide ban on chemical weapons is to be proposed by America, Secretary of State George Schultz said yesterday. A US treaty will contain safeguards against cheating, he told a 35-nation peace conference in Stockholm.]
Last week Moscow proposed the elimination of chemical weapons in Europe only but the United States is determined to make the new treaty world wide.
[The plan takes a stage further a ban on chemical weapons in the Europe proposed by Russia last week.]
In his opening speech George Schultz also urged Moscow to resume the Geneva peace talks which the Russians broke off last year when NATO countries began installing Cruise missiles. But East German Foreign Minister Oskar Fischer set out a tough Warsaw Pact stance demanding the removal of Cruise and Pershing II missiles.
The tough stance by the East Germans was not welcomed by the Western allies who fear the talks between Soviet Foreign Minister Gromyko and George Schultz due to take place today (Wed.) may not be fruitful.
[Shultz also urged Moscow to resume the Geneva peace talks which the Russians broke off last year when NATO countries began installing Cruise missiles. But East German Foreign Minister, Oskar Fischer took a hard line on behalf of the Warsaw Pact countries, demanding the removal of Cruise and Pershing II missiles. His tough

stance raised fears of deadlock when Soviet Foreign Minister Gromyko meets Shultz today.]

The last three paragraphs were deleted in the third and later editions, leaving only the first three. The early edition headline, 'BAN WAR CHEMICALS', was revised later to 'SCRAP WAR CHEMICALS'.

Wednesday Night, 18 January

In the wake of Mr Heath's rebellion, the editor decided in the morning to devote most of the front page to a 'Mirror Comment' on Mrs Thatcher's sacked ministers, or government-in-exile. It was to be written by Joe Haines, and the editor himself later in the day provided a sketch of the layout he wanted.

CHART 6.4 *Editor's design given to night desk*

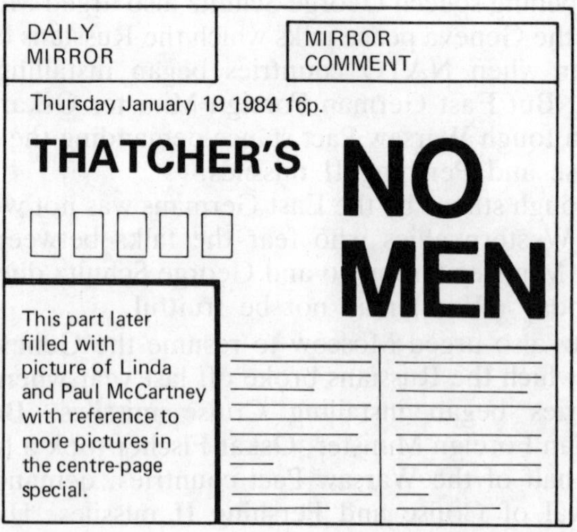

DAILY MIRROR

MIRROR COMMENT

Thursday January 19 1984 16p.

THATCHER'S NO MEN

This part later filled with picture of Linda and Paul McCartney with reference to more pictures in the centre-page special.

While the *Mirror* was leading on its 'Comment', the *Mail* had pulled out of a bottom drawer its exclusive on penal reform and was also giving prominence to the inquiry by Tim Miles into drug-selling in London. *The Times* and the *Guardian* led on more exchanges between Mr Schultz and Mr Gromyko, the *Telegraph* on the print union NGA preparing to purge a contempt of court, and the *Sun* in later editions on the wedding ban on a crippled soldier.

Also on the *Mirror*'s list had been 'Koo back in town'. Koo was an actress and model, Koo Stark, then featured frequently in popular newspapers because she had been a friend of Prince Andrew and had shared a Caribbean holiday with him after his Falklands war service. As someone on the news desk said, 'When Koo farts we are there.' A reporter had been on her doorstep since 6.30 a.m. A short story appeared on page 2 about stolen audio tapes, with the implication that Andrew's voice might be on them.

The general feeling on the *Mirror*'s night desk was that the pops were at an advantage over the heavies on days when there was no big story. As one man remarked 'We can easily make up a front page. We can take a human interest story from one of the inside pages, get a bigger picture and put it on the front. The rest of the page can be filled with a "See centre pages" ad. I feel sorry for the heavies on a slow day. What does the *Guardian* do for example – "Three more die in Lebanon"?'

SOURCES, STORIES USED AND NEWS SPACE

Exactly where and how the first spark was lit on some topics is easier to trace than on others. Here are a few:

Monday/Tuesday	McCartneys – for the *Mail*, Bahamas 'stringer', hearing from police; for the *Mirror*, UPI 2½ hours later.
	Ford closure – company PR and inquiries by industrial staff.
	Queen's pay – Treasury and Lobby briefing, Reagan speech – White House.

Cairngorm rescue – for *Mail*, Manchester office; for *Mirror*, Glasgow office.

Tuesday/Wednesday   Heath – Commons proceedings.

McCartneys – reporters at Heathrow to meet them, and Metropolitan police tipoff to crime correspondents, late p.m., on further drugs charge.

Jaguar aircraft crash – Salisbury 'stringer'.

Premature babies (*Mail* only) – news desk/forward planning idea for following up previous day's story on abortion studies.

Wednesday/Thursday 'Make crooks pay up' (*Mail* only) – chief crime correspondent, through private contacts.

Hard drug sales (*Mail* only) – Tim Miles, who was assigned a fortnight previously to follow up material received through 'Femail' (women's features section).

NGA to purge contempt – NGA had said beforehand that its executive would be meeting, so industrial correspondents were there.

Church refuses marriage – Nottingham 'stringer'.

As to numbers of news items, taking Tuesday 17 January as a typical day, the number (not counting features, arts news, formal obituaries, weather forecasts, City, sport, radio/TV programme trailers, bingo, etc.) and the aggregate of texts (not including headlines or pictures) were as shown in Table 6.1.

Big headlines, big pictures and space for bingo mean that the popular papers have fewer and shorter news items. But since

TABLE 6.1 *Numbers of news items*

	Number of items over 2 col. cm text	Number of 'brief' under 2 col. cm text	Aggregate news text (col. cm)
Express	28	2	490
Guardian	76	27	1980
Mail	31	6	630
Mirror	17[a]	6	215[a]
Sun	30	11	355
Telegraph	68	28	1750
Times	75	20	1550

[a] Not including the *Mirror*'s NHS special, with text of 350 col. cm.

they have almost as many news sub-editors and as many reporters as the 'heavy' papers, more man/woman-hours go into each item. Almost all the news at the *Mail* and a large proportion at the *Mirror* is staff originated. Of the 31 items in the *Mail* on the Tuesday (not counting 'briefs'), 28 were written by staff correspondents or reporters. Only three – all foreign – were news agency material. The staffing ratios also mean that, to an extent not practicable in the heavies, every story has been selected after special attention.

As to usage of staff stories, an analysis was made on two days at the *Mail*. The proportion used was high, though often the item was heavily cut. Thus on Monday, 16 January, used in one or more editions were 35 stories (or 57 including 'add' and 'new intro' copy); not used were 15 stories; held over was one story. Not included are telephone calls and other inquiries which produced no copy. Of the 35 stories, 20 were cut by more than half while in 15 above half the original copy survived. On Tuesday, 17 January, used in one or more editions were 25 stories (or 52 including 'add' and 'new intro' copy); not used were 20 stories; planned for late edition use but prevented by production difficulties were five stories (follow-up of other first editions). Out of the 25 stories that were used, 14 were cut by more than half, in 7 above half the original copy survived, and with 5 no copy was available for study (all being late stories of which the duplicates were not kept).

SOME CONCLUSIONS

The *Daily Mail*'s news values are, above all, Sir David English's news values. The paper's style and character have been shaped by him since 1971. He leads and directs his staff, who respond to him. His values are based on an instinctive judgement of what will interest his readers. The paper aims chiefly at a Conservative middle-class market, although not exclusively at that sector.

The *Daily Mirror*'s news values are an amalgam based on the commercially successful style built up by Hugh Cudlipp. Entertainment of its readers, variety of topics and occasional campaigning are components. The paper holds back from the extremes of popular journalism; it will not, for example, fabricate interviews or distort pictures or use page three nudes. For 40 years the paper has been loyal to the Labour movement, but that loyalty has lately been strained by the rise of the militant left.

In both papers, news is only one ingredient, their success depending as much on their sports services, general features, bingo and other 'millionaire' inducements, and in the *Mail* also on its financial pages.

Both newspapers stand within the broad band of 'sociocentralism', in that both believe their readers to want only orderly and gradual changes in society and to dislike terrorism, violence and physical confrontation.

While the *Mail* is politically partisan, as English readily admits, that is not always evident in the treatment of news. On many days its political approach is to be seen only in feature pages, not in news – though the force of its features must often reinforce Conservatives in their existing outlook. During elections or a Falklands crisis, its political view will influence its presentation of the news, and will do so also on long-running events such as the Greenham Common women's camp. Its fierce loyalty (so far) to Mrs Thatcher did not prevent it from giving maximum coverage to the plight of her protégé Cecil Parkinson in October 1983 or to the blunderings of her choice as Coal Board chairman in 1984.

The *Mirror*'s commitment to Labour is evident day-to-day in the prominence given to news favourable to the party or to the centre-left. Its 'shock' issues are also aimed at campaigning for the centre-left. But its tactical phasing of the paper's contents can mean long periods with comparatively little political or economic news.

'Personalities', especially the Royals and those seen often on television, rate high in the news values of both papers. It is not uncommon to find four page leads in the *Mirror* all related to television events or television people. Executives at the *Mail*, however, are unanimous that high priority must always go to stories of 'significance' – that is, to the reporting of events that are judged to be of political, economic, social or human importance to their readers. The *Mail*'s attention to political and economic affairs is more consistent than the *Mirror*'s, since it wishes to remain midway between the 'heavies' and the more boisterous end of Fleet Street. While judgements of what is

TABLE 6.2 *Content analysis, Tuesday, 17 January*

Final	Express	Guardian	Mail	Mirror	Sun	Telegraph	Times
Reagan speech, Soviet reaction	6/1	1/1	4/1	2/2	2/a	1/1	1/1
McCartneys on drugs charges, Barbados	1/2	28/a	1/1	2/1	1/1	24/a	—
4% pay rise for Queen	1/3	1/6	1/2	2/3	2/a	1/4	1/5
Ford to close Dagenham foundry	1/1	1/3	1/3	2/4	2/1	1/2	1/4
Liverpool 'sex trap' row	—	3/1	2/1	2/1	—	3/2	3/a
Mirror's NHS special	—	—	—	1/1, 3/1 and 5/1	—	—	—
Reactions to choice of Benn at Chesterfield	2/a	2/2	2/a	2/5	6/4	24/3	2/5
Snow, and Cairngorm rescue	7/1	28/a	13/1	4/1	2/a	1/3	1/2
Angela Rippon off to Boston	2/3	2/a	3/3	9/2	3/4	—	3/a
BBC blackout risk, Selina birthday	2/1	2/a	3/2	—	11/2	1/5	1/3
Threat of Tory revolt on rates Bill	2/2	1/2	2/2	—	2/3	1/a and 2/2	1/a
China's plans for Hong Kong	6/a	8/3	—	—	—	24/1	28/1
Hussein invites Arafat	5/a	1/5	—	—	—	4/1	1/a and 6/1
Tax burden heaviest in Britain	—	1/4	—	—	—	—	—
NUM and overtime ban	5/2	2/1	9/1	9/a	4/2	1/6	2/3
Rail engineering contracts	—	28/1	11/a	—	—	7/4	4/3
Winchester murder trial	5/1	2/5	11/1	9/1	7/2	3/1	3/a
Council helps sextuplets	3/1	—	11/2	15/1	7/2	—	3/a
Blandford's drugs cure	7/3	—	3/1	—	—	—	—
Doctors want lower time-limit on abortions	—	—	9/3	—	—	—	3/1
Bingo, Jackpot, Casino, etc.	22/1	—	24/1	20/1	1/2 and 2/2	—	—

a=minor story, downpage.
NOTE: 1/1=page 1, splash.
   1/2=page 1, second story (in order of typographical prominence).
   3/5=page 3, fifth story (in order of typographical prominence).

'significant' remain subjective, it is a mistake to underestimate the intellect, thoroughness and experience which are applied to these decisions.

TABLE 6.3 *Content analysis, Wednesday, 18 January*

	Express	Guardian	Mail	Mirror	Sun	Telegraph	Times
Heath's rebellion, Commons vote	2/1	1/2	1/1	2/1	1/3	1/1	1/1
Schultz, missiles and Warsaw pact	6/1	1/1	4/1	—	—	1/2	1/2
Linda McCartney on drugs charge	1/1	1/4	1/2	1/1	1/1	1/4	2/8
PSA corruption charges	1/2	—	—	—	—	—	—
Scott-Lithgow near closure	2/a	1/3	9/a	—	2/a	2/1	2/1
Porton Down plane crash	5/1	—	1/3	11/3	2/2	1/6	1/5
US antisatellite weapons	—	6/1	4/2	—	—	—	—
Scargill on coal board losses	10/a	26/2	9/1	2/a	2/1	30/1	2/5
Jessel, MP, in car chase: banned	3/a	—	13/1	4/1	7/3	1/5	2/a
One twin born after accident	—	—	—	1/2	—	—	—
US video recording is legal	—	1/5	4/a	—	—	1/7	—
Benn: early date for Chesterfield?	—	—	—	—	—	—	1/4
Lighthousemen lifted out	—	—	—	—	—	—	1/3
Royal computer links	—	—	—	—	—	6/2	1/7
Better betting shops	2/2	—	—	—	—	—	3/3
King of Rock, Michael Jackson	5/2	—	—	—	11/2	—	—
Cardinal rebuked by Dublin govt.	—	2/1	—	—	C	2/6	—
Doctors call for abortion time-limit	—	2/2	Y	—	—	—	X
Bingo, Casino, Jackpot, etc.	26/2	—	34/1	17/2	1/2	—	—
Solihull grammar school plans	—	3/1	16/a	—	—	15/1	1/8

a=minor story, downpage. X carried Tuesday.

NOTE: 1/1=page 1, splash.

       1/2=page 1, second story (in order of typographical prominence).

       3/5=page 3, fifth story (in order of typographical prominence).

7 Decisions (4): the *Guardian* and *The Times*

Because this is a study of news – what is news and what is not, who decides, how they decide – it concentrates on newspaper front pages and television's leading topics. These serve to show most clearly the priorities and the reasoning behind the choices. The front page, however, is only one of many news pages. It is important because most readers glance at it first and because it is on the counter of shops and kiosks. The popular papers regard the choice and presentation of the 'splash' as of high importance, as noted by David English (in Chapter 6). The heavies also regard it as important, but in context. Thus Peter Preston, of the *Guardian*, making a point with which Charles Douglas-Home of *The Times* would surely concur:

> It would be wrong to give the impression that all one spends one's time agonising over is 'is that a better lead than that?' It's part of it but not the solitary focus. As editor I'm just as much concerned to make sure that there's a good follow-up from a Puerto Rican coffee plantation or a piece about the probability of a Scottish pit strike as anything else. The paper builds itself by being a good balance that fits the regular readers. You must have a bit of a blend.

Nevertheless, because the choice of news for the front page gives insight on newspaper priorities, let us follow the decisions on the nights of 13–15 February 1984.

For both papers, as already indicated, the prime influence is the editor. His intentions are interpreted at *The Times* by the chief night editor, David Hopkinson, in consultation with whoever of the senior staff (deputy editor, executive editor and others) is at hand. Similarly at the *Guardian* the choice is made by the night editor, Phil Osborne, in consultation with Preston or whoever is 'duty editor' that night. Decisions for the back page follow from the front, since 'turns' or continuations take much space. But there is always an endeavour to place one or more fresh stories on the back, and *The Times* whenever possible places a pictorial feature there.

MONDAY NIGHT: CHERNENKO v. PRINCESS DI

On the Monday night, 13 February all the heavy papers except the *Telegraph* led with the choice of Chernenko as the Kremlin's new leader, while all the populars except the *Mirror* led with Princess Diana's pregnancy. The *Mirror* and the *Telegraph* divided their front-page tops equally between the two, the *Mirror* giving foremost place to Chernenko and the *Telegraph* to Diana.

The headlines for the first and second stories:

Times	Chernenko takes over with firm pledge on detente
	Princess expects September baby
Guardian	Hopes of West are dashed by Chernenko
	Princess expects autumn baby
Telegraph	September baby for Princess
	Chernenko of the 'old guard' takes over
Mirror	The man who rules the Kremlin
	DIANA – a baby in September
Mail	Secret behind that smile . . .
	A baby!
	Maggie asks to see Chernenko
Express	Smile that says it all [with half-page picture]
Sun	Happy Di wants a girl!
	Kevin Keegan to quit

While neither the *Guardian* nor *The Times* had any hesitation about leading with Chernenko, there is a marked difference in the character of the two reports. Hella Pick in the *Guardian* said in her first sentence that the new Soviet leader 'has dashed the hopes of Western leaders . . . that the change of leadership in the Kremlin can be converted into a turning point for East–West relations'. She went on to summarise and analyse his first public statement. Richard Owen in *The Times* said in his second sentence that Chernenko 'immediately pledged himself to a policy of detente abroad and continuation of the late President Andropov's domestic reforms'. A short biography of Chernenko followed, and a listing of the day's events in Moscow. *The Times* centre pages, however, carried a long feature from Owen on how 'the sagging figure' of Chernenko had had new life breathed into it, on the disappointment of the younger liberal intellectuals in the Kremlin over the choice, but suggesting that Chernenko had a commitment to *détente* and peaceful coexistence.

When questioned about these divergent interpretations, both Hopkinson at *The Times* and Osborne at the *Guardian* were quick to defend their writers. Hopkinson not only regarded Chernenko's pledge on *détente* as the proper and inevitable page 1 lead, but expressed admiration for Owen's performance under great pressure in Moscow – so much so that judgement might well be swayed in Owen's favour next time he was contending for the front page.

> Richard Owen was enormously stretched. He was unlucky – having just come home to this country on leave and having to turn round and go back on Friday. He offered that feature and another and the title page lead. He's had a terrific day and coped magnificently.

The foreign news editor shared that view and had no qualms about accepting Owen's interpretation. He had seen the copy just before it went to Hopkinson and they had discussed it briefly.

Osborne at the *Guardian* justified both the choice of lead and Hella Pick's treatment of it by saying that, with a new Soviet leader, 'it's signs, signals, any shift of policy that you're looking for'. Pick had done that, indicating a continued tough line. Had she been given any advice on treatment? None at all. Was her report not too hard in its summing up? Not really, though it was probably harder than it might have been in less competitive days 10 or 15 years ago.

The deputy foreign editor on duty that evening, John Gittings, had a parallel reaction. No, he had not given any advice. He would have done so only if Pick's copy had been unclear or if there was other contradictory evidence. (Gittings himself is a specialist on China.)

The Tass text didn't start coming in until after 6.30. Hella was here, having watched the television. She was rewriting and revising as the text came in. The story wasn't complete until after 8, and by then page 1 was breathing down our necks, tearing pages from the typewriter. We can't sit around indulging in lengthy analysis or Kremlinology.

Why had she not been in Moscow instead of London? Because it had been impossible to obtain a visa after Andropov's death. Only those with existing visas could get in.

The royal story provoked a different kind of argument. Both Preston and Douglas-Home at first had reservations about giving it much prominence, while acknowledging the public curiosity about it. The editor of *The Times*, indeed, placed it seventh in his 4 p.m. priorities. Preston at 6.15 thought it was an interesting story with a nice picture, but never conceivably a lead. 'The child's not even first in line for the throne: we're getting into the second division.' Still, it was a jolly story and worth a good place. (Martin Wainwright, the reporter who had written it, said he'd simply been handed the PA copy and left to get on with it; he knew the paper's approach to such events, 'no grovelling, some gentle mocking'; he thought he'd been chosen partly because his wife, too, was due to have a second baby in September.)

At *The Times* it took a little mild persuasion before Hopkinson convinced his editor that the Princess of Wales should be the second lead, but Alan Hamilton had written a very readable account of the Princess expecting a baby and it made a happy change from heavy news. (The comment from Douglas-Home that I overheard in the newsroom about 6.35, as he leafed through the copy, was 'Alan does go on a bit, doesn't he?') Anyway the Princess won second place, with bold type for the text. Hamilton's own retrospective comment next day: 'They're ambivalent about the royals on *The Times*. It was a story that excited everyone in the office, and the executives all had their special points. I put them all in, knowing it would be cut by half.' And the editor:

I have an instinct against the spasm 'ra ra ra' reaction to royal stories. It was the lead on BBC radio all night, I think, and a lot of papers splashed it. My philosophy to the lead to the paper, though this sort of philosophy isn't written in tablets of stone, is that it should if possible be a news item that has implications. The first-born child to the heir to the throne has implications in a way that the second-born doesn't. Given a choice, I prefer to lead on a story with implications . . .

That *Times* front page had three other stories with implications, in addition to Chernenko – Robert Fisk's report from a Druze hamlet of how a US warship brought terror to a village, Peter Hennessy's on secret talks between the Cabinet Secretary and the Civil Service unions, and Philip Webster's on an impending free vote on the Matrimonial Proceedings Bill. All three, although not claimed as such, were *Times* exclusives.

Fisk's was the first eye-witness account in the British media of the villages bombarded by the battleship *New Jersey* at the end of the previous week – a straightforward and painful report on the civilian casualties, with many men and women wounded or dead and screaming children carried away in ambulances, though also with a guarded hint at the end that some Syrians and perhaps some Russian officers had been killed there. It provided a partial answer to a question that many British and other television viewers must have asked themselves the previous Friday, as they saw news film of the *New Jersey's* colossal salvoes: what on earth was it achieving? To obtain his report Fisk had had to take risks, both in travelling through the fighting areas and because the bombardment might be renewed. 'He's a man without concern for his own skin', Hopkinson said.

Hennessy's front-page report followed a news desk initiative. His weekly Whitehall brief, written for an inside page, revealed that over the weekend there had been secret talks between the Cabinet Secretary and the Civil Service unions; these were on the government's banning of unions at GCHQ, Cheltenham. The news editor thought that that was worth the front page in its own right. (In the office it was assumed that Hennessy had talked to the Cabinet Secretary, Sir Robert Armstrong, though it was thought better not to ask him outright.) The revised front-page report said that Sir Robert was about to put to the union leaders a 'toughened' version of their compromise proposals, and if that could be agreed he would put it to the Prime Minister on her return from Moscow. Next day it was followed up by nearly every other newspaper, as by television and radio, and indeed proved to be correct – although Mrs Thatcher eventually turned down the proposal.

The source of the third 'exclusive', on the Divorce Bill, was simpler: alert realisation by one of *The Times* political staff of the implications of allowing MPs a free vote on the floor of the House which would give opponents of a clause allowing divorce one year after marriage a marginally better chance to defeat it. (In the end they failed.)

Quite evidently *The Times* choice of third, fourth and fifth for its front page was influenced to some extent by the 'exclusive' nature of each of the three, but much more by the character and 'implications' (Douglas-Home's word) of each.

Comparable thinking was taking place at Farringdon Road. The *Guardian* gave third place to a City Office report on the future of a cross-channel hovercraft company – in itself not momentous, but thought to be significant because British Rail might sell its share, parallel with its impending loss of Sealink by 'privatisation', and it was probable that the *Guardian* would have the story to itself. Fourth place, however, went to a report which proved to be extraordinarily prescient, though that was not realised at the time. In Edinburgh a press conference being given by the NUM's vice-president, Mick McGahey, had been broken up by miners from Polmaise colliery in Stirlingshire – angry because they believed that their union executive was 'selling them down the river'. This was three weeks before the National Coal Board announced the closure of Cortonwood colliery in Yorkshire, thereby sparking the Yorkshire miners' strike and all that followed from it.

According to the news editor, the northern industrial correspondent Peter Hetherington (no relation of the author) had 'self-started' his report on the Edinburgh event. That is to say, he had gone north from his base in Newcastle on his own initiative and in the late afternoon had warned the London news desk that he had a strong story. Osborne thought it curious that Scots miners should be giving their man McGahey a hard time, and to Preston it was something unexpected. So at 6.15 it was judged worth a good place on page 1. As it turned out, no other Fleet Street paper gave the event the attention it received in the *Guardian*. It was not reported in *The Times* or

Telegraph, and mentioned only briefly in the *Mail* and *Mirror*; it was the fourth item in the BBC's Nine o'clock News, with a 1½ minute item, but was not reported that night by ITN. Yet the Coal Board's decision to close Polmaise and the resulting strike by miners there were the first shots in what became the most extensive news event of the year.

Asked months later whether he had any premonitions of this, Preston said no. It was simply the unexpected nature of the event that, in his eyes, made it news that night – plus Hetherington's insistence that it was something worth watching.

At the foot of the *Guardian*'s front page was a mildly frivolous piece about farmers in Wales trying to cash in on the high price of truffles (£100 or more a pound). It was, in *Guardian* conference shorthand, a 'basement' – one of those agreeably written, non-political pieces of which the news desk tries to generate two or three each day. They are part of Preston's 'blend', designed to offset a heavy political diet. Sometimes they work, he said, sometimes they don't. This one he liked.

For the inside home news pages, at the *Guardian* items are chosen primarily by the deputy night editor and at *The Times* mainly by the chief sub-editor in consultation with the executive editor or his deputy. That Monday night page leads chosen by the *Guardian* were on the opening day of the Chesterfield by-election, with Mr Tony Benn as Labour candidate; a foretaste of Labour's budget for the Greater London Council, which turned out to be another 'exclusive'; Church groups withdrawing from the so-called Video Inquiry Group, examining video 'nasties', because of uncertainty about its methods; and a partial breakdown of the cancer scanning service for women in south London. *The Times* opened its first home page with a dispute between the BBC's *Panorama* and the Conservative party chairman over a programme on right-wing infiltration of the party, together with the start of the Chesterfield by-election. Its second home page (page 3) began with a court case about women smuggling gold in their underwear on day trips from Jersey – a lightweight story, but judged to be 'readable'. Since the days of Harold Evans, page 3 has been treated as a relief from the heavy politics and economics of the main news pages, with a 'his and hers' character, lighter stories and more court cases or crime than *The Times* had traditionally carried. In the office it was generally thought a success, and the experiment of the Evans era had been developed. It is not, however, allowed to go as far as the *Sun*'s page 3.

TUESDAY NIGHT: EROTIC ICE

Andropov's funeral took place in Moscow, and afterwards visiting statesmen had individual talks with Mr Chernenko. At *The Times* at 4 p.m. the editor had no hesitation in placing this first, and no other lead was ever contemplated. At the *Guardian* two other possibilities were discussed. From early in the day, the news editor had been pressing both the drama and the importance of two government reports on the discharge of radioactive waste into the sea at Sellafield in Cumbria – 'devastating' reports, he said – and in the evening the night editor was interested also in the Druze offensive against Beirut.

In both papers, nevertheless, the talks in Moscow became the lead. But the *Guardian* in all editions carried a narrow 'strip' across the top of its front page on the Sellafield affair; while *The Times* in later editions replaced its Moscow photograph of Mrs Thatcher meeting Mr Chernenko with a large one of the ice-skaters Torvill and Dean, erotically kissing at the climax of their performance which won them the Olympic gold medal at Sarajevo. It was a memorable picture which caused some controversy in *The Times* office next day.

For *The Times* from Moscow Richard Owen sent early in the day a 'colour' (i.e. descriptive) piece about the funeral, and in the evening a diplomatic report on the talks. At 4 p.m. Douglas-Home said that the funeral should go either as second lead or on the back page, while the talks must be the lead. On the telex to Moscow in the morning, the foreign desk had agreed tactics with Owen. In fact, three stories were planned – the colour sketch of the funeral, which could stand alone all night; the main story with the bare facts of the funeral at the end (but to be sent early), and the East–West exchanges as lead to the report (to be sent later); and a side-bar (secondary) story on Mrs Thatcher's meeting with Chernenko, also to come late. That way *Times* production needs could best be met. Thus Ivan Barnes, foreign news editor:

> Owen had exactly my concerns – that when we started to update the main story with Mrs Thatcher it would become a Thatcher story. It seemed to us that this was an international story, the Soviet Union and the superpowers, with Mrs Thatcher an important element but not the most important. We were concerned that in 'renosing' the story late the international element might be lost. Owen was pleased with the idea of sending a side-bar story – the iron lady meets Genghis Khan or whatever, so that Thatcher could have her own headline – but he could keep the nose to whole thing in an international context.

These well-laid plans, however, foundered on a go-slow in the composing room. For reasons noted later, the NGA printers' union were demonstrating their displeasure and only minimal changes could be made in later editions. Of Owen's new nose for the main report, only a few fragments appeared; and of his side-bar story on Mrs Thatcher only three sentences. The disappointment was the more bitter because Owen had again stretched himself to the limit – and because the midnight and morning radio news programmes had Mrs Thatcher herself giving her own version of the Chernenko meeting.

Reading Owen's unused side-bar story late that evening, personally I thought it would have made a strong splash. As a taste, here is its second paragraph:

> Had there been a meeting of minds in the Kremlin? Well, the Prime Minister said cautiously, Mr Chernenko talked a lot about 'peaceful co-existence', while the equivalent concept on our side was peace through security, with lower levels of weapons. She smiled her dangerous smile. 'When you're in power you need a touch of steel, although it is only one touch. I am as fierce as ever in defence of the things in which I believe.'

In retrospect, however, the Barnes view that this must be treated as an international – not British – event appeared sound.

In early editions the title page carried a large picture of the Prime Minister shaking hands with Mr Chernenko. At the editor's request, a third figure in the background was toned down, to leave the two leaders in high relief. In the late editions, printing from 2 a.m. onwards, Torvill and Dean took over. Among the newsroom top tier, that night and next morning, there were divided opinions: those who thought the Prime Minister's first encounter in the Kremlin was an historic occasion, deserving a picture; and those who welcomed Torvill and Dean as a change after three days of Moscow and as a wonderful excitement. The first school was willing to admit that if Mrs Thatcher had had a headline as well, the page would look like *Pravda*. But wasn't the fuss over Torvill and Dean, they asked, a bit of British parochialism?

The editor's view? 'I was relieved to see any paper.' The ice-skating picture, which he liked, had been printed in only 60 000 copies when it ought to have been in 120 000. 'We not only had a late print but we did no changes that weren't absolutely essential.' Now, next morning, his primary preoccupation was how to get a better start to the print that night.

At the *Guardian* next day there was some chagrin over that picture. 'If we'd had it we'd have used it', Preston said. He was 'cross' that a technical fault had prevented his office from receiving it. When he first saw it in *The Times* he had suspected that, as sometimes happened, a 'sports' picture had bypassed the night desk and had gone to the sports desk. That was not the case: it had never been received. But he too was bothered about production problems. 'Cosmetic changes' were resented by the composing room, he said; but one would have been ordered if the picture had been there.

The Sellafield story, which the news editor had offered for the lead, was in Preston's view a strong one. All the beaches near the nuclear plant had been closed to the public since mid-November, and were to remain closed for many months. 'Peter Cole was pressing at an open door.' Preston also shared the view that, after three days of Moscow, it would be good to change to a home story. But he thought the compromise of 'stripping' Sellafield across the top was satisfactory. Osborne had some reservations: 'Moscow was a big occasion and we ought to give it gravitas.' In the end, though, he was happy with the result.

Cole had read advance copies of the Sellafield reports overnight and had kept close to reactions in the Commons and elsewhere during the day.

> It's one of those areas which the *Guardian* is best at: nukes and the environment. Interest groups and pressure groups had been going on about Sellafield for years. On the news desk we're as sceptical as anyone, but here was a story where a lot of us had had suspicions that all was not well. It was a terrific example of official secrecy – the government, the Atomic Energy Authority, BNF and others saying 'all is well'. Then suddenly you've got radioactive beaches. Suddenly the government – which has been conspiring in the cover-up and pretending it's all alarmist – admits that there was a leak and tremendous incompetence there. With Three-Mile Island in the background, I feel that appalling things are going on, that there will be a massive nuclear accident somewhere . . .
>
> It has happened here. That's why we had three people working on the story.

In addition to parts of the front and back pages, the *Guardian* gave the topic half of page 2 and a leader. *The Times* restricted its coverage to a long report on its page 2. The editor, visiting the newsroom soon after 6 p.m., had decreed that there would not be room for it on page 1. The chief sub-editor accepted it gladly as his page 2 lead, saying it was 'fascinating, slightly chilling, and sure to hold people's interest'.

One other Tuesday topic: the visit to the United States of the Opposition leader, Neil Kinnock. The *Guardian* on Tuesday morning had carried a mildly satirical report from Washington of Kinnock's meeting with Jesse Jackson, one of the potential Democratic candidates for the presidency, and of other visits around the capital. *The Times* had had nothing, because its printers' go-slow had prevented use of a report that came late the previous evening. Douglas-Home at the morning conference said that they must make sure of something that night, the more because the radio in the morning had reported a row between Kinnock and George Shultz, the Secretary of State; and Kinnock was due to meet President Reagan that afternoon. As a result the front page next morning carried a straightforward report, though with little about the White House meeting. The *Guardian* carried a whimsical 'basement' to its front page, discussing a phrase used by Mr Kinnock about Mr Shultz: 'he went off his pram' (a phrase said to be of Welsh origin and used by Mr Kinnock about a discussion of US policy in Central America).

The *Guardian* also carried on page 6 a short account, based on Washington briefings, of what had been said at the White House meeting about nuclear defence. Preston remarked later that Kinnock's entourage had not been happy about the *Guardian*'s reporting of the visit. They had wanted someone to be sent from London to travel with the party, but he had not thought it a sensible use of £1500 when there were two good *Guardian* staff men in Washington. Overall, he said, the paper had given Kinnock more extensive and sympathetic coverage from the US than any other British newspaper.

WEDNESDAY NIGHT: NO RETREAT ON GCHQ

At last a home story as indisputable lead in both papers – a Commons Select Committee calling on the Prime Minister to withdraw her ban on trade unions at the Cheltenham 'spy centre' (the Government Communications Headquarters or GCHQ), and a clear indication from Downing Street that Mrs Thatcher would not alter her stance. For both papers that was a welcome change after days dominated by Moscow and the new Soviet leadership. Less welcome was that both papers were still having production difficulties – *The Times* especially, with the 'go-slow' among printers threatening more late running and a further loss of distribution.

That indeed was the dominant point at the morning conference at Gray's Inn Road. The editor was determined that whatever else happened, the first edition must go to press on time. His opening words at the morning conference were that the flow of copy, 'even and early', was vital that night. The paper had failed to reach readers in the north and other distant destinations last night. 'It's more important to get the paper into readers' hands than to worry about critical points.' Later, out of conference, he told his senior executives that if necessary, standby whole-page advertisements could be substituted for two or three news pages, to get away on time. It was a painful and drastic expedient. It carried the risk also that if the printers were to hear that such measures were being contemplated they might go even slower.

From mid-morning it was known that the Select Committee report would be available later in the day, though little was known of its contents. The strength of its criticism came as a surprise. A copy reached *The Times* office soon after 5 p.m.; the *Guardian*'s political editor, Ian Aitken, received one at Westminster a little earlier. Already, both papers had picked it for the lead. At his 4 p.m. conference, Douglas-Home said it was sure to be important. So also, he believed, was the Prime Minister's reaction which was likely to remain unyielding. At the *Guardian*'s informal gathering about 5 p.m., Cole and Osborne agreed that it was the best prospect. Ian Wright, the second deputy editor and that night's duty editor, concurred. 'It was a collective decision', he said, 'as it often is. We had all come to the same view.'

Unlike Douglas-Home, however, the *Guardian* group thought that Mrs Thatcher might be about to shift her ground. Ironically, they had been influenced by what *The Times* man, Peter Hennessy, had written in his exclusive earlier in the week. Even the night editor at *The Times* was keeping an open mind, in spite of his editor's private hint. When copy arrived from their political reporter, Philip Webster, Hopkinson was worried by its opening phrase. It said that the government 'last night signalled its determination to go ahead and ban trade unions at the Cheltenham headquarters despite a call from Conservative and Labour MPs to drop its plans . . .' Telephone calls were put in both to Webster and to Julian Haviland, the political editor, to check whether the report was not 'too hard'. Haviland replied that the emphasis was 'correct'. By implication. the line had come from the Prime Minister's press secretary. Hopkinson then instructed that Webster's text should stand as written.

For the *Guardian*, Aitken also wrote that Mrs Thatcher had 'no intention of giving way', and that after her return from Moscow and a meeting of ministers that morning, the Cabinet Secretary, Sir Robert Armstrong, had 'dismissed' detailed plans put forward by the Civil Service unions. Compromise was not in the air, after all. Aitken also had to file, later that evening, a long report on the Prime Minister's reply to questions about her son Mark's commercial activities in Oman at a time when she had been there on an official visit. That, too, made the front page in later editions. Not so at *The Times*: the printers' go-slow prevented it.

With his first edition almost ready, Hopkinson summed up his evening's choice, still retaining some scepticism about the future at GCHQ.

The nearest rival to GCHQ is the exchange of letters between Peter Shore and the Prime Minister [on the Oman contracts]. If we hadn't GCHQ, that would have been pressing – and possibly the deal with the TUC on the political levy. I can envisage days when the levy would have made a respectable lead.

GCHQ matters because of the suspicion that the government will end up with egg on their faces. It really does seem that the Select Committee have got to the heart of the thing, and it's significant that all the Tories on the committee were as censorious as their Labour counterparts. In spite of what she's saying, that she'll ignore the call to lift the ban, it's inconceivable that there won't be some kind of climbdown within the next week or two. It's interesting on that level as well as on the 'spy HQ' dramatic level. It's a natural lead tonight . . . and it's part of the saga of banana skins.

At 10.48 Douglas-Home telephoned from home. Were they printing yet? Hopkinson was able to reassure him: the machines had just started up in spite of a foundry chapel meeting. The cost, however, was high: two full-page advertisements replacing news pages, to get the paper on its way. The newsroom by now had a somewhat forlorn and inactive air. Very few changes, if any, were going to be possible. Even the Wall Street prices exceptionally did not get on to the title page, though eventually one City page, one sports page, the arts review page and the two lost news pages were replated.

Two more cheerful footnotes, indicating an editor's involvement. When visiting the newsroom soon after 5 p.m., Douglas-Home was shown a picture of Princess Diana at Coventry – a long, thin side view, and a possibility for page one. He ruled it out at once: he did not want on the title page 'a picture simply designed to show that, although we all know that the Princess of Wales is pregnant, she cannot be seen to be pregnant'. By 6.15 Flynn and Hopkinson had found another picture, a smiling face-forward shot of the Prince and Princess. Hopkinson said that the page would benefit from 'vibrancy', and the picture could provide it. This time the editor capitulated.

At the morning conference there had been another exchange deriving from a picture – this time the theatrical one of Torvill and Dean kissing as they danced. Douglas-Home referred to it towards the end of the morning meeting: a pleasing picture, he said, and doubly so in getting away from the Moscow funeral. Did anyone want to 'know more' about the pair, and if so what? There was a slight snickering among the assembled executives but no response until Sarah Hogg, once of Channel Four News and now *Times* economic editor, said 'yes'. The editor went on 'I mean about the kind of money they can expect to earn – and who supported them while they were training?' Since he is well known for his horror of all kinds of public subsidies, as Sarah Hogg explained to me afterwards, she found the opportunity for editor-teasing irresistible. Torvill and Dean, she said, were 'a triumph for public expenditure' – they'd been able to train to this peak because they'd had a small grant to live on from the (socialist) Nottingham council. 'Oh Lord', said Douglas-Home, taking the joke against himself, 'you mean they're a quango.'

It did not end there, though. Next day *The Times* carried a feature from Sarajevo about the pair, skirting delicately around the question whether their relationship was sexual or platonic, for they were still denying that they intended to marry. That topic provided two of the popular papers with their splash – 'True love!' in the *Sun*; and 'Marry Torvill? Well, not this week says Dean' in the *Express*. A day later *The Times* also carried a long extract from a biography of the pair written by its former sports editor, John Hennessey. My own guess, when Douglas-Home mentioned the picture at his morning conference, was that he too was responding to it with normal human curiosity.

NEWS EDITORS AND REPORTERS

In common with other news editors, those at the *Guardian* and

The Times are in charge of the reporters and specialists. Hour by hour they are choosing the topics to which reporters are assigned – and choosing the men or women for the job – as well as keeping in touch with the specialist writers. They initiate or approve investigative inquiries, whether by specialists or reporters, and when necessary will bring together a small team for the task. As already outlined, they brief and advise the night editors and chief sub-editors.

In the spring of 1984 *The Times* news editor was David Blake and the *Guardian*'s Peter Cole. Blake had then been in the post about 18 months and Cole about seven years. Blake in his previous 10 years with the paper had been successively in business news, economics correspondent and then economics editor. Cole had been about nine years with the *Guardian*, having served on the political staff at the House of Commons before becoming news editor. In the autumn of 1984 Cole became one of the *Guardian*'s two deputy editors.

Although the work of the news desks is similar, there were two immediately evident differences. The layout of *The Times* newsroom is inconvenient – it is probably the worst in London, although in a fairly new building – and the atmosphere is more tense than at the *Guardian*, mainly because of the way higher executives monitor the work of the news desk.

The layout is a legacy of bad planning when *The Times* moved to its expensive new building in Gray's Inn Road at the height of the Thomson era. The management upstairs is luxuriously housed; for working journalists the environment is poor. From where he sits the news editor cannot see his reporters and must either telephone to them or leave his desk to discover whether or not they are at hand. He has his back to the night-editing and sub-editing complex, with a barrier in between; the foreign desk, the features desk and the business news desk are equally remote. Only someone with no sense of how a newsroom works could have devised such a scheme.

The *Guardian*, by contrast, has a large open-plan newsroom with a central complex common to the news and night desks, while the reporters and City office stretch out on one side and the sub-editors and foreign desks on the other. It is fairly compact and convenient, though the proximity of individual reporters' desks to each other can bring distracting noise. *Times* reporters have rather more space around them.

As to atmosphere, the difference derives from a determination at *The Times* to be extremely thorough both in 'postmortems' on what may have been missed in the previous night's paper and in seeking clues or ideas from other papers, radio and television on what to pursue during the current day. Blake usually arrives in the office about 8.30 or 8.45 – an hour or so earlier than the *Guardian*'s news editor – and with a list of points to pursue already prepared. Soon after arrival he will have a session with the executive editor (news) or his deputy – Charles Wilson or David Flynn – who will also have a list of questions and proposals. Part of the executive editor's role is to see that nothing slips, checking that whatever is ordered has been done and that nothing is neglected. Wilson and Flynn are accustomed to long days, up at 6.30, in the office two hours later and often not leaving until 10 p.m. or later.

At the *Guardian*, by contrast, the editor himself tends to deal direct with the news desk and on a more informal basis. Both the editor and the news editor do a good deal of telephoning from home before going to the office, and they too will have absorbed the other 'heavies' among the newspapers as well as the early radio news. They will also have skimmed through the popular papers. But Peter Preston does not believe in intensive postmortems, regarding them as often too time-consuming and unconstructive. He prefers to let the news desk get on with its job, visiting it himself from time to time and making occasional suggestions.

Each paper, of course, believes that its own system is the best. One veteran, with service both on the *Guardian* and *The Times*, on the whole preferred the latter.

At the *Guardian* they're too ready to dismiss some failure with a quip. That happened in your time [the author's] and it's still true today. It's a weakness . . . When Haley was editing *The Times* he fired off ten or fifteen memos to reporters and others every morning. Reporters would dive for their pigeon holes – they welcomed the feedback, whether it was a plus or a minus . . . *The New York Times* used to have a system of a cyclostyled sheet in which the editor or deputy editor commented on the day's paper. Something like that about once a week is what you need.

Asked about the frequency of postmortems at *The Times*,

David Blake said that they are essential but unpopular. You must build into the system, he said, the belief that if someone says 'do a story' either it's done or you convince people that it should not be done. 'It's too easy to slip back into the old world [of some years ago], with things slipping through the net time after time. Even when you think you've got everything going beautifully you still have to keep nagging away.'

It cannot be entirely a coincidence that in *The Times* office Wilson is sometimes mentioned by a title that, in a joking moment, he invented for himself – 'the arse-kicking machine'. That, however, gives too negative an impression of his role. Although treated with much suspicion when he first arrived from Scotland in 1982 – a surprise appointment by Charles Douglas-Home – he quickly earned a great deal of respect. He is relentless in asking questions and swift in picking on the aspect of an event that matters most. Either he or Flynn, together with David Blake, has a session with each of the specialists about once a fortnight to discuss recent work and future plans. The news lists, also, are more formal at *The Times* than at the *Guardian*, as explained in Chapter 3.

A few overheard fragments of Blake's conversations on those four February days give a taste of his news desk activities.

Talking to Alan Hamilton about the pregnancy of the Princess of Wales: 'yes, gynaecology and genealogy, and something about her public engagements. Talk to x and y.'

Discussing Hennessy's Whitehall diary: 'it's the strongest thing tonight. Rewrite an extract for the front, keeping it in context.'

On telephone to local 'stringer' who had provided unchecked information about electronics companies trying to recruit GCHQ staff: 'you injured a good story by wrong identification [Plessey instead of Marconi]. You must check every detail, not rely on someone else. *The Times* will not run stories that are "walking on soggy ground".'

To another staff man working on GCHQ: 'check whether there was a non-union agreement two years ago at Faslane, with £950 paid.'

On telephone to Anthony Bevins in Chesterfield: 'how do computerised electoral rolls affect the parties? What's happening to the little old ladies who used to address the envelopes? . . . Yes, we must rotate: not Benn all the time.'

To political staff about Commons questions on BBC row: 'do a "new readers start here"!'

Briefing night news editor on Chesterfield: 'it's all second-division stuff, Hattersley and Biffen not Kinnock and Thatcher.'

Talking to David Flynn about *Express* exclusive on Lloyds: 'it's a fake. They dug it out of the files, removed the names, and re-ran it. It was the same with their PSA "scandal": all old trial material reprocessed.'

Was Blake bothered by the thought that news editors and others may narrow the agenda, sharing a common vision with other journalists but excluding new concepts? On the whole, no, though he acknowledged the risk. He said that each of the competing papers is seeking 'new lines' and that some of them 'strike chords which then spread to others'. He believed that *The Times* must cover 'all the main political developments every day' together with 'a good mixture of social trends'. He insisted that every story must be comprehensible, with the greatest clarity, and that writing should be 'short, sharp, clean'. There should be greater readiness to explore an interesting subject even without a conventional news peg – 'conventional journalism', he said, 'anaesthetises people against going out and digging away' – but he is wary of interpretation for its own sake. For *The Times*, he said, one of the most serious obstacles is still the squeeze on home news space.

Shortage of space is a problem shared at the *Guardian*. Although in 1984 that paper was averaging about 30 per cent more space for home news than *The Times*, it was still cutting reporters' copy, often drastically. 'Almost everyone overwrites to some extent', Peter Cole said. The paper tries to maintain its tradition of giving writers freedom and minimising sub-editorial changes, but it does not always succeed. Some of the staff reporting from the coalfields during the 1984 miners' strike were aggrieved by the way what they regarded as relevant detail was being knocked out of their copy and by the way separate reports from different locations were at times clumsily merged into a single story.

The *Guardian*'s news editor appears to exercise rather more direct influence on the final choice of priorities than is usual at *The Times*. With Peter Cole that may have been partly because of his seniority, though it must also have been – and continue to be – because of the *Guardian*'s more informal system, which leads to a longer consultation each evening between the news editor and night editor. With news lists which are not a statement of priorities, it is inevitable that the night editor will heed the news editor's verbal account of what he believes to matter most.

As at *The Times*, a few of the overheard conversations on the newsdesk.

A call from the *Guardian*'s Scottish correspondent (herself a former news editor) to say that all but one of a group of East European trade unionists, due that day at a conference in Glasgow, had failed to turn up because the Home Office had refused to grant entry visas. Ironic, she thought, when Mrs Thatcher had lately come back from Hungary saying she wanted more freedom of exchange. Only one East German had got through. The Scottish correspondent was encouraged to go ahead with a substantial story.

Some chat about whether or what to do about Princess Di's second pregnancy. In the face of sardonic comment from some others, Cole held to the view that *Guardian* readers had a right to be told what was going on.

A Charlton Athletic soccer player was reported to have been deprived of his driving licence in a court case. Cole remarked that the club itself might be in the High Court later in the day, in bankruptcy proceedings. Was it worth putting someone on to write a 'bad day for Charlton' story? In the end it was dropped, because the club's case was postponed.

Readers rang up to ask why some CND demos had not been reported. Had they been subject to D-notices? Not at all, the news desk replied; it's just that you can't report every demo, not even every big one. It depended whether there was any fresh aspect to it and what else was happening. There was no ready yardstick by which to determine what would get in one day or what another.

The political editor, Ian Aitken, on the phone from the House of Commons with an assessment of the day's prospects. (He usually calls about three times during the day for an exchange with Cole.)

One substantial matter, discussed between Cole and Osborne – and with the reporter Martin Linton – was the timing and placing of a long account by Linton of the Young Conservatives' own study of far right infiltration of their party. First mention of the YC report, a private document, had appeared very briefly in the *Sunday Telegraph* two weeks earlier. The Conservative Central Office had evidently decided to bury the document, so far as possible, by putting out a short press release at 5.45 p.m. on the Saturday afternoon – too late for the Sunday papers and too soon for Monday's. They had done it, what was more, by simply placing copies of their press statement in the Commons press gallery, knowing that hardly anyone would be there on a Saturday evening.

Linton had followed up the Sunday story with a brief piece of his own which appeared in the *Guardian* on 31 January. That brought a 'flood of brown envelopes', with much more detail from the YC report and of its embarrassing appendices. Linton had asked Cole for time to pursue and check as much of this as he could; and the story was given impetus by the BBC's *Panorama* on 6 February – a programme that brought protests to the BBC from the Conservative party chairman, John Gummer. Now Linton's full account was ready. Since so much effort had gone into it, Cole did not want it used unless most of a page could be given to it. Osborne was sceptical at first, but agreed. It was, after all, a good story and immediately topical because senior Conservatives at Central Office had been discussing the problem of infiltration that day. So Linton's report was awarded its page.

Linton's own comment is of interest both because of the way
the Conservatives 'massaged' the news and because of what it
tells us about the interplay of television and newspaper news
judgements.

Panorama gave it momentum. It was an uphill battle until
then because people's [journalists'] news values are so much
dependent on what the judgements of other newspaper and
television people are . . . In the office you have to persuade
others that there are special circumstances to justify going
back to what is otherwise 'an old story'. It's a system that
leads to some very good stories being lost and forgotten . . .

It tempts organisations like the Conservative party and
other parties to massage the news – though I've never seen it
done so blatantly as this, by pushing a major report into the
one real media blind spot in the week. That's late Saturday
afternoon when nobody's interested in watching television
news at night and television news itself is not interested in
heavy stories – and when you're into Sunday it's already a
day old.

The value of Linton's work was to bring into the open much
more of the YC inquiry than Central Office, *Panorama* or
other newspapers had published, including some of the
evidence of systematic infiltration by ultra-nationalist and
neo-fascist groups. The decline of the National Front had left
extreme right-wingers with nowhere to go, and they had found
entry to the Conservative party easy. The YC report was
critical also of MPs who were prepared to use race and
immigration in emotive ways, whipping up bigotry and
prejudice. It recommended withdrawal of the whip in certain
cases.

To close this section on the work of news desks, some words
from the *Guardian*'s deputy news editor, John Gardner.

Students ask absolute questions: it's difficult to get over the
point that there are no absolute answers. It depends on the
strength of what you have – what you had yesterday, what
you have today, the strength of the stories. There are no
absolute values. A story that only yesterday you'd be happy
to page-lead with is lucky next day to get two paragraphs.
The day's different. That's all.

That indeed is the answer to many inquiries about coverage of demonstrations, job losses, trade figures and other repetitive topics. Each day is different, and each has its own news values.

POLITICS, BIAS AND TEXTS

Senior *Times* staff believe that *Times* reporting should be politically 'down the middle'. Senior *Guardian* staff believe also that reporting should be down the middle, though with particular attention to the well-being of the less affluent and less privileged. Some senior BBC news staff, while respecting the standards of both *The Times* and the *Guardian*, take the view that in tone and character the first is too obviously 'establishment' and the second too 'nonconformist'. They are talking here of news coverage – the choice of topics, the headlines, the opening paragraphs.

On the days studied here, both *The Times* and *Guardian* are 'down the middle' on every major news topic with the possible exception of the Chesterfield by-election. Even there the difference is not great. *The Times* gave less extensive coverage than the *Guardian* or *Telegraph,* but was factual, while the *Guardian* was more freewheeling, colourful and interpretative. Some textual quotations follow. On GCHQ, there is little to choose between their reporting, apart from the head start that *The Times* gained by its Tuesday report on the secret talks between the Cabinet Secretary and the unions. On the Moscow meetings, the *Guardian*'s Tuesday interpretation of Chernenko's first speech might be seen to have been too pessimistic; but next day it reported Mrs Thatcher's version of her talks mainly verbatim, in the later editions, while *The Times* had next to nothing. *The Times* failure, however, was caused by the printers' 'go-slow'. On the questioning of Mrs Thatcher about her son Mark's involvement in Oman, the two papers ran parallel. On Neil Kinnock's visit to Washington, the *Guardian*'s coverage was more thorough though sometimes whimsical. Again, the omissions in *The Times* were partly because of production constraints.

Even on these days, however, there are pointers. The *Guardian* carried substantially more about the Greenham Common women, the threats of eviction there and the bailiff's action at one of the camps. It carried more than twice as much on the Sellafield beaches and the government criticism of the management at the nuclear plant. It was a day ahead of *The Times* in giving prominence to the Duncan Campbell case and the Metropolitan police retention of his personal papers, though *The Times* gave deliberate prominence to the topic thereafter. These may be no more than straws of evidence, but they indicate the secondary differences of character.

Let us take Chesterfield in more detail, as the most controversial topic of the week. The parties regarded the campaign as starting on Monday, 13 February, and each held a press conference. The opening shots were covered, for once, by all the popular papers as well as the heavies – though for two or three days after that only the *Daily Mail* among the tabloids continued to give much space to the by-election.

Thus the Tuesday morning headlines, main content and space were as follows. (All text measurements are equated in standard column centimetres, not including headlines and pictures.)

Times, p. 1: 'Tatchell asked not to aid Benn'
Peter Tatchell, Labour's controversial left-winger who lost at Bermondsey, arrived in Chesterfield to support Benn but was asked to leave lest he diverted coverage. Text total *6 col. cm.*

　　　p. 2: 'Benn promises to support the leadership'
Report of 'crowded meeting' with Benn supported by Roy Hattersley; also of press conference at which Benn said that the Greenham Common women could claim most of the credit for Mrs Thatcher's decision to go to Moscow. 'Scathing attack on the press' by Hattersley and Benn reported, with *Times* singled out particularly for 'trivialising' and 'personalising'. The real issue', Hattersley said, 'is whether or not Chesterfield is prepared to aid and comfort Mrs Thatcher.' The press 'obsession' with Labour's divisions on defence 'hid' the extent of agreement in the party on education, health, the economy, employment, welfare, race, the police and data protection. Brief report (4 col. cm) of Home Secretary supporting Conservatives; and 1 col. cm on need for a moderate MP. Total text *36 col. cm* plus large picture of Benn and Hattersley.

Guardian, p. 1: 'Poll pals' – trailer for p. 3　*1 col. cm*

p. 3: 'Labour fields new pals' act'
Report of Hattersley and Benn canvassing after 'a public
display of spiky friendship that must rank as a connoisseur's
piece in recent political friendship . . . Differences were not
altogether buried. How could they be without massive dis-
sembling? But somehow they got through . . .' Report
thereafter covered the opening press conference, including
Hattersley's pledge that 'Labour has ended the years of
self-destruction and will from now on fight as a united body
loyal to a balanced leadership.'

Also 4 col. cm given to Dr David Owen supporting Liberal
and saying Benn 'was the architect of the policies which cost
Labour the 1983 election'; and 2 col. cm to Home Secretary
opposing 'extremism'. Text total *53 col. cm* plus large picture
of Hattersley and Benn.

Telegraph, p. 8: 'Benn makes a meal of unity in the works
canteen'
Report of press conference, Hattersley acknowledges some
policy differences but says Labour will fight as a united party.
Nearly half the report is taken up with exchanges on disunity
but includes Hattersley comment on party 'wholly and totally
united' on economic policy, education and other issues. Report
of lunch-time meeting in factory canteen, with Hattersley
saying Benn will be an MP of 'character and calibre'.

Also 2½ col. cm on Dr David Owen criticising Benn, and 4
col. cm on Home Secretary criticising Benn. Total text *37 col.
cm* plus picture.

Of the popular papers, the *Sun* on page 3 under 'Benn in poll
clash' said that Hattersley 'made it clear that he was at
loggerheads with Benn's anti-Common Market stand' (8 col.
cm). The *Daily Mirror* on page 2 under 'Big hit Benn' said he
attracted a crowd of 1000 for his opening meeting (4½ col.
cm). The *Daily Express* on page 7 under 'Divided we stand!'
reported the press conference with emphasis on points of
disagreement (30 col. cm). The *Daily Mail* on page 9 under
'They're off' gave exactly equal space in three parallel boxes to
Benn pledging to fight for Kinnock, the Home Secretary saying
that extremists must not be 'smuggled in', and David Owen
criticising Benn (30 col. cm).

On Wednesday morning:

Times, p. 1: 'Benn attack on BBC journalist'
Vincent Hanna accused of playing the role of SDP candidate.
     p. 2: 'Tatchell would be welcome, Benn says'
Benn dismisses reports that Tatchell was asked to leave. *The Times*, he says, 'very often tells lies'.
     Also 2 col. cm of Roy Jenkins press conference, and 1 col. cm on Conservative candidate. Text total *20 col. cm* and picture of Conservative with supporting MPs.

Guardian, back page: 'Benn hopes that Tatchell will go back to help'
Benn campaign 'went into a damaging skid yesterday after it emerged that Mr Peter Tatchell had been sent out canvassing . . . by the Chesterfield Labour headquarters'. Benn's denial that he had been asked to leave and willingness to welcome him back, which *Guardian* man says 'is bound to provide a whole cache of ammunition for the Liberal Alliance and the Conservatives'. Liberals quick to claim that 'the raggle-taggle Red Army is on the march again' and that Checkpoint Charlies were being set up outside Chesterfield. *Guardian* man says Tatchell arrived on Monday, was sent to canvass in New Whittington, a ward unexpectedly lost in a recent by-election, and may have encountered there 'some hostility in the streets, possibly from a Labour worker', before returning to London in the evening 'as he had planned'. Remainder of the *Guardian* report devoted to Benn's attack on Vincent Hanna. Text total *37 col. cm.*

Telegraph, p. 2: 'Benn says TV man is pushing for Alliance'
Criticism of Hanna reported; also Tatchell controversy. Short note on Hattersley speech accusing government of increasing unemployment 'as a central item of its economic policy', and on Conservative reply. Text total *46 col. cm.*

On Thursday morning:

Times, p. 2: 'Benn tries fitting jobless to work'
Benn suggests a way to match skills of Chesterfield unemployed with the community's needs – a local register of skills

and needs. Labour, he says, will sponsor such a scheme nationally. 14 col. cm on that, and 3 col. cm on Hanna. Also statements on Hanna from Conservative and BBC. Text total *22 col. cm* plus picture of Benn.

Guardian, p. 2: 'Second thoughts on first loyalties'
Both Conservative and Labour campaigners 'are nervously aware that many voters have begun to question their political loyalties'. The mood is easily detected, *Guardian* man says. Benn 'is an unsettling factor'. Among Conservatives there is 'outspoken criticism' of Mrs Thatcher's harsh approach to policy at home and of their party's 'seemingly timid' campaign at Chesterfield. Conservative candidate goes out of his way to describe himself as moderate and says GCHQ dispute should be settled by consensus. Liberals also having some problems over their 'slightly raw edged and over zealous candidate', but running 'a cool campaign'. Mention of Benn's plan to mobilise unemployed and of BBC reply on Hanna. Text total *34 col. cm*, plus large picture of Liberal canvassing.

(*Guardian* also has leading article on tactical voting at Chesterfield, with jocular aside about Vincent Hanna and his critical treatment of the SDP candidate in Darlington by-election.)

Telegraph, p. 2: 'Plan by Benn to cut town's unemployed'
The job-creation plan; supported by John Cunningham, advocating powers for local council to promote municipal enterprise. Brief note on Hanna affair and BBC reply. Conservative critical of Benn but himself disagrees with government on gas and electricity prices and GCHQ. Text total *30 col. cm,* plus big picture of Conservative at disco.

Sun, p. 6: 'Vegie Benn angling for votes'
Benn now a vegetarian, preferring fish to meat. Also on fringe candidates. Text *10 col. cm.*

Dail Mail, p. 15: 'Once upon a by-election – can Labour live happily ever after?'
News feature on 'the politics of make-believe' – voters not being told of contrast in policy between Benn and previous MP Eric Varley. Voters really being asked to 'stand on their heads' to support Benn. Kinnock's hard task in pretending that

Labour is 'one big happy family'. Article goes on to accuse Conservative and Liberal candidates of 'telling fairy stories too'. In their hearts they want Benn to win. Tories need Benn at Westminster 'as a bogy', and for Alliance there is nobody in his class as a recruiting sergeant. Further waspish comments on the Liberal and Conservative candidates. Text total *52 col. cm*, plus small pictures.

Fair coverage or foul? However unprejudiced, any political reporter was bound to take account of the wounding rift in the Labour party in preceding years and of Tony Benn's share in responsibility for it. Not to do so would be naive or wilfully misleading. The policies advocated by Benn and others on defence, the Common Market and Labour's own constitution had contributed both to the birth of the SDP and to Labour's poor showing in the 1983 general election. Chesterfield was a legitimate test of Labour's standing and of the likely consequences of Tony Benn's return. In any event, whoever the Labour candidate had been he was bound to be front runner in defending a large and safe majority.

The Tatchell episode may be seen as an irrelevant diversion. *The Times* at first saw it as a political curiosity, worth a short mention on page 1 but taking only a fraction of space in its opening day's report. It was an indication of continuing left-wing loyalty to Tony Benn and of the embarrassment that that could bring to the party leaders. Of the truth of its report *The Times* was never in doubt. Anthony Bevins, its man in Chesterfield, is described by Charles Douglas-Home as 'a very practised reporter', a hard news man with no prejudices and 'a relentless checker of stories'. Bevins had never said that it was Benn who asked Tatchell to leave. Another point was that, because of a libel action three or four years previously, when *The Times* wrongly said that Benn had a bank account in the Bahamas, there had always been 'electricity' between *Times* reporters and Tony Benn.

Tatchell himself had been the victim during the Bermondsey by-election not only of character assassination by some of the popular papers – partly brought on by his own conduct – but of the 'snowball' effects of press coverage. At Chesterfield again the snowball rolled, and after *The Times* story other newspapers took it up, along with radio and television.

Equally, however, when Benn launched his proposal on a Chesterfield 'skills and needs' register – as a forerunner to a national register – that was picked up and given prominence by the heavy newspapers and the broadcasters. For *The Times* and *Telegraph* it was the main Chesterfield story of the day. If Benn believed that his constructive points were neglected on the two opening days of the campaign, by the third they were receiving attention.

Looking back, the candidates with the greatest cause for complaint were the Liberal and the Conservative. Because attention was so intently focused on Benn, understandably and properly, their parts in the campaign were neglected. In the opening days only the *Guardian* and the *Daily Mail* attempted any assessment of their performance and prospects – and both papers were as sceptical about them as about Labour's showing.

Television coverage of the campaign's opening maintained a more clinical balance. Although Benn still received more attention than the others, the Conservative and Liberal candidates each enjoyed about two-thirds of the exposure awarded to Benn. Both Channel Four News and *Newsnight* suggested that the Liberal was likely to come second, both had film of Dr David Owen supporting the Liberal, and *Newsnight* spoke of tactical voting against Benn. *Newsnight* also treated the event with an agreeably wry humour, which may not have endeared it to Labour.

Two further political indicators, both linked with civil liberties. The previous Thursday a well-known freelance journalist, Duncan Campbell, had been knocked off his bicycle in Hampstead and taken to hospital. He was well known for revelations about defence and security matters, and he had been prosecuted two or three years earlier under the Official Secrets Act – an unsuccessful prosecution, and consequently an embarrassment to the government. The *Guardian* on the Wednesday reported that Campbell's lawyers had protested to Scotland Yard that documents which he had been carrying at the time of the accident were being held by the police, and had demanded their return.

During *The Times* morning conference that day, the news editor proposed 'a story a day' until the documents were returned or Campbell was charged with some offence. Douglas-Home concurred, and his wish was minuted in the morning circular. Similarly on the Conservative 'threats' over the BBC's *Panorama* programme on infiltration of the party: Douglas-Home wanted a continuing watch on that, with more details of precisely what the Conservative chairman was complaining about. He wanted both sides of the conflict fully covered and suggested a further attempt to tap *Panorama* sources. As asked, the reports were written. Unfortunately the incapacity of *The Times* composing room again knocked out much of the detail.

On both topics, the *Guardian*'s coverage was thorough. If 'down the middle' is a tenet of *Times* reporting, the principle was well observed on these days – and by both papers. In both newsrooms, admittedly, mention of Arthur Scargill or Ken Livingstone might bring a barbed aside. So might mention of Mrs Thatcher or John Gummer.

PRINTERS: AGGRAVATION AND FRUSTRATION

In 1984, both *The Times* and the *Guardian* had a bad year with their printers. Altogether the *Guardian* lost its whole print on one day and lost part of its print on 56 other days. *The Times* lost the whole print on 11 days and part on 21 others. Not all of those losses were because of trade union troubles: one day's print for each paper was prevented by a fire in the London machine room which they share. (The *Guardian* rents three lines of presses at *The Times–Sunday Times* plant, but employs its own staff to run them.) Mechanical failure was also responsible for a few of the days of shortfall.

For *The Times*, the week of our study was a particularly unhappy one. Three weeks earlier the paper did not appear at all for six nights because of action by members of Sogat '82 in a dispute over appointment of a library manager. Again, for one day at the end of February it did not appear because of action by a few engineers on the TUC's day of protest over the union ban at Cheltenham. Readers were told about both stoppages and one exasperated subscriber, after an anguished *Times* leader on the latter stoppage, wrote to ask why the management hadn't the guts or ingenuity to publish without the engineers.

Readers were not, however, told anything about the difficulties that plagued the paper in the middle week of February. Only the most perceptive might have deduced that something was wrong. On the Monday night a backlog of setting, because of an extra-large *Sunday Times* two nights earlier, delayed the first edition start and restricted edition changes thereafter. If computer setting and photocomposition were being employed properly, there need have been no difficulty – but, as in other offices, the transition to new technology has worsened performance instead of improving it. That has come to be accepted in Fleet Street. If not exactly an old Spanish custom, it is now a well-established new one.

On the Tuesday night there was an additional complication. For more than two months the management had been discussing with the NGA what it regarded as a minor change of format on the Stock Exchange prices page, with a change of column width, and agreement was thought to have been reached. The composing room chapel, however, still wanted extra payment for what it regarded as a major change. That was refused, and a 'go-slow' began. As a result of a very late start, much of the Scottish and North of England distribution was lost.

That in turn led the editor to give his Wednesday instruction (noted above) that the first edition must go on time even if finer points had to be sacrificed – and privately to tell Flynn and Hopkinson to use standby whole-page advertisements, if necessary, as substitutes for the last inside news pages. Two such substitutions had to be made. Douglas-Home's view was that, to maintain goodwill among buyers, the paper must reach them regularly. While a proportion of readers would remain loyal whatever happened, a number would not. Already the February sales figures were almost certain to be down because of the January week's stoppage.

The damage of such incidents is not only to sales but to editorial morale. As one senior executive said: 'Night news editing has been killed by the unions. So little setting is possible, and so few page changes, that late reporters and the sub-editors have almost given up. The effort has been made so often, only to be frustrated.'

On the three nights I listed only the most obvious losses:

Monday for Tuesday's paper
Report from Washington on Neil Kinnock's visit
Late additions from Moscow on arrivals for Andropov's
    funeral and informal talks

Tuesday for Wednesday's paper

Richard Owen's report on Mrs Thatcher's talks with Chernenko, and new lead to overall Moscow story

Details of GCHQ story, cut from first edition and not able to be placed later

Detail on Gummer's complaint against BBC, similarly cut and not placed later

Defence correspondent's report on marines who have to buy their own rucksacks, severely cut and not replaced later (annoying because it had begun some months earlier as a *Times* exclusive; now a page lead in the *Telegraph*)

Torvill and Dean front-page picture in only 60 000 copies instead of 120 000

Wednesday for Thursday's paper

Two new pages lost on early editions (pp. 3 and 5)

Back page feature on Paddington station deferred

None of this will come as a surprise to anyone working in Fleet Street. The *Guardian* not long afterwards lost part of one day and the whole of another because of a dispute over which union should refill the chemicals in a new phototypesetting machine – a task required about once a month. In the first six weeks of 1985, the *Guardian* had an even worse time because of NGA go-slows in the composing room, with up to 30 per cent of its print lost almost every night; then, after management warnings, there was a period of normal working. Journalists are bitterly accustomed to the anarchy of the printing unions and the inability of managements, individually or collectively, to cope with it. It is a costly and demoralising cancer, perceived only infrequently by readers or outside observers.

TIMES AND GUARDIAN: SOME CONCLUSIONS

The claim that *Times* reporting is politically 'down the middle' was generally justified in the week studied here. The *Guardian* can equally claim that its reporting emphasises straightforward factual information. Both papers were striving to provide comprehensive coverage of the main political, economic and social events of the day. In determining news priorities, the senior staff of both papers constantly try to assess the significance or possible repercussions of an event.

There is, nevertheless, a difference of character. Although not prominent in the front or back pages of the week we studied, it could be seen. (The difference is, of course, more marked in feature pages and leading articles, but they are not part of this study.) The *Guardian*'s front-page display of the Sellafield story – official criticism of the way radioactive waste was allowed to reach the Cumbrian beaches and sea – is an indication of its 'nonconformist' character. Douglas-Home had relegated the story to an inside page, though mainly because of preference for reports from Moscow and Washington. The more 'establishment' aspect of *The Times* could be seen in its choice of secondary topics. It was *The Times*, however, which made the most of Torvill and Dean, their Olympic gold medal for ice-dancing and the picture of their lips almost meeting as they danced – a touch of the frivolously popular amid politics and diplomacy.

Political bias was not evident in the week's reporting. *Times* coverage of the GCHQ affair, potentially embarrassing to the government, is one example of an impartial approach. The *Guardian*'s unsolemn reporting of Mr Kinnock's visit to the United States – displeasing to the Labour leader's entourage – can be seen in the same light. Politically the most controversial event of the week was the Chesterfield by-election. *Times* coverage was less extensive than in the *Guardian*, but that was mainly because of lack of space and production difficulties. *Times* reporting at the start of the campaign was criticised both by Mr Roy Hattersley and by Mr Tony Benn, but their charges appear to have been weakly founded. Given Mr Benn's previous share of responsibility for wounding rifts in the Labour party, there was legitimate interest in where the party would stand at Chesterfield on issues such as defence and the Common Market. On the positive side, politically, initiatives by the editor and others at *The Times* are noted in Chapter 1, for example on Duncan Campbell's papers being held by the police and on Conservative 'threats' to the BBC over *Panorama*. The Campbell papers were a topic on which the *Guardian* had got in first.

'Exclusives' were a daily occurrence in each paper. They

covered a wide range of topics, mainly political. They also illustrated the point that, contrary to an occasional academic assumption, there is much news that does not derive from news diaries or Press Association lists.

Were there 'silences' – areas of public concern which either paper was avoiding for political or commercial reasons? If any, in the week we studied they were not apparent. There may be occasions when *The Times* chooses not to give prominence to facts or figures damaging to a Conservative government: Murdoch's objection to Evans over prominence given to reports critical of government economic policy (*Good Times, Bad Times,* pp. 286–9) ought not to be forgotten. Of such intervention, however, there was no evidence.

Both papers are catering mainly for a public that is prosperous, educated and interested in world affairs. Of the two, *The Times* assumes greater affluence among its readers than the *Guardian* in its public – and there was a curiosity in the apparent popularity of the latter among pickets and police alike during the 1984–5 coal dispute (Chapter 9). In their choice of news, both papers are influenced by their perception of their readers. That both are catering successfully for their readers' interests is a reasonable assumption, given rising sales in 1984–5 and improved advertisement revenue. There is, however, little direct contact with readers apart from tele-

TABLE 7.1 *Content analysis, Tuesday evening, 14 February*

	C 4 N	BBC 9 o'clock	ITN, 10	Newsnight
New hope of East/West thaw	} 1/18.10	} 1/5.43	1/3.47	} 1/14.00
Andropov's funeral			2/3.53	
Torvill and Dean – Gold	—	12/4.36	12/4.09	a
Kinnock upsets Shultz	4/5.31	3/1.27	9/3.51	3/12.29
GCHQ – Select Committee, talks, etc.	—	6/1.05	—	—
Sellafield – Reprimand over errors	a	2/2.05	3/2.16	2/13.33
Couple tortured by gang	—	4/1.47	—	—
Beirut/Lebanon fighting	2/3.09	9/1.05	6/0.44	a
Elton John marries	a	15/1.02	14/1.53	—
Shooting tests on animals	a	—	10/0.58	—
Second Scott Lithgow rig cancelled	a	—	5/0.35	—
Industrial output up in December	a	8/0.12	8/0.54	—
Not in newspapers, Wednesday				
Amsterdam riots (brief in some papers)	—	11/0.32	7/0.30	—
Umaro Dikko in exile	—	10/1.59	—	—

a = minor story

phone calls and casual encounters in clubs, pubs, golf courses and so on.

Each editor is a strong influence in shaping the paper most days – as much as, for example, at ITN, if less flamboyantly than at the *Daily Mail*. This may be seen both from the conferences and from their other interventions.

The 'new technology' of production is painfully unsatisfactory. It is not being employed properly, and readers are told only a fraction of the truth about it. As elsewhere in Fleet Street, the managements in 1984 appeared incapable of coping with the combined difficulties of technologies and trade unions – and this was a perpetual frustration for journalists (pp. 180–2). That the journalists achieved so much nevertheless is a tribute to their patience and persistence.

TABLE 7.2 *Content analysis, Wednesday, 15 February*

	Express	Guardian	Mail	Mirror	Sun	Telegraph	Times
New hope of East/West thaw	1/2 & 6/1	1/1 & 26/3	1/2 & 4/2	2/2	2/1	1/1 & 36/3	1/1 & 32/2
Funeral of Andropov	6/2	1/2	4/1	4/1	2/1	3/1	32/1
Torvill and Dean – Gold	1/1, 2/1 & 36/1	1/6 & 22/1	1/1 & 43/2	1/1	1/1 & 13/1	1/2, 33/1 & 36/1	1/2
Kinnock upsets Shultz	2/2	1/5	6/1	2/1	4/2	*	1/3
GCHQ – Select Committee, talks, etc.	—	26/1	2/4	4/2	—	2/6	1/5 & 32/3
Sellafield – reprimand over errors	—	1/3, 2/1 & 26/5	13/1	5/3	16/2	1/6 & 8/1	1/8 & 2/2
Couple tortured by gang	2/1	2/5	11/1	5/1	1/2	1/3 & 2/2	2/9
Chesterfield by-election	—	26/2	9/3	—	—	2/4	1/9 & 2/1
Beirut/Lebanon fighting	2/3	1/4, 6/1	—	—	—	6/2	1/4
Gummer denies 'threat' to BBC	—	26/4	—	—	—	2/7	1/6
Hell's angels horror killings	7/1	4/2	—	11/1	7/1	10/1	3/4
Elton John marries	7/2	—	3/1	14/15	4/1 & 5/1	—	—
Shooting tests on animals	2/6	2/7 & 21/6	2/1	5/4	11/1	1/4 & 15/1	4/5
Second Scott-Lithgow rig cancelled	—	2/2	—	—	2/a	1/5	2/6
Industry output up in December	—	18/1	—	—	9/a	23/2	1/3
Greenham evictions begin	—	4/1	—	—	—	—	—
Supply of donor kidneys	—	—	2/3	—	—	2/3	—

Telegraph late enditions, Tuesday.
a   minor story, downpage.
Note: 1/1=page 1, splash.
      1/2=page 1, second story (in order of typographical prominence).
      1/3=page 3, fifth story (in order of typographical prominence).

8 A Deeper Dimension

The biggest television news programme each weekday lasts fifty minutes – Channel Four News, at 7 p.m. Since it was started in November 1982, it has brought a deeper dimension and a broader perspective to British television news. For three years before that, the BBC's late-evening *Newsnight* had begun to develop a more thorough exploration of particular topics, concentrating on two or three each night. *Newsnight* is a hybrid – part news, part current affairs or documentary – but it too had already helped to broaden the concepts of what is news.

The nature of these two programmes can be seen by comparison with the main television news on three nights in November 1983, as described in Chapter 5. The priorities are similar; the treatment differs. It may be remembered that that was the week when American marines were mopping up after their invasion of Grenada, and when the first Cruise missile components arrived at Greenham Common.

The Monday's Channel Four News, taking its decisions more than three hours earlier than ITN's News at Ten, also picked the events in Grenada as its leading topic. But it concentrated chiefly on an interview in Washington with the US Assistant Secretary of State, Richard Burt, on the implications of the American intervention for the future of the Atlantic alliance – his theme being 'we can disagree and yet go on and work together' – and then linked this with the Commons debate on the coming of cruise missiles. It noted Mr Heseltine's admission in the Commons that the events in Grenada marked a 'damaging disagreement' with the United States, together with his insistence that cruise would still come and that there was no need to demand a 'dual key' control over firing of the missiles. This was followed by studio interviews on dual control with Mr Heseltine, Dr David Owen (Alliance) and Mr Enoch Powell (now Ulster Unionist but a former Conservative Cabinet minister and a critic of the government view).

Altogether Channel Four News gave 22½ minutes to this, compared with News at Ten's 4½ minutes on Grenada and 3½ on Cruise. In its total of words, Channel Four New's coverage was the equivalent of more than three full columns of print in the *Guardian* or *The Times*. Later in its bulletin it devoted eight minutes to a preview of the South African referendum, aimed at giving voting rights to blacks while keeping all real political power in the hands of Afrikaaners; and another eight minutes to an interview with Sir Peter Hall, of the National Theatre, on the number of American works currently on show in London. The Hall interview was one unlikely to be carried by the mainstream television news, or – if carried – to be treated briefly as a light tailpiece.

Newsnight, like the BBC's Nine o'clock News, chose Cruise as its first topic – but it, too, linked the Commons debate with strains on the Atlantic alliance because of Grenada and with the unlikelihood of progress in the East–West disarmament talks at Geneva. It included a studio discussion with Mr Winston Churchill (Conservative), Mr John Cartwright (SDP) and Mr Denzil Davies (Labour). In all, sixteen minutes was given to that, compared with four minutes on the Nine o'clock News; 13½ minutes went to a preview of the South African referendum, compared with 3½ in the earlier programme; and 5½ minutes, compared with 3½, to the election of a democratic government in Argentina.

Length in itself is no guarantee of a deeper dimension. The summaries above, however, may give at least some indication of the more critical examination by Channel Four News of the background to events, the endeavour to explain both the causes and the possible consequences, and the readiness to give an airing to opposing views on a greater scale than is possible in a 23- or 25-minute news bulletin.

On the following night, similarly, 21 minutes were given by Channel Four News to the continuing debate on Cruise, after the Defence Secretary's warning that intruders at Greenham Common risked being shot – and that item included interviews by a woman reporter with women at Greenham, and studio interviews with Mr Heseltine again, Mrs Joan Ruddock of CND and a Soviet journalist live from Moscow. Later, 8 minutes went to Grenada, including an interview with the Governor, Sir Paul Scoon, on why he had sought American rather than British intervention; a report from Washington on criticism there of the American action, and an analysis of US casualties showing that more than half the dead had been killed in accidents or by fire from their own side. Newsnight gave 20 minutes to the 'warlords' of Lebanon meeting in Geneva, 10 to a new British design of 'supership' and 9 to local authority planning for 'life after the bomb'.

Stewart Purvis, after becoming editor of Channel Four News in the summer of 1983, extended the concept of a strong first item to be examined in depth, and he revised the pace and rhythm in the grouping of items in the remainder of the programme. In explaining his approach, he said to us that the choice of first item could put 'tremendous' nervous pressure on him or the programme editor. The first item must derive from one of the major events of the day; and that meant taking risks. There must be enough material to justify at least seven or eight minutes. Normally, a second topic also of up to seven or eight minutes follows, and then the 'newsbelt' in which a number of other news items are summarised in a series of items each of anywhere between 15 and 70 seconds.

After the first commercial break – two come within the programme – there is usually what Purvis called 'a hard feature'. This need not necessarily have a news 'peg'. It can be on industrial or scientific development, on conservation or on the arts. A feature, for example, on destruction of parts of the old Caledonian forest in the north of Scotland can be carried – having been filmed some days earlier as a result of inquiry into the inadequate powers of public bodies to prevent such destruction. Or it can be used by one of the arts specialists to preview an exhibition at the Tate Gallery, with explanation and critical comment on the paintings and their history. Or it may be taken up with a report by the science correspondent, using computerised graphics, on research into remote planets.

Television programmes have to have a pace and rhythm of their own [Purvis said]. Channel Four News has a pace of its own in the sense that normally the first item is quite long and the second item can be quite long and there may be a third item, and then there's the 'newsbelt' to pick up the pace. Then the idea is that you can settle down, feeling that you have been briefed on the stories of the day, and then after the break go into other subjects which are not part of the day's news. But in planning that slot, you have to discuss how it will feel after what's gone before.

If the newsbelt contained killings in Northern Ireland, for example, Purvis felt that there must be care in the choice of what followed immediately after.

The routine at Channel Four News begins about 9.30 a.m. with an informal discussion among a small group, led by Purvis, of the previous night's programme and the coming day. At 10.30 there is a large gathering – up to 40 people – of everyone involved that day. It is chaired either by the programme editor of the day or by Purvis. Taking as an example Wednesday, 7 March 1984, the prospects were outlined by Mike Sheppard, programme editor. Obvious events were the miners, with the NUM executive due to meet next day and the Yorkshire area having already decided to strike from the end of the week; a meeting of NEDC ('Neddy'), the consultative body bringing together government, industry and trade unions – but about to be boycotted by the unions because of the government's ban on unions at GCHQ in Cheltenham; and the future of the Scott-Lithgow shipyard on the Clyde, which Channel Four News's industrial editor, Ian Ross, had visited two days earlier.

At that stage, there was general reluctance to look to the NCB and NUM as top of the programme. Their differences and the Yorkshire decision to strike had led Monday's programme, at about 14 minutes, with some of the economic background filled in (decline of demand for coal, overproduction, high stocks); and on Tuesday it had had a further 8 minutes, reporting the NCB decision to cut production, with interviews with Mr Scargill and Mr MacGregor and a series of 'vox pop' interviews with miners on a bus. Purvis, Sheppard and the home news editor were looking for a new angle – possibly the constitutional position within the NUM – but Ian Ross was needed both for 'Neddy' and for Scott-Lithgow. Ross was out at the time, interviewing the former director-general of 'Neddy', but he was to be consulted about all three topics as soon as he returned.

A wide choice of secondary items was available for later in the programme. The front runner was an interview, recorded late on the previous evening, with an American colonel visiting London. He was to be one of those in charge of security at the Los Angeles Olympic games, and in 1979 he had been ground commander of the abortive attempt to rescue American hostages in Tehran. Others were a pre-Raphaelite exhibition at the Tate, known to be a colourful piece in preparation by the arts correspondent; a report on 'video nasties' which, according to the science correspondent, was 'crap'; a Commons Select Committee report on immigration; Princess Diana visiting a health centre; and one of Prince Andrew's girls appearing in a television series.

The decision to lead with Scott-Lithgow was taken in mid-afternoon. It well illustrates Purvis's comment about having to take risks with the lead. Soon after 3 p.m. there was word through Ian Ross that two of the competing bidders for the shipyard – which the government had said must be privatised or closed – were coming together in a joint bid. That was what Ross had expected, after his Clydeside visit two days earlier, but confirmation was still needed. At first he had only one tip to go on. The most encouraging sign was that the Secretary of State for Scotland, when his office was approached in the late afternoon, replied that he was ready to be interviewed live at Channel Four News at 7 p.m. Most unusually for a minister, he was also prepared to take part in a live discussion with a shop steward from Scott-Lithgow, who would be in a studio in Glasgow.

That clinched it for Purvis, Sheppard and Ross. It was a stronger and more active story than 'Neddy' and the union boycott, and very much stronger than video nasties.

Scott-Lithgow is rather a story we've made our own from the beginning [Sheppard said]. It fits very well our brief to cover the nuts and bolts of industry, not just the disputes. Ian [Ross] has very good contacts up there, and this coming together of Trafalgar House and Howard Doris could be the final chapter, though it may not . . . It's important in showing the government's relations with nationalised industries. It's important to us in the sense of looking at Scottish employment generally. It goes with a story we did – we gave prominence to it the other night – on a thousand new jobs at the 'silicon valley' near Greenock . . .

For Purvis it had the added attraction that Ross on the Monday had shot some very good new pictures of the Scott-Lithgow yard, the offshore oil platform under construction and the new naval vessels being fitted out there.

The item as broadcast lasted 7½ minutes, with Ross recounting the news of the joint bid and explaining, over his Monday pictures, that without such an offer the yard was in imminent danger of closing. There were short interviews with the chief executive of Trafalgar House and the deputy chief executive of British Shipbuilders, both of whom were hopeful that a deal could now be done, including renegotiation of contracts with BP and Britoil for whom platforms were under construction.

Then came the live interview – conducted by Trevor Mc-Donald, who was presenting the programme – with the Secretary of State for Scotland, George Younger, and the Scott-Lithgow steward. Mr Younger welcomed the offer, saying it was good news all round and that the new company intended to develop the yard. Pressed by McDonald on whether the government had obtained guarantees from the private investors, he replied 'I think we have.' It was a new company, he said, dedicated to developing the business. The shop steward, Duncan McNeil, agreed with Mr Younger that the workforce must be 'stable and cooperative', but he was cautious about the prospects, saying that they did not know the details yet. Anyway, he said, why could not British Shipbuilders and the government have preserved 'a national asset'? George Younger had the last word, saying that the more orders the yard could obtain the more jobs there would be. Purvis afterwards thought the item particularly worthwhile because the Secretary of State had been seen, on air, to say that the government would back the scheme. He was pleased also that the discussion with the shop steward had been constructive.

Among the other items, he also thought the video nasties had been worth doing, in spite of earlier doubts. It was important that there had been an open debate in studio both about the validity of the research – which claimed that one child in three aged eight had seen a video nastie – and on the implications of censorship in the Bill going through Parliament. Trevor McDonald had been advised to let the two antagonists in the debate put their points directly to each other, Purvis said, and it had worked well. (The item was, in all, 9½ minutes long.)

He agreed that uncertainty remained on the validity of the research behind the video nasties report. As one of the staff round the news desk had said, it was not enough to build an item on the basis of suspect statistics, sourcing it as 'a report out today says . . .'. But the reporter, Jane Corbin, had compiled a very competent summary, and the discussion had followed.

The science reporting, the medical reporting and the arts reporting were all important to Channel Four News, Purvis said. On foreign news, they were trying to extend the coverage with occasional features from Third World and other countries not normally in UK bulletins. Anyone regularly viewing Channel Four News would know that that policy was being carried through.

His own background? Graduate of Exeter University; worked for a local news agency in Exeter, then joined the BBC as a trainee journalist in 1968. He became scriptwriter in radio news, then moved to ITN in 1962. By 1976 he was a chief sub-editor and a weekend news producer, and by 1979 one of the three programme editors at News at Ten. He was responsible for a number of special programmes, the eventual release of the Tehran hostages being one and the SAS storming of the Iranian Embassy in London another; the Pope's visits to Poland, Britain and Central America followed, and Princess Diana's tour of Australia. In the summer of 1983 he was put in charge of Channel Four News.

Another primary influence at Channel Four is Peter Sissons, the chief programme presenter. The whole of his working life had been with ITN, since he went there from Oxford in 1964 as a trainee. He was for ten years industrial correspondent and then ITN's industrial editor, and for five more the anchorman of News at One before the starting of Channel Four. He is one of the most experienced of television interviewers, with the ability to persist with difficult questions but without aggression or discourtesy towards the person being interviewed. Of that, more will be heard in Chapter 10 on the coal dispute.

On the day before the one described above – Tuesday, 6 March – Sissons had been the presenter. The two leading items were on the questioning of Mrs Thatcher in the House of

Commons about a bank account to which payments were made in connection with her son Mark's activities in Oman, and the NCB–NUM meeting at which Mr MacGregor had told the miners' union that production must be cut by 4 million tonnes. The programme had led with Oman, giving it 12 minutes, and coal followed with 8 minutes. Apart from the fact that the coal dispute had been the lead the previous day, with 14 minutes, were there other reasons for putting Oman above it?

When asked about it, as one of those who took part in the decision, Sissons said that the Commons exchanges were 'an extraordinary drama'. The decision was taken after Purvis and he had heard the Prime Minister's replies, relayed from the Commons from 3.15 onwards.

> Suddenly we became aware of two new elements. The first was a particularly offensive question by Willie Hamilton [MP for Central Fife] where he suggested that the Thatchers were on the make, which if he'd said outside the House would probably have been the subject of a writ, and it was a particularly effective and nasty question. And secondly Norman St John-Stevas, former Leader of the House, got up and made the first really effective defence of the Prime Minister that one had heard during the saga – an extraordinary eloquent defence by someone that she had sacked.

Asked whether, nevertheless, it was an event of sufficient importance to head the programme, Sissons replied: 'It's generally enough for me if politicians regard it as of inherently great importance . . . Some politicians can be stupid and think that trivial things are important, but in this instance the fact that it was getting a lot of people concerned is enough.' Eleanor Goodman, the political correspondent for Channel Four News, had spoken to Purvis soon afterwards and persuaded him to take a 'spot' from Westminster colouring in some of the background to the exchanges; and there had been studio interviews with St John-Stevas and Peter Shore (Opposition front bench), in which Sissons had 'asked Stevas one or two, I hope, tough and searching questions and then bounced off that to Peter Shore'.

On a wholly separate matter, Sissons was asked about coverage of the return of the McCartneys from Barbados two months earlier (Chapter 6).

If I'd had my way it wouldn't have appeared at all. It's no secret that on the day he came back and did his famous piece at Heathrow – saying why not legalise it, it doesn't do any harm – I argued at the meeting here against us using it . . . The whole McCartney statement was used in full at about 8½, as on practically every news programme in the country. I said why don't we break the habit and take the view that what this guy says about legalising pot is only of zoological interest; and if it had been anyone else saying it, we wouldn't have run it, and it can only be the thin end of the drugs wedge, encouraging a lot of young people perhaps to experiment. I was heavily outvoted. I still think I was right!

There is in this reply an implied sense of social responsibility, which, though probably not many journalists would admit to it, can be an underlying and unstated factor in news judgements. On this occasion, Sissons was outvoted. For most of his colleagues, the instinct that this (McCartney's Heathrow comment) was too good a story and too popular to miss prevailed. But on other occasions the counter-instinct, not to make too much of drugs cases, may prove stronger.

Peter Sissons also commented on the concept of a 'seismic scale' for measuring news values, as outlined in Chapter 1. His reply was indirect but revealing of the way Channel Four News works.

You may recall, I think it was the *Washington Post* a number of years ago – they have an enormous staff and they polled them all about who they were actually making the newspapers for, and they all decided they were making it for themselves, primarily; that they regarded themselves as a good cross-section of society, the sort of people that they wanted to read the newspaper, and they basically made it for themselves.

It would, he said, be dangerous to carry that approach to extremes; but he found something of the same character in Channel Four News's approach.

The sort of cross-section of people you have working on our programme is pretty well a sort of cross-section of our audience. We've got some highbrow people, some lowbrow people, some sporty people, some funny people – some are intensely interested in politics, and I don't know if you've noticed but this is the only ITN programme when the morning meeting is a meeting of everybody involved. If there are 40 people, all 40 people are there, and that's what it's been since the beginning. I think it's extremely effective.

The framework of the programme, he said, was not the work of one person alone. Everyone could be involved, and it was an extremely healthy development.

Coming back more directly to the seismic scale, Sissons said this:

> Anyone who says that you can make a journalistic judgement in a sort of sterile bath is talking bunkum, twaddle. You make a judgement because of all your empirical knowledge store; you make it because of your family, because of the society in which we live. I hope I don't make judgements because of my political views . . . party politics does not figure at all in my make-up; my views go right across the parties; I'm with one party on one thing and against them on another. I hope that no one thinks that that comes into my judgement because it doesn't.

Finally, on the responsibility of a reporter to 'point up' the significance of an event, Sissons said that this was 'what you employ specialist reporters for'. It was often mistaken for 'imposing a view' on a story; but a specialist must say to readers or viewers 'look, this is important because it puts at risk your freedom of speech, or freedom of access to information or your rights as a citizen'. Some decisions had to be taken against 'some sort of background of the kind of society one wants to see', but such perceptions must not be tightly drawn. He believed that much of the criticism of journalism, whether lay or academic, was basically criticism of bad journalism.

CONCLUSION

Channel Four News, building on the precedent of *Newsnight*, has brought a deeper dimension to television news. Where the main news bulletins are almost the equivalent of the front and back pages of newspapers – headlines, summaries, detail of no more than two or three of the biggest events – Channel Four News has had the time and space to develop an equivalent to the inside news pages and some of the features. But its contribution has been greater than that. It has shown that interpretation of an event is a legitimate part of reporting, sometimes even the most important part. It has tried to let people speak for themselves, as will be seen again in Chapter 10 on the NCB–NUM dispute. And it has made a conscious effort to widen the agenda of news, bringing in coverage of scientific, medical, arts and Third World news.

9   The 1984–5 Coal Dispute: Newspapers

Innis Macbeath

The coal dispute lasted just one year, from March 1984 to March 1985. It was the dominant news story in Britain throughout that time. It had been preceded by an overtime ban, enforced by the National Union of Mineworkers from 1 November 1983. At its peak in the spring and early summer of 1984, more than 140 000 men were out on strike and about 30 000 had gone on working five-shift weeks. By December some 40 000 of the strikers had gone back to work, and by late February the National Coal Board was claiming that over half the NUM's membership were no longer on strike. Hardship had driven many men back.

This chapter describes the year's dispute from the vantage point of reporters and labour specialists for newspapers. The activities of other journalists and broadcasters and of actors in the dispute itself appear only as needed to clarify the position of the news writers. This treatment avoids the need to comment extensively on (although not the need to read) the mass of material which was purely propagandist. Some important matters are touched on only lightly – the battle of terminology, the use of statistics and the extent to which an individual journalist can distance himself from the other productions of the newspaper that employs him or her.

The research involved dozens of interviews and attention to hundreds of thousands of words in a few weeks, but the balance of attention has been on the process of news production, the variety of persons and roles involved and the interplay of pluralism and consensus. It has been difficult to comment on the coverage while reserving judgement on the substance of the dispute – especially for someone who has

197

been a labour academic and consultant as well as having played many journalistic roles; the attempt has been made.

From the start the air was full of conflicting allegations and disputed statistics. Thousands of police from other parts of the country had converged on mining areas to assist local forces in controlling picketing. There were violent clashes. The national funds of the union, subject to sequestration orders for contempt of court, were pursued through foreign banks. The form that the dispute took from March 1984 onwards came as a surprise to specialists as well as other journalists. Even to the most knowing, there appeared to be an unusual combination of familiar elements, and as the months passed there were fresh surprises. At the same time, coverage of the dispute settled down to an appropriate routine in most offices, and non-specialists became bolder in contributing to the huge bulk of commentary and conjecture.

This complex series of episodes involving many thousands of people, most of them far from London and mistrustful of the media, was a searching test of the assumptions of 'factual reporting'. Ernest Dimnet once commented that news is history written by people who are not historians.[1] It would be more illuminating to say that news is history written without the benefit of hindsight. The ideal assignment for the ideal reporter is a self-contained incident witnessed in detail by the reporter and capable of precise description in what Feibleman calls 'actual-object language', although the language of logic (generalisation) and qualitative judgement (values) keeps creeping in.[2] In highly controversial affairs like industrial disputes, participants may be inordinately sensitive to innocent attempts to put the facts succinctly or freshen up a tired topic.[3]

REPORTERS ON THE GROUND

For the individual reporter, assignments of this kind limit responsibility to specific work on a specific story. It cannot be complete; but in a narrow sense it can be accurate, and it can be written in plain terms.

In covering the coal strike this kind of reporting, whether by labour specialists or not, was confined almost entirely to action stories about pickets and police or demonstrators and police, and contained no examination of the issues. For a television reporter the priority is to get good pictures, and if his team manage that, then neither radio nor print can hope for the same impact. Radio reporters, with their greater frequency of news broadcasts, are concerned principally with succinct updating of the main known incidents, with occasional short descriptive pieces and interviews. Local radio came into its own during the coal dispute, and earned praise from several national newspaper reporters.

From the print journalist, this sort of work is taxing and frustrating. Patrick Wintour of the *Guardian* described the routine: watch picketing at 5 and 11 a.m., exchange notes with other journalists at a pub they frequented, listen to *The World at One* on BBC Radio 4, telephone the police and perhaps fit in a nap before filing a report to London. For about two weeks when there was intense interest in the picketing, Wintour spent most of his time covering the Nottinghamshire beat – for that is what it rapidly became, with several reporters on the same track.

Reporters are gregarious. They have to be; if you are always working against time, you cannot afford to waste time on elaborate rituals of acquaintance, and if you do not hit it off with one contact in reasonable time, you try another. The easiest contacts of all are others in the same trade. Besides, natural caution helps to keep journalists on the same assignment within the same broad lines. It is, of course, possible for an individual to be right when most colleagues are wrong ('Normal vision', Bernard Shaw once said, 'is extremely rare – and I have it'), but that does not mean that what he writes will be printed. Worst of all is to miss what everyone else reports, when it appears important to the 'gate-keepers' – the editors, editorial executives and sub-editors – who have the final say on what is actually published.

'One of the things that was quite remarkable was the tendency we had as journalists to all go to the same place', Wintour told us. 'There was a fantastic sort of sense of security: if we all go there at least we've *all* missed the story – or we've all got it. I think it was just a group mentality that all people develop.'

Wintour was London-based. His colleague, resident in Yorkshire, Malcolm Pithers, had much the same experience.

He covered the clashes at Orgreave coke plant in June, and explained something else:

> Most of the journalists have tended to stay behind police lines. I mean, we even have a nickname: there's a part of the field we call 'Cowards' Corner' where most of the journalists congregate. You can see what is happening, particularly if the police are moving forward . . . but it does imply that you are with the police and not an impartial observer.

Clearly the miners and their supporters did not expect anything else; the assumption was that the media were against them. Radio and television people were particularly visible and vulnerable, and experienced kicking, jostling and rowdy abuse, even occasionally spitting. Much of the exchanges were no more than banter, but sometimes there was specific anger, especially against the *Sun, Daily Mail, Daily Express* and less often the *Daily Telegraph*.[4] At the least, reporters were assumed to be hostile until they proved otherwise. The main physical risk was of being caught up in a skirmish, particularly if there was a police charge, and reporters had to see to their own safety. Besides, in the thick of things you can neither observe much nor record it.

Peter Hetherington, the *Guardian's* northern industrial reporter based on Tyneside, always tried to talk to picketing miners. Sometimes the response was so unreasonable and so hostile that the only thing to do was 'walk away' – though Hetherington blamed the hostility largely on the press. The police on the whole he found helpful; but it was always important to get the mood of the pickets.

> You find middle-aged people who seem incongruous on the picket lines. It's worth bringing out that there are a good number of people who in their own way are deeply patriotic, who've never been involved in this kind of action before and who clearly don't take a picketing decision lightly. They feel threatened, that their whole future is at stake . . . People from some threatened mining communities do look around them and see the results of industrial closures and they're asking where do they go from here. It's politicising them to a very great extent.

In his home area of the north-east, Hetherington found that he had few difficulties in talking to miners. In Yorkshire and Scotland it was tougher. Malcolm Pithers, being himself a Yorkshireman, had fewer problems there; he also mentioned the need to dress to fit the occasion.

Away from the confrontations, relations were much easier. Any journalist who wanted to could find some set of pickets to take him in their car and experience police surveillances. The road blocks and similar measures that kept Yorkshire pickets out of Nottinghamshire had immense coverage for a week or two, and then disappeared from the papers except for passing references. 'We dropped reports about road blocks because they were no longer news', Wintour said. 'By then people accepted them as part and parcel of their daily lives.'

For particulars of the numbers of people deployed, arrested and injured, reporters had to depend on official sources, usually the police. (Their helpfulness varied: Pithers found South Yorkshire very helpful, West Yorkshire slow and Nottinghamshire very unhelpful.) The National Coal Board had a press office with three or four officers in each area, and systematically correlated figures of pits open and miners at work. There was no equivalent on the union side, and although area officials were on the whole very open with all comers, they were very busy and had to be waited for. The NUM head office in Sheffield gave little help to reporters in the area, although its oddities were felt more deeply at another level, as we shall see.

To what extent reporters on the ground could make much of what they had seen themselves was largely a matter of luck. However carefully observed, action that has been reported with moving pictures on midday television loses its attraction for a newspaper long before the next morning. There was also little room in the news columns for any other kind of personal-experience reporting: 'sketches' and 'colour pieces' have fallen into disuse in the television age, or retreated to the features pages.

THE STRIKE AS SEEN BY NEWSDESKS

The spread of incident geographically and its episodic nature caused difficulties of a different kind. 'The whole thing's so

diffuse you just don't know where to deploy your resources',
said Paul Dacre, news editor of the *Daily Mail*. 'The whole of
Fleet Street was catching up desperately at Orgreave.' David
Blake, news editor of *The Times*, put it this way:

> It's a terribly difficult dispute to cover. Not much actually
> happens, but it's terribly important. You can't compete with
> television for action, and quite frankly in day-to-day terms
> it's quite boring most of the time. Our readers are basically
> southern; most of them have never met a miner. From
> reading most of the papers, it's clearly impossible the strike
> has lasted as long as it has, because for most papers it's
> obvious the miners shouldn't be on strike, they should go
> back to work and they will be beaten.

When he spoke, the stoppage had lasted 14 weeks. Six months
later, when 'action' had largely given way to a campaign of
attrition as winter set in, Blake still saw the problems in much
the same light.

In the event, reports from staff journalists in the field were
often incorporated in news round-ups, with or without a shared
by-line. If they were to see their work in the paper, they were
obliged to incorporate a great deal that they had not observed
personally. That does not mean that they necessarily accepted
hearsay uncritically; most reporters check with as many sources
as they can, but it is not easy afterwards to remember details of
one's own working behaviour on a crowded day.

The extreme intensity of news reporting against a deadline is
often underestimated by commentators (sometimes by editors)
who have never experienced it. In an ideal world, reporters
would never be given nine hours to fly from London to a
country whose language they do not speak to write the paper's
lead story for the following morning about a crisis of which
they know nothing, or dictate a front-page news report without
notes because there has been no time to write before the
edition deadline. These are extremes – but in fact a sudden
order to Yorkshire from London has elements in common with
the first; the old saying that Britain and the United States are
separated by a common language has some relevance also for
an abrupt move to Notts or Yorkshire. The experience is
always tiring, often exasperating and usually too concentrated
for the writer to recall for long in detail.

This sketch of 'front-line' activity and of newsdesk control illuminates some of the observations in Chapter 1. In a general sense, there was never any difficulty about 'agenda-setting'; conflict in the coal industry was clearly well established on the agenda already. But at the start of the dispute news desks were slow to perceive the dimensions of the event and its possible duration; and few in London at first saw any need to project the implications for miners' families and mining communities. Hetherington at the *Guardian* was able to secure some space for his reporting of the human implications, particularly in south-east Durham. In the early days, that was exceptional. Hetherington himself noted at the time that the Scottish press were quicker to appreciate these aspects – and more sympathetic to the miners – than were the nationals in London.

Later the reporters in the field contributed to the detail of the agenda in two other ways; by their judgement on what was still remarkable – 'police roadblocks are not news any longer' or 'when you've seen one picket you've seen them all' – and by the cumulative effect of their common reporting from the same or similar incidents.

From the later comments of news editors one derives at least some sense of the 'highly organised, systematic response' to a confusing situation, as mentioned in Chapter 1. It took the form of searching for something relatively predictable or administrable. This cast of mind almost always demands quantifiable information whenever it seems possible and seeks to establish a general shared understanding of what is going on – in this case, what had changed in the continuing coal affair and how the developments of 1984 had become a 'big story' in their own right.

WHAT INDICATIONS OF DISTORTION?

How far are there indications of distortion, as McQuail feared in his notes for the McGregor Royal Commission (see pp. 44–9 of his working paper), from primary emphasis on action, personality and conflict, and from the 'snowball effect' when one newspaper follows another and a dominant 'news angle' is established? The implication of the question is that newspapers may neglect the essentials of a development to run after some lively side issues that can be dramatically presented, and that they will all tend to do so together. Certainly, as David Blake's comment indicates, avoiding boredom is a consideration even for traditionally staid papers, and front-line reporters also frequently have long periods of simply hanging about.

More often than not, decisions about what would be significant in these reporters' area of operation are laid down for them. They are posted where they are to look for activity that is significant in terms of their remit. Such activity as comes their way may not be typical in any grand sense, and they may underrate lack of a particular kind of activity or overlook indications of change that would be more obvious to a specialist. On the other hand, an observer unencumbered with much prior knowledge may sometimes report more shrewdly than a blasé specialist and journalists in the field cannot wholly disregard the evidence of their own senses.[5]

Again, an industrial dispute is a conflict and the emphasis on personality was already well established. Ian MacGregor, chairman of the NCB, and Arthur Scargill, president of the NUM, had been individuals of particular media interest for a long time, although for different reasons. Journalists who have to deal with them consider them both secretive men who use rather than inform the media, with Scargill more effective in doing so than MacGregor. By 1984 they had certainly become celebrities in the sense of being talked about more than their accomplishments warranted, perhaps than any person's accomplishments would warrant.[6] How far the media lead and how far they respond to current celebrity and 'public opinion' is an open question, but both have certainly existed in some form as far back as records tell; modern technology has speeded up and concentrated the puffing process.

These were all established themes for the reporter in the field. We have to look elsewhere in the newspapers' organisation for change in them. By far the most difficult theme, in terms of assessing what is actually going on, is that of violence and intimidation. In a light-hearted moment Arthur Marsh once defined industrial relations, as practised in Britain, as 'mutual intimidation', and in certain circumstances this is true enough.

Paul Routledge, labour editor of *The Times,* had this to say about mass picketing:

When miners go on strike they don't sit at home all day doing their knitting. What was significant this time was the speed of the police response. Within 48 hours they had sealed off the county of Nottinghamshire. When this strike is over, it will have been Charles McLachlan [Chief Constable of Nottinghamshire] who did most to reduce its effectiveness.

On a long view, the scuffles of 1984 were a throwback to an older day. In 1912 police borrowed from other counties were deployed in the first national coal strike, and in 1929 the late Will Paynter, eventually general secretary of the NUM, lost his front teeth to a blow from the police and learnt shorthand during his ensuing prison sentence.[7] All experienced labour reporters have seen scuffles and worse; Geoffrey Goodman, labour editor of the *Daily Mirror,* recalled when he talked to us outright fighting in the British Motor Corporation dispute of 1955, but there was no police presence and no media presence more stimulating than a young man with a notebook. At the other extreme, the Grunwick affair 20 years later was immoderately emphasised simply because it was in London. The picture of the policeman knocked out by a bottle, with blood running from his head, was powerfully memorable.

The taste of violence reported may not be representative of anything more than the incidents themselves – usually involving too many people to be repeated often. Scargill was injured in the biggest incident – at Orgreave on 18 June – just as he had been arrested at Grunwick. (At Grunwick, it is said, the arresting officer either did not recognise him or had not heard the instruction that his visit was to have no publicity.) There is simply no body of evidence to put the reported incidents in context, and there is no mechanism to record systematically the amount of small-scale, back-row suffering and intimidation. The *Guardian*'s Hetherington saw some of it and heard about more.

Some of the most bitter and violent scenes have taken place out of the glare of publicity – because you don't know about them at once, because it hasn't been Notts, it hasn't been Ravenscraig. If you look at various little opencast sites up and down the country you'll find quite a few incidents of fairly serious violent picketing – Tow Law in County Durham, Blyth power station and others. They've received no publicity at all because Notts has been seen as the main trouble spot.

Although anything approaching absolute truth is impossible, there can be no doubt that in 1984 there was a great deal of shameful behaviour by some miners and some policemen. Discussion was clouded by the refusal of Scargill and his colleagues to repudiate violence by NUM members; they criticised the police and the government instead, whenever the matter was raised. Police spokesmen in turn tended to say that they would not even have been there if pickets had not been massing first.

THE PHASES OF GETTING IT INTO FOCUS

On 5 March 1984, when the Yorkshire area council of the NUM decided to call out the 56 000 members in this biggest area of all, none of the national newspaper specialists was there to report the decision at first hand. The occasion was the announced intention of the local area director to close Cortonwood Colliery near Doncaster within five weeks, although the agreed appeal procedure usually took months. The report was picked up in London and incorporated in round-up reports including coincident but separate items like an appeal by MacGregor for an end to the overtime ban and some stone-throwing at another colliery in Yorkshire where there was a dispute about maintenance.

This was only one of several disputes in Yorkshire at the time; the most serious had begun as an attempt to prevent the managers at one colliery from changing the mealtimes of 14 men (an attempt, the union said, to circumvent the effects of the overtime ban) and went on to stop work in the whole South Yorkshire 'panel', a quarter of the coalfield. There was continuing unrest in Scotland, and Hetherington's report of a demonstration at an area council meeting in Edinburgh against the closing of Polmaise had been on the *Guardian*'s front page in mid-February.

All the same, local problems had been contained before, and in London stepping up of industrial action was not expected.

Routledge of *The Times* was actually abroad on sabbatical leave. The overtime ban had kept unrest simmering – directly over pay, but with an element of unrest about pit closures – but the election of Peter Heathfield as general secretary in January had been by the narrowest of margins, suggesting that the militant faction to which he belonged had at best failed to increase its dominance. Three times Scargill and his supporters had been unsuccessful in a ballot for a national strike, and they seemed to have no more prospect of success in 1984.

'In view of the worsening situation in Yorkshire and the demands for action over the Lancashire pits', wrote David Felton in *The Times,* 'the NUM executive will be under pressure on Thursday to step up industrial action. Mr Scargill and his supporters have been reluctant to do this because they believe the overtime ban is effective.' In the *Daily Mail* David Norris referred to the danger of a national strike, but by June 1984, when he was interviewed, he could no longer recall the source of this uniquely prescient comment.

The next six weeks or so saw a shakedown cruise for the media in general. The scrupulous constitutionality and respect for balloting in the NUM were taken for granted. Rule 43 of the NUM required that a national strike should not take place until after a ballot of the membership in pursuance of a resolution of the national conference. Rule 41 gave the national executive committee discretion in respect of local disputes. A ballot of all members before a strike of all members is a requirement in several union constitutions, including the biggest, the Transport and General Workers' Union. The difference is that the TGWU, with 20-odd trade groups party to more than 150 national agreements, never has occasion to bring out all its members. The NUM requirement, first followed in 1970, had become almost an annual event; it was a condition of the settlement in 1944 that had made the unitary NUM out of the assorted regional unions in the old Miners' Federation of Great Britain. No one had suspected that anyone would look for a way round Rule 43 by declaring a nationwide cluster of local action under Rule 41.

The NCB, led by MacGregor, met NUM leaders in London on 6 March for a long-arranged meeting, and announced their intention to cut back mining capacity by 4 million tonnes in 1984. In view of the fact that for several months Scargill had been claiming, and the board denying, that there was a 'hit list' of pits to be closed, this seemed as provocative as the zero per cent pay offer that led to the national steel strike four years before. Two days later the NUM executive in Sheffield – with rowdy demonstrators in the street outside – authorised area industrial action in advance if the area chose to take it. There was no precedent that anyone could recall for such a general interpretation of the phrase 'previous sanction' in Rule 41. (When the Electrical Trades Union was led by Communists, all strikes were deemed official until the national executive decided otherwise.) Mick McGahey, the NUM vice-president, said: 'Area by area will decide, and in my opinion have a domino effect.' This phrase was widely reported – both in *The Times* and *Guardian,* for example – but without commentary it seemed more a prediction than a statement of intent.

On 12 March the Yorkshire strike began. It was supported by Scotland, Wales, Kent and the north-east; Lancashire and Derbyshire were uncertain and Leicester and Nottingham reluctant or opposed. From then onwards there was a steady flow of inquiry about how things had happened as they did; some questions were answered in one newspaper, some in another. By the end of April a certain consensus had developed about what were the salient facts, and a general agreement about the issues involved, although not about the merits of the issues. The consensus did not include agreement on what was clearly a matter of fact but was not clear from the public record: the behaviour and motives of the miners' union leaders, senior managers of the coal industry and the government. Any or all of them could have been guilty of opportunism, readiness to bend rules and deliberate deception of the public or one another. What is interesting from the point of view of this study is the limit beyond which the conscientious news reporter feels he cannot go.

One firmly believed that the confrontation from March onwards was provoked by MacGregor at the government's bidding, and at a propitious time to defeat the miners' leadership and make deep cuts in capacity quickly. He did not try to get this view into the paper, although it was not Conservative.

If I put that in, it would be deleted anyway – considered

biased, just a personal opinion . . . The best you can do is get someone else to say it, and that's weak: 'Union leaders believe . . .' This is not Scargill's strike. But you've got to admit that the government has handled it quite brilliantly as a propaganda exercise.

Another, working for one of the anti-union papers not in this study, said he 'considered Arthur frankly impossible, and if I were a miner I'd never forgive him, but I'm here to do a reporting job and I leave the filth to the professionals'. No doubt to some people this repudiation would be morally precarious, and ineffective as well if they believe that 'the public' derives an overall impression of an event from a newspaper rather than, in separate compartments, attested fact here and what the paper thinks about it there. Critics of journalists as a class are inclined to catch them both ways, accusing them of mixing up news and comment on the one hand, and claiming, on the other, that it is an artificial distinction – a convention to ease reporters' consciences.

Away from the 'front-line', reporting of the dispute is determined by the interplay between gate-keepers and specialists. Some tension here is a useful safeguard against the 'snowball effect'. It is a commonplace for the specialist and, say, his editor to be at least in different snowballs; they keep different company. There are certainly mutual influences among journalists of a less rudimentary kind than the get-togethers in the coalfields, but they usually look on one another's work with a critical eye, particularly if they are specialists. They check where they follow, if their own reputations depend on special knowledge. They have a variety of reference groups – 'people like me' – with whom to discuss, cooperate and make comparisons, and they have various less intimate contacts.

Most labour specialists are in the industrial group of journalists – a consortium of newspaper and broadcasting staff correspondents. Being a labour or industry specialist in a recognised house is a necessary qualification but does not automatically ensure membership. It confers the same advantages as membership of other organised groups, such as joint briefings and some increase in credibility among those in the know. Most trade union officers accept that members of the group are better informed and more reliable than 'any old journalist'; most trade union members have never heard of the group. Its officers sometimes make representations on behalf of the group; for example, in June 1984, they discussed with Peter Heathfield whether the NUM could improve its methods of distributing information.

Journalists also often form working partnerships, with two or more cooperating to share more potential sources of information than one could manage alone. These partnerships may last for a few days, when reporters meet on the same story and hit it off, or for years, so that it is well known that X of the *Blade* and Y of the *Beast* work together. The partners are usually not in the same organisation, and sometimes their employers are in direct competition.

These are supports in what can be a formidable task in a crowded business like the coal dispute. The reporters must first select from an overload of data. They must then check what they have selected and put it in a form which will be right for what they believe to be their readers; it must also be right for what gate-keepers believe to be their readers. 'We are conditioned by the newspapers we work for', said David Norris of the *Daily Mail*. 'It would have been slightly different for the *Guardian,* but I would say our reports have been fair.' Geoffrey Goodman detected in his senior colleagues on the *Daily Mirror* the assumption that other working-class readers were out of sympathy with the miners, and he believed that as a result the paper had failed to bring to life the social reality of the mining areas. He considered none of the other tabloids nor the *Daily Telegraph* had even tried, and none of the 'heavies' had really succeeded.

At every point there are evaluations – of institutions, of persons, of themes. During the shakedown, the preponderant emphasis in most of the coverage was on the development of confrontation with its political and commercial implications, although from the beginning Routledge in *The Times* rehearsed Scargill's emphasis on saving mining communities, and Hetherington, Pithers and Jean Stead (Scotland) in the *Guardian* supplied some excellent social observation, first as back-up in the news columns and later as features, as the importance of this aspect of the dispute loomed larger in London. They should have earned the paper exemption from

Goodman's criticism. *The Times,* by contrast, was relatively way-ward, with a much higher proportion of opinion to observation.

There is bound to be some friction between the comprehen-sive second-hand overview available to the head office and the observations of the field reporters. Only a few journalists have enough experience as both gate-keeper and reporter to see the difference in the round (Jean Stead, as a former news editor, is one of them), and the question, 'How do you know?' is all too easily overlooked in assessing distant realities.[8] The centre does not always know best.

What makes a report plausible? The source, the medium in which it appears and (before it is published or broadcast) the form in which it is presented; the dexterity of the writing and the standing of the writer – all these are influences; so is the quality of the authentication. There was nothing new in the view that the government was deeply involved in the strategy of the coal dispute, and it was certainly plausible; the intervention of the photocopier provided the *Daily Mirror* on 7 June with an authentic statement that the Prime Minister had let it be known that she wanted a settlement of the railway-men's pay claim so that they would not be on strike at the same time as the miners.

Plausibility depends on the receiver as well as the transmit-ter. Among journalists, plausibility seems to be accorded to abundant detail and avoidance of declamatory comment – in this case displayed in the *Financial Times,* which consistently gave more words to the developing situation than any other medium, even at some risk of duplication and repetition from day to day, and also gave the impression of earnestly trying to make sense of what was going on. Broadcast news and tabloids had acute problems of trying to summarise without distortion. The text papers had another advantage over television. Moving pictures of actual events and important participants are offset by deficiencies in explanation. Not only is it confined to relatively few words, but the talking staff head is somehow less convincing than the direct material elsewhere in the broadcast.

Television journalists (or their researchers) read the news-papers in their field and expect to get leads from them. Conversely, newspaper journalists watch television and listen to the radio for 'one-liners' about where the action is and for possibly significant comments by leading figures. They do not expect to get much information from such broadcasts, which, like tabloid newspapers' reports, are boiled down to a minute proportion of available data.

Natural caution operates for specialists too. Experience may be reluctant to admit novelty. For example, Goodman, when interviewed in June, played Ecclesiastes,[9] emphasising the familiarity of many features of the dispute. Interviewed again six months later, he wondered if the country was indeed facing collapse of the structure of industrial relations as Britain had known it for half a century. Identifying a new trend, or a convergence of what seemed separate trends (such as rising unemployment, centralised government, 'positive' policing and industrial confrontation) has its own special difficulty. 'When you look back', said Keith Harper, labour editor of the *Guardian,* 'you didn't know it was the start of a gigantic strike; it was an important local news story. Only when it starts developing do you look around for all the angles.'

When thousands of other miners came out with the Yorkshiremen on 12 March, the 'looking around' began in earnest. *The Times* and the *Financial Times* had coverage by their energy correspondents from the middle of the month onwards, yet it was the *Guardian* who first reported worry about paying for the oil being used in the power stations to save coal. Someone from the generating board phoned late one evening to speak to the energy correspondent and got Harper because he happened to be still at the office. It was, he recalled, a little haphazard. On 22 March Wintour reported from Cortonwood a rational, localised explanation of events there. The area director had been asked to contribute 400 000 tonnes to the national reduction of 4 million tonnes' capacity. Production at Cortonwood was 400 000 tonnes, the pit made a loss by Coal Board accounting conventions and the local market for that grade of coal had gone with the cutback in manufacture of special steels. Rapid closure would meet the deadline of the end of the financial year. This was certainly plausible enough; it still left a confused impression about how the NCB operated and what its standards were.

THE CONFLICT OF STATISTICS

Some aspects of the affair could not be checked because of the work it would have involved, like assessing coal stocks at power stations. Again, there were constant reports of coal coming into the country by small east coast ports and taken inland by fleets of lorries, but no one would acknowledge being the buyer and only mass surveillance could have produced much information. Figures were another problem. Usually the reader had little to help him to make sense of the difference between a government estimate that the dispute had cost £400 million and Opposition estimates as high as £3000 million. No estimate was available of the change in cash flow to the mining areas, naturally, although it was obviously important and not summed up in any official figures. Probably the total funds raised for miners' families will never be more than a rough guess; they might be some sort of record, too.

The uncertainty was illustrated in a round-up by Philip Bassett in the *Financial Times* on 31 October. He recorded that the miners had lost £577 million in wages, including £502 million since March; the NCB had lost 55.5 million tonnes of production, including 8.2 million during the overtime ban, with an additional loss of ('it is roughly estimated') £700 million; the government ('it is thought') had an extra borrowing requirement of £850 million with some estimates much higher, British Rail's loss from running only 40 coal trains a day instead of 300 was about £140 million, and benefit paid by the Department of Health and Social Security was £21 158 406. The lunatic precision of the last figure makes an astonishing contrast with the others.

In February there were estimates that the overtime ban had increased the NCB's loss by £25 million. In mid-March the figure everyone printed was £135 million – based apparently on NCB draft accounts. When MacGregor announced the 4 million tonnes' capacity cut, all the papers printed the estimate that it would close 20 pits and end 20 000 jobs. The NCB neither confirmed nor denied these figures. Where did they come from?

David Norris, who had been a labour specialist only since November, explained that he had accepted the figure of more experienced specialists who had a formula. It seems to have been put together from past experience. For example, the tally of the NCB proposed cuts in 1981 (when the government had been obliged to give in) had been 23 pits and 4 million tonnes, and in June 1983, the *Daily Mirror* had got hold of a memorandum from Norman Siddall, then chairman of the NCB, presenting options to Nigel Lawson, Secretary of State for Energy. It had equated 70 pits and 70 000 jobs. Scargill claimed that the job losses and probably the capacity cuts would be much larger – and so far as one can judge from different reports, the actual outcome would not follow a precise formula. The NCB press office was cautious, but it was generally believed that it would deny any estimate that was wildly wrong. By common consent the most reliable press office in any nationalised industry – perhaps any industry in Britain – it retained the confidence of most journalists, but it was stretched. 'If you don't believe either side you just have to put down what they both say', said Terry Pattinson of the *Mirror*. 'You haven't the time and resources to go round and check whether pits are open or not, when the NCB say 117 are closed and Scargill says 135.'

THE ROUTINES OF MIDSUMMER

By midsummer each paper had developed a routine. At *The Times* and the *Guardian* the senior specialist handled the 'top of the news' and attended the principal press conferences and lobbied the meetings of the NUM executive and any negotiations. They each had two assistants and colleagues in the field, but whereas Keith Harper in the *Guardian* felt that he or his deputy maintained reasonable control over total news coverage, at *The Times* it was much more in the hands of the news editor and the other editorial executives. One effect was a greater coordination and apparent tidiness in *The Times* coverage. Another was some submergence of nuances.

On the *Mirror,* Pattinson spent much of his time in the office, checking a mountain of copy by telephone and reducing it to '15 to 17 sentences'. He went to Sheffield for the NUM executive, and had a couple of forays out of London to do feature articles, but had few opportunities. Goodman wrote a background feature from time to time, and colleagues in Manchester and the sister paper the *Daily Record* in Glasgow sent material. Norris was similarly tied down with the *Mail*. A colleague in Manchester covered some of the northern end, and features were written by some of the paper's 'top writers' sent north from London. Reporters seemed to have least autonomy in the tabloids and most with the *Guardian.* 'The *Mirror*'s very much a bureaucracy', Pattinson said. 'Local reporters wouldn't do something like a day in the life of a picket unless they're instructed.' Pithers and Hetherington, in the regions for the *Guardian,* generated more of their own material but felt they were not always kept in the picture about what was required in London.

Harper observed that for a labour correspondent the dispute was the nearest thing to a general election. Indeed, politics and personalities were handled with more assurance than technological facts and figures. This tendency was stimulated by what Routledge called the 'small daily surprise' which was a feature of the dispute, punctuated by big ones.

> On the train going up to Sheffield we'd say, 'What'll be the White Rabbit today?' What with the bishops, the courts, the role of the women, the relationship with the Labour Party and the TUC, the comings and goings between unions, law and order, new labour legislation and old-fashioned litigation, the police presence, dissent in the management – there were so many angles it's virtually inexhaustible.

'Something always happens to bring it back to the front page', Harper said. 'People will say almost with relief, "So we can give the coal strike a rest today", and we'd always say, "Just wait, there'll be something", and there nearly always has been.'

The parties to the dispute also seemed to have settled into certain norms. The government had embraced the 'law and order' aspect with great relish, successfully fastened the label 'uneconomic' on pits which were not commercially viable and described the presumed cost of the dispute as an 'investment', presumably on the assumption that industrial power and political authority are commodities. They also emphasised the 'right to work', a novel usage in Britain in respect of strike-breakers and a very powerful one; it may have developed spontaneously or been imported from the United States, where state Acts outlawing the closed shop are usually known as 'right to work laws'. The Labour party was relatively tormented, partly because a prospective alternative government cannot condone inefficiency and violence, or repudiate 'work'. In an odd way, simplicity was easier for the government. The union's constituent parts – the striking majority and the working minority – were hard for journalists to get at. More remarkable, the management began to rebel, although it was not until the autumn that the revolt came to a head.

The intervening period might be called the time of the eclipse of the professionals – including both specialist writers and other industrial relations practitioners; among them would be the professional conciliators of the Advisory, Conciliation and Arbitration Service whose help proved unsuccessful by the beginning of November. Once the stoppage began, few specialists expected it to be settled quickly. In the shakedown phase several doubtful points were clarified: the extent of support from other unions, the government's and management's resolution, the pressure on coal stocks and the effectiveness of steps to supplement them or find substitutes. The steel industry, the railways and the docks were seriously affected. The dockers' leaders had two bites at a dock strike; the first, in July, apparently worried the government but the second, at the end of August, was half-hearted and simply petered out – although the TGWU leaders represented it as an internal matter to do with blackleg labour, dockers in ports that refused to strike made it clear that they felt they were being 'bounced' by Scargill. The surprise to the specialist writers was that the NUM leaders and their sympathisers in the docks should have put things to the test at that point.

Specialists' calculations are naturally governed by precedent and shared notions of sensible solutions. Because so much was still being resolved in power terms in May and June, few expected results from the intermittent talks. A settlement seemed closer in early July, especially after nine hours of 'constructive' talks at the Rubens Hotel in London on 6 July. 'I wonder why that chance was squandered by Scargill', Harper said. 'He would have had a very good settlement in the middle of the summer while the miners were still full of fight.' Routledge, a Yorkshireman himself, saw it differently. Of the form of words on offer he said:

The NUM saw through·that. The board would continue to

have the right to close pits pretty well as and when they
wanted . . . There were very different formulations, but
much the same concept. I didn't believe there was going to
be a settlement. Neither side was close enough to defeat to
have to make that climbdown.

For the core coverage of this phase of the dispute a different set
of journalistic skills was required. One in particular is the
patient plod round contacts, putting to them a developing
notion of an event or situation, taking in fresh material and
knocking out what is too readily deniable. For example, after a
meeting behind closed doors, the formal press conference or
statement is often unsatisfactory. The reporter must wait until
the participants he knows are available somewhere else, and he
meets or telephones them in turn. 'I'm trying to check on the
meeting tonight. Did Jack really say? . . .' 'Yes, I know it's
confidential, but . . .' 'I have what Jill said, and . . .'
　　Naturally the ability to master documents and take a long
view is useful too; the specifically journalistic expression of it is
managing to do so unusually rapidly. Equally important is
remorseless inquisitiveness about those who choose positions
of public responsibility. There are risks in being too close to
any one contact, or small group of contacts; a reporter loses a
lot of credibility if he is known to 'fly kites' for his friends.
Paradoxically, the ability to honour a confidence, not only
about the source of information but about the substance, may
be important. It may also hamstring a reporter, or even the
whole newspaper.[10]

THE SPLIT IN THE NCB

The eclipse of the professionals took roughly from the
beginning of July to the ACAS failure at the beginning of
November. Dissension just below board level on the management side was already apparent and soon came to a head. A
strike by the supervisors (the National Association of Colliery
Overmen, Deputies and Shotfirers) had been barely avoided;
their position is pivotal, because a pit cannot operate without
their members' working. A few days afterwards, on 4
November, the British Association of Colliery Management

publicly criticised the board's approach, and the BACM membership included all middle and some senior management. Journalists had been aware of stresses for months. ('Peter Heathfield had been saying to anyone who would listen', Routledge recalled, ' "There are managers on our side, too." ') Open dissent by managers and their dismissal in the course of a stoppage are very rare; in the nature of the situation, managers tend to leave comment to the official mouthpieces while union members may become more vocal. If the settlement appears a severe reverse, of course, dismissals of managers afterwards are commonplace but rarely publicised.

Before the trouble began, MacGregor had concentrated authority in the office of the chief executive – run by himself and his deputy, Jimmy Cowan – and he reconstituted the board with a majority of part-time members. The industrial group of journalists had concluded early on – probably, like the NUM, as soon as his appointment was announced – that he proposed to try in the coal industry what had apparently succeeded in steel, and address his employees over the heads of their unions and regardless of the advice of his subordinates. Already in 1983 the *Financial Times* had published from an American correspondent a devastating 'hatchet' article pointing out that Amax, the corporation through which MacGregor had made his reputation, was losing even more than British Steel, and as a result his reputation in the United States had declined. In moving from steel to coal he met a hail of hostility. 'Even the Nottinghamshire miners consider him a professional butcher', Routledge said. 'The miners believe Arthur rather than the board, largely because of MacGregor's blasé, off-hand manner.'

As early as May both Harper and Routledge had written about management dissension. The industrial group had witnessed the altercation between Cowan and Ned Smith, industrial relations director, about a television broadcast, with Smith saying, 'I will not, sir; I will not' in full sight and hearing of journalists in the foyer of Hobart House. There were indications as well of forms of news management that bypassed the usual channels. Goodman, although not most of the group, was conscious of a decline in NCB reliability by June. MacGregor was concentrating the flow of 'information' through his own office, advised by external consultants, and becoming choosy about whom he talked to. Harper was one journalist to whom he refused an interview; Harper thought it was because of a *Guardian* leader, but it may have been because of a radio interview in which he seemed critical of the board's redeployment promises to South Wales miners whose pits were closed.

Meanwhile, Scargill's highly idiosyncratic news management at the NUM caused intense annoyance. No one at head office was allowed to give press statements except Scargill himself and his press officer, Nell Myers, who lived in London but had to commute regularly to Sheffield. Most reporters had despaired of receiving any information from Scargill's press conferences, which were clearly designed for direct public consumption; his ready flow of statistics was impressive but unhelpful.

Outside the control of the industrial group, there were effective pressures on some of the papers. The *Guardian* and the *Mirror* both followed a fairly consistent line, deprecating violence and the extremity of the NUM's total resistance to pit closures and (which was unprecedented) its refusal to accept an interpretation by the courts of the union's rules;[11] this allowed the *Guardian* freedom to criticise MacGregor's clumsiness and some of the government's enthusiasms and hypocrisies. The *Mail* was a solid supporter of the government's line from the start (although it too eventually joined the chorus of criticism of the chairman). Most notable was the editorial approach of *The Times*. When massed police were first used in March, *The Times* was uneasy, saying that the civil courts and not the police and criminal courts were the better remedy. By 12 May the tone had changed – 'How long must we tolerate what should be intolerable in a country which has always prided itself on being law-abiding?' – and by 27 July an editorial referred to 'this undeclared civil war which has defaced Britain this summer'.

During the fortnight in October when Nacods leaders were negotiating with 82 per cent authority for a strike which would probably have ended all coal production, there were two notable incidents. The first concerned *The Times*. The main headline in the first edition of 18 October read: 'Deputies predict total strike in Notts pits'; and the first paragraph of a four-paragraph summary read: 'The coal industry is set to come to a complete halt on Thursday after pit deputies, including those in Nottinghamshire, voted to back their leaders' strike call.' The story was attributed to Paul Routledge (labour editor), Barrie Clement (labour reporter) and Craig Seaton (a reporter who had handled much of the coverage of picketing). The final edition had instead the heading 'Midland deputies' disquiet over pit talks failure' and the summary: 'The Nacods executive's strike call has prompted the Midlands Area to agree to meet on Saturday to seek "clarification" of the reason for the pit peace talks breakdown.' The story was attributed to 'Our Labour Staff'. Where the original story by Routledge and his colleagues said that officials of Nacods predicted a 100 per cent response to the strike call, the anonymous one said: 'It became clear last night that there is considerable disquiet among the 17,000 Nacods members.' In effect it made a total stoppage in Nottinghamshire seem much less likely than the early edition had done. Other members of the industrial group were puzzled; most of them had heard of the proposed Saturday meeting, but did not think it worth mentioning.

The next week the *Daily Express* carried a report that the NCB would concede to Nacods all that they asked for, to keep them at work and isolate the NUM. Cowan, the deputy chairman, authorised a denial to the *Express*. Sir Larry Lamb, the editor, laughed when he heard about the denial and commented that it seemed even MacGregor's own office now were not told what he intended. How did the editor know? Evidently because he had talked directly with MacGregor. It was against this kind of background, and some weeks of verbal hair-splitting and cross-country negotiation, that the press heard about the dismissal of Geoff Kirk, director of public relations, who had been with the Coal Board for nearly 40 years and shared much of the credit for its reputation for openness and honesty.

Although Michael Eaton, an area director from Yorkshire, had been brought to London as NCB chief spokesman, this was generally considered an acknowledgement by MacGregor that he needed a good 'front man' and not a criticism of anyone else. For months Kirk had been uneasy about MacGregor's publicity decisions and about some of his informal advisers.

However, Kirk had given no indication of his discontent to any of the journalists we interviewed. On 29 October, the day before he was sent home, he had had a brisk argument with MacGregor, who was trying to make the most of a visit by an NUM official to Libya and apparently could not make up his mind about Eaton's position; Eaton had already been withdrawn from media contact once.

The Libyan business illustrated MacGregor's difficulties. Jon Swain's revelation in the *Sunday Times* that the NUM had sent an emissary to Libya looking for 'trade union support' had important repercussions. In particular, it gave Labour politicians a 'political escape hatch' (as one privately described it) from being locked into support for the NUM leadership – in view of the odium incurred by the murder of a police woman in St James's Square. For an experienced publicist such as Kirk, the Libyan visit was a perfect instance of a story that needed no elaboration by 'the other side'; it had its own momentum. But the experienced publicist was ignored by MacGregor just as the experienced industrial relations practitioner had been ignored four months earlier in the despatch of a 'personal letter' to tens of thousands of miners.

As a result, newspapers that had been denouncing Scargill one day were deriding MacGregor the next. On 30 October the *Express* front page had a headline 'Fury at Libyan link – Scargill at bay' and the *Mirror* 'The poisonous embrace', with a still picture from Libyan television (relayed by ITN and the BBC) of the NUM man being welcomed by Colonel Gadaffi. On 31 October the front-page headlines were 'The Coal Board scores yet another own goal' (*Express*) and 'Chaos at the Coal Board' (*Mirror*). Other front-page headlines included 'Coal Board rift seen as MacGregor silences spokesman' (*Telegraph*) and 'Scargill off hook in Mac bungle' (*Sun*). The *Mail* carried a feature on page 6 by Peter Paterson under the heading 'Is MacGregor turning into Mr Magoo?' Paterson commented: 'Mr MacGregor has been destroyed by Mr Scargill, whose mastery of television has shown up his most glaring inadequacy – a complete inability to communicate.'

On the afternoon of 30 October, Harper was interviewing Eaton with Kirk in attendance when MacGregor's secretary called Kirk away. 'I was whisked off down the corridor', Harper said, 'not knowing that the clamp had been put again on Eaton and that Geoff was going to be sacked.' Within a week Kirk had retired early, telling a press conference that Mac-Gregor had ignored professional advice, and it was announced that Ned Smith would also retire early at the end of January.

The year ended without further negotiations and with more mutual contradictions. From time to time Scargill predicted that coal stocks would run out at the power stations (as he had been doing since May). The NCB predicted that the strike would be over by Christmas, as the miners drifted back to work. The NCB began to issue regular weekly and then daily counts of the number of men back at work for the first time since March, and the NUM continued to deny them. By the end of the year they disagreed to the tune of about 30 000 men whom the board said were working and the union said were out.

At the end of November a report that some academics had found the NCB's accountancy methods wanting was reported in the 'heavies' and on Channel Four television.[12] The writers accused the board of the elementary error of assuming that closing a pit would save its attributed overheads – that is, the proportion of the overall cost of the coal industry and the servicing of its historic debt conventionally assigned to that particular pit. The NCB, the *Guardian* reported, had persuaded *Accountancy* magazine to delay publication because the article contained 'numerous inaccuracies and privileged information' and because of the 'politically sensitive time'. However, the criticism spread and more and more papers questioned the validity of the board's calculations. The *Guardian,* in a leader on the *Accountancy* affair, saw a need for an independent committee to review 'the real economic position' of the mines the NCB wanted to close. NCB rejoinders tended to concentrate on procedures rather than substance.[13] Whatever the score in public relations with the community at large, unquestionably the credibility of all parties with the media had dropped sharply. Geoffrey Goodman saw it as a kind of mutual suicide of reputations.

A RETROSPECTIVE VERDICT

All the journalists we interviewed thought that anyone who seriously wanted to know would have derived a clear view of the issues involved from studying the media. This is fair, so long as one remembers that the serious inquirer would also have to evaluate and put aside a great deal of mere background noise – some of it necessarily reported because it came from an important person, some of it generated by the media themselves. It is also true that people as well informed as the writers and broadcasters could make them might still reach diametrically opposite views about the merits of the dispute. It would be absurd to blame the press for that, nor is it reasonable to expect from it analysis of data that no one was collecting or a definitive proof of which of the large, powerful and secretive parties to the dispute was furthest from the truth.

John Lloyd, industrial editor of the *Financial Times,* won the Granada award of journalist of the year for his coverage of the dispute. In an article in the *New Statesman* on 21 September he offered a robust defence of the press under the heading, 'It's our job to be a nuisance'. He was writing just after a series of cross-country drives by NCB and NUM leaders, claiming they wished to negotiate free from media attention. He commented sardonically that at least the media had got MacGregor and Scargill to agree about something, and he expressed in rather different terms and perhaps more optimistically Goodman's idea that a familiar structure was on the way out. Lloyd wrote:

> Labour reporting is, in the UK press, its own specialism, uniquely powerful among the world's press. With a 40-year history, it has acquired some traditions which can make it stiff: a strike like this one, breaking the rules, throwing up new formations, can at times by-pass reflexes trained to respond to other stimuli.

Goodman, as it happened, won the Gerald Barry Award for services to journalism at the same ceremony. He is in his sixties, Lloyd in his thirties – and it is unprecedented for two labour specialists to take the chief awards in the same year. One might say that all it proves is that fortune favours the person in the right role at the right time – and perhaps with the right newspaper. There is more to it than that. If you don't know the rules, you cannot tell who is breaking them. At the very least, without the industrial group the public would have been much less well informed. One need only look at the files for 1926, when there was no labour correspondent, let alone an industrial group. What passed for reporting before and after the General Strike would win no awards in 1985.

TABLE 9.1 *Selected background or explanatory items: newspapers and television*

This list includes some only of the more notable contributions to a better understanding of events, and some notable initiatives.

Tuesday 6 March

Newsnight. History of 1972 and 1974 strikes; Scargill's three failures to get a strike by ballot; atmosphere and expectations in various NUM areas. Approx. 20 mins.

Thursday 8 March

Guardian. Projection of collieries and areas where closures now most likely, with criticism from BACM (British Association of Colliery Management) on proposed closures at Polmaise (Scotland) and Herrington (Durham). Peter Hetherington. 46 col. cm.
Times. Projection of collieries at risk. David Felton. 29 col. cm.
Channel Four News. NUM constitution; two routes to a national strike. Ian Ross. 2 mins.

Monday 12 March

Channel Four News. Miners with mortgages and other commitments. How the dispute will differ from 1974. A report from Grimethorpe, Yorks. Patrick Bishop. 4 mins. 45 secs.

Tuesday 13 March

Guardian. Wives on the picket lines. Impressions from South Yorkshire and Nottinghamshire. Malcolm Pithers. 57 col. cm.

Wednesday 14 March

News at Ten. The Welsh coalfield; history and solidarity. Ken Rees. 2½ mins.

Thursday 15 March

Channel Four News. Why the Yorks and Notts coalfields differ; their characters, prosperity and prospects. Jane Corbin. 7½ mins.

TABLE 9.1—*continued*

Friday 16 March

Times. Yorks NUM assets £8m: more than NUM centrally. Paul Routledge. 21 col. cm.
Nine o'clock News. First report on mobilisation of National Reporting Centre at New Scotland Yard. Bill Hamilton. 2½ mins.

Saturday 17 March

Times. National Reporting Centre to track union trouble points. David Nicholson-Lord. 16 col. cm. (late editions only).

Monday 19 March

Guardian. The NRC at work. Nick Davies. 41 col. cm. (cut to 20 in late editions).
Guardian. Analysis of NUM area voting; comparison with past votes; critical study of Scargill's figures. Patrick Wintour. 38 col. cm.
Times. Why Britain's coal industry will be booming by 2000 AD, when gas and oil are less plentiful. David Young. 47 col. cm.
Channel Four News. 3 a.m. on the road with Yorks pickets, going into Notts. Jane Corbin. 4 mins. Reactions of Notts miners. Edward Stourton. 3½ mins. Is police interception on roads legal? Alistair Stewart. 6 mins.
News at Ten. Early morning on the picket lines, at three collieries. Ken Rees. 2½ mins.

Tuesday 20 March

Guardian. BACM's concern over misjudged pit closures: case studies at Herrington and Polmaise. Peter Hetherington. 52 col. cm.
Times. Costs of police mobilisation. Stewart Trendler. 52 col. cm. (cut to 16 in late editions).
Nine o'clock News. With a miner's family at Polmaise: will they have to emigrate? Mike Smartt. 1½ mins.

Friday 23 March

Channel Four News. A colliery electrician from Yorks is flown to Pittsburg, Pennsylvania, to visit a privately owned pit (once MacGregor's favourite) and compare impressions there. Andrew Manderstam. 6½ mins.

10 The 1984–5 Coal Dispute: Television News

From the first day of the one-year strike, television news was under attack. That day the miners' president, Mr Arthur Scargill, accused BBC news and ITN of 'distorted coverage', and he kept up the barrage to the end. Yet he loved to appear on television himself, as the radio journalist Nicholas Jones soon noted, and he made astute use of his opportunities.[1] He knew that television was his most effective way of reaching both the NUM membership and the public as a whole. His opponent, Mr Ian MacGregor, also complained of bias – against management – but shrugged it off as one of life's inevitable injustices.[2] Journalists found him a less adequate communicator, lacking the dexterity and appeal of Mr Scargill.

Such attacks and opinions are relevant though peripheral to the main questions that we must try to answer. Was the reporting fair, accurate and non-partisan? Was the background to the news adequately explained? Were the implications for the future explored? In particular, were the NCB's pit closure policy and the NUM's response fully covered? Was there excessive emphasis on violence? And was there a tendency to play down anything damaging to the police? How far did concentration on immediate events tend to exclude the reporting of longer-term trends? Looking back, what was missed?

If the dispute had lasted only two or three weeks, these questions would have been difficult enough to answer. With an event lasting a year, and with the most intensive television cover ever given in the UK to any happening – apart from the Falklands War, general elections and the Olympics – they are much more difficult to answer. On controversial aspects such as violence, the whole truth will never be established: with

226

picketing potentially at up to 200 sites and with incidents also in villages and on roadways, no reporter or historian or group of observers could hope to gather a complete picture. As Peter Hetherington (Chapter 9) remarked, much violence went unreported because no outsider was there to witness it. With policy issues, too, it was hard to arrive at the objective truth – even about a single point such as how the Coal Board chose the Polmaise and Cortonwood collieries for closure.

Nevertheless we must try to examine and assess the way television news went about covering the coal dispute. To make the study manageable, we concentrate as before on Channel Four News, the BBC's Nine o'clock News and ITN's News at Ten. This still means nearly 1000 programmes during the year, of which we have looked closely at some 200. Although standard content analysis and the techniques of semiology (the study of verbal and visual signs) can be helpful, in themselves they are not enough. A form of narrative analysis has therefore been adopted here, to bring out salient aspects.

That narrative and the interviews with journalists provide some understanding of how the messages of television news are prepared and of their validity. How they are received, intellectually and emotionally, is harder to tell. A vivid example of this came at the Edinburgh International Television Festival in August 1984, when two people of opposing views chose almost identical extracts from one bulletin – BBC news of Tuesday 8 May – to illustrate their interpretations. For that reason, it is also used for analysis here. The other days used in our opening section are Monday 5 March 1984, when the Yorkshire area of the NUM decided to strike; and Thursday 21 February 1985, a week before the Coal Board claimed that half the NUM's members were not on strike. Studies of other days have been done, but they would take too much space to be reproduced here. Those included in this chapter are fairly representative of the news programmes.

The proposition that emerges is this: that the main television news channels have done their best to present a fair, balanced and accurate account; that there were occasional mistakes, misjudgements and inadequacies; but that, in the face of real difficulties, they offered their audiences a generally reliable and dispassionate news service.

MONDAY 5 MARCH

Channel Four News

[Headlines, Peter Sissons to camera, with still picture of pithead behind, right.]

> The Yorkshire coalfield is called out on unofficial strike over pit closures. The National Coal Board abandons another Yorkshire pit after a controversial incident on a picket line – 1400 jobs are put at risk. And the Coal Board chairman [still of MacGregor] appeals to miners to stop harming the industry and themselves. We hear [back to Sissons to camera] from both sides in this latest deterioration in coal's industrial relations.

[Other headlines follow; then back to Sissons to camera with logo of pithead behind.]

> First, the tensions in Britain's coal-mining industry, where feelings are running high because of the national ban on overtime. These tensions came to a head today in Britain's biggest coalfield, Yorkshire. There were two principal developments. In Barnsley, the Yorkshire area executive of the National Union of Mineworkers called an all-out strike in the coalfield from the weekend over two pits [map displayed] that are to be closed on economic grounds. And in Doncaster 1400 jobs were put on the line by a management decision to abandon a pit that was being picketed. The decision followed another controversial picket line incident. An engineer was allegedly hit by a stone.
>
> In London the chairman of the Coal Board upped the temperature by warning the miners that they'd had their final pay offer and telling the union that they were out of touch with their members. He said that too many unions lived by intimidation.

The item then moved to Alistair Stewart's voice over extracts from the day's news film, setting out the background both to several separate local disputes in Yorkshire and to the main issues of pit closures and pay. The news clips included the

NUM's Yorkshire president, Jack Taylor, who said his members were frustrated – feeling that unless they made a stand now, the Board would escalate the dispute further. Stewart went on to speak of a meeting due next day between NCB and NUM, where warning of more pit closures was almost certainly coming.

Next there was an interview with Ned Smith, industrial relations director of the NCB, who agreed that there was frustration among the miners after loss of pay during the 18 weeks of overtime ban; but he said that stocks of coal were high both at pitheads and at power stations. Jack Taylor, from a studio in Yorkshire, was then interviewed by Sissons. He said that the Yorkshire area had held an individual ballot of all its members in 1981, and pit closures had to be resisted. Cortonwood was a 'purely economic closure'. He regretted the hardship that the strike must bring, but the alternative was to finish up with 'no industry'. Whether by accident or design, each interview lasted 2 minutes 40 seconds.

Finally Professor Gerald Manners, adviser to the Commons Select Committee on Energy, was interviewed. He said there was a horrendous problem of adjusting the industry to its markets, and that did require closure of the high-cost, most expensive pits. At the same time, capital investment was going on at a high rate. The problem was aggravated because in the late 1970s and early 1980s the industry did not take notice of its changing markets. A strike now was bound to drive consumers away.

The item lasted 14 minutes.

Nine o'clock News

[Headlines, with voice of John Humphrys over the day's pictures of miners outside Yorkshire area headquarters and then MacGregor walking through the lobby of a hotel, surrounded by reporters.]

56 000 miners to strike – and Ian MacGregor takes a tough line.

[After other headlines, Humphrys to camera with inset, right, still picture of miners going down a pit and caption 'Strike call'.]

Good evening. Yorkshire's 56 000 miners have been called out on strike from Monday, and as confrontation grows in the industry the union has challenged the Coal Board to come to its senses and talk seriously about pay and pit closures. Bitterness is increasing on both sides.

On the most disruptive day since the overtime ban began 18 weeks ago, miners' leader Arthur Scargill [still of Scargill] accused the Coal Board of bullying tactics. The chairman [still of MacGregor] Ian MacGregor said too many unions live by intimidation. At Yorkshire Main colliery [map] near Doncaster an engineer was hit by a stone as management tried to cross picket lines.

[Voice of John Thorne over pictures of miners outside NUM area headquarters, some carrying placard cartoon with caption 'WOT NO PIT? SAVE CORTONWOOD'; Thorne introduced interview with area president, Jack Taylor, who began:]

I hope that the strike won't take place. I hope the Board come to their senses and say 'Well, all right, we'll have meaningful talks and we'll stop closing pits.' If they do that we'll consider our position. But at the moment you can't talk to Board. Their attitude is very intransigent. They've got a take-it-or-leave-it approach; and our members aren't that sort of people.

Next, Thorne's voice over pictures from Yorkshire Main colliery, with huge graffiti on colliery entrance 'Scargill rules OK'. About the incident earlier in the day, Thorne said of the injured engineer 'a missile caused facial cuts that needed three stitches'; he then interviewed pickets, who denied throwing anything, one saying 'that man must have fallen down while he were sneaking in round the back'. Thorne next interviewed the NCB area director, who said that the pit could soon become too dangerous to enter and that he was not prepared to put management through picket lines in the face of violence.

Finally the BBC's industrial editor, Martin Adeney, filled in some of the background speaking to camera in studio. He said that the dispute was about two issues, pit closures and the Board's 5·2 per cent pay offer. An extract from MacGregor speaking at the Coal Society lunch was included, with MacGregor saying that the pay offer was final and 'cannot be increased', because 'the Board hasn't the money to pay'. Adeney said that recent attempts to bring out the South Wales, Kent and Scottish coalfields had failed, so it was not clear that Yorkshire would fare better in trying to bring out others now; but under the Coal Board plans, due to be spelled out next day, there were 'perhaps 20 pits to go'.

The item lasted just over four minutes.

News at Ten

[Headlines, preceded and followed by Big Ben 'bong'; voice of Sandy Gall over library pictures of miners coming off shift at pithead.]

Yorkshire miners are told to strike from Monday.

[After further headlines and bongs, Gall to camera with still picture of miners at pithead, inset top left.]

Good evening. Yorkshire's 56 000 miners have been called out on indefinite strike from next week to protest against pit closures. Their leaders are asking miners across the country to join the stoppage. The Yorkshire coalfield produces up to half Britain's coal, but the Coal Board said that with high stocks the strike wouldn't have an immediate effect. The strike call comes on the eve of a crucial meeting on the future of the industry between the Coal Board's chairman, Mr Ian MacGregor, and the miners' leader, Mr Scargill.

Today [map of Yorks coalfield] the Coal Board announced that it had abandoned the 'Main' colliery near Doncaster after pickets [pictures of pickets] prevented a management team carrying out safety work there, but the threat was lifted tonight after pickets let safety men through.

[Voice of Giles Smith, ITN's industrial editor, followed over library pictures of miners coming off shift.]

On a day that the overtime ban crisis in the industry worsened – a Commons Select Committee highlighted the mounting financial losses, £135 millions so far – miners in Britain's biggest coalfield, Yorkshire, were called out as the spearhead in the union's dual fight over closures and pay. The Yorkshire miners' president explained his members' mood . . .

[Jack Taylor in his office, being interviewed to camera.]

They say that unless they stand up now and be counted, the Board will escalate it further and further and further; and as one delegate said, you know, you can eat grass while you get used to it – and I think that that was the general mood, that they're going to stand and fight for the industry.

Next Giles Smith, to camera, reported MacGregor's speech at lunchtime – with extracts of MacGregor saying that the wage offer had 'nothing to do with pit closures', that the two issues were entirely separate and that the pay offer was final. Smith summarised his later comments, saying that MacGregor called that day's violence in Yorkshire 'sad' but regarded it as a matter for the union. Smith omitted MacGregor's general comment about unions relying on intimidation. In conclusion Smith said that at next day's meeting the Board Chairman was not about to withdraw the backdated pay offer – or at least had not intended to before today's events. He had been planning an attempt at conciliation with Mr Scargill.

The item ended with Gall's voice over a still of Scargill saying that 'tonight' Mr Scargill had said he was lodging an official complaint with the BBC and ITV over what he called 'distorted coverage' of the day's events. Some days later it turned out that the complaint was over the midday bulletins accepting as fact that the engineer at Yorkshire Main colliery had been hit by a stone thrown by a picket, whereas the pickets said that he had fallen over.

The item, in all, lasted three minutes.

Commentary

All three bulletins put the coal item first, although as we know from our interviews none of the newsrooms had any premonition that this marked the beginning of a prolonged national stoppage, with only Nottinghamshire staying at work. Two of the three programmes made clear that there was frustration among miners after their 18-week overtime ban; and all three made clear that there were two issues – pay and, more important, pit closures. All three made clear that among Yorkshire miners there was genuine anger over the sudden decision to close Cortonwood, and that the Yorkshire area was calling on others to follow its lead.

Audiences were given the salient facts and pointers to likely consequences. The background was more fully filled in by Channel Four News than by the others, through its interviews with Jack Taylor, Ned Smith and Professor Manners. The dilemma over 'uneconomic' pits was explored by Channel Four News, though the term 'uneconomic' was not directly used; others only mentioned the Coal Board's current financial losses. None of the bulletins, at that stage, said anything about the possible implications of closures for whole mining communities.

A semiological study of language used in the bulletins, as noted earlier, is difficult because of the very wide range of events and issues. Examination of the texts above, however does not indicate bias or prejudice in the presentation. Objection has sometimes been taken to the BBC's use of introductory captions in which the word 'strike' frequently occurs: on this day 'Strike call' was an apparently reasonable way of pointing to the main news, though the repetitive use of 'strike' or 'miners' strike' on later days may as reasonably be seen as having been excessive.

Objection may also be taken to Channel Four News's use in its opening sentence of the word 'unofficial', as applied to the Yorkshire strike call (a word repeated again next day). That raises a fine constitutional point, in that NUM areas are authorised to take local action but they must obtain national executive approval immediately afterwards, as Yorkshire did three days later. When asked about use of that word, Sissons said that at the time it was believed to be correct and they were trying to be as accurate as possible.[3]

On the semiology of pictures, the Coal Board's chairman was seen in the sumptuous surroundings of a top London hotel's banqueting suite, whereas the pickets at Yorkshire Main were seen out in the cold at the colliery gates. On the whole, to any viewer who made the comparison, the hidden (or not so hidden) meaning was that MacGregor and management live in luxury while miners have a hard life. It is improbable, however, that any programme editor or video editor was consciously making that contrast; they used the pictures that were available, and Mr MacGregor's statement happened to be made in a luxurious London hotel.

About the controversial incident at Yorkshire Main, over which Mr Scargill complained of 'distorted coverage', an open verdict is inevitable. When a man has had three stitches in his face and says he was hit by a stone, there is a predisposition to accept his word unless there is contrary evidence; but there is no way in which anyone not there can be certain of the truth.

TUESDAY 8 MAY

Channel Four News

[Coal was the second of five headlines, Sissons voice over library pictures of offshore oil platforms.]

> How Britain's oil could last well into the next century – is there a message here for the coal industry? We talk to the minister.

[The item began with Ian Ross summarising the Energy Department's report, out that day, on the greatly increased estimate of oil reserves off British coasts, putting the recoverable reserves of oil at 5280m tonnes and of coal at 45 000m tonnes. It went on to explain the way the CEGB, since the start of the strike, had stepped up electricity generation at the five big oil-fired power stations. Professor Manners was then interviewed again, saying that oil was now fuelling 30 to 40 per cent of electricity, compared with 4 per cent before the strike, but that the cost was very high. The Minister of State for Energy, Mr Alec Buchanan-Smith, was next interviewed by

Sissons in studio with the opening question 'have the miners nothing to worry about from the latest projection of oil production?']

I think we've got to realise on our energy policy that we are very lucky in the United Kingdom that we have a very wide range of energy resources – and certainly the government regards our coal reserves as very important indeed, and that's why we are investing at the rate of nearly £1 billion a year; and I think it would be deeply unfortunate not only for the UK economy but for the miners themselves if anything happened in this dispute that affected our making the best use of these reserves, because we do believe that there's a very big future in coal and we must not jeopardise it.

Answering later questions Buchanan-Smith said that efforts were being made to win new customers for coal, here and abroad, but that Britain must produce the coal to get those customers. There was, he said, more oil round Britain's coasts than previously thought, the revised estimates being thanks to drilling, exploration and seismic surveys during the past year.

The item ran to just short of eight minutes; and in the 'newsbelt' there was also a brief mention of 5 pickets being injured and 65 arrested at Hunterston on the Clyde.

Nine o'clock News

[Coal was the fourth of five headlines, the line-up being Russia pulling out of the Olympics, an attempt to assassinate Gadaffi, three dead in a siege at a government building in Canada, coal and the Queen opening the Thames barrage. The coal headline had Sue Lawley's voice over pictures of a police cavalry charge.]

1000 pickets, but the coal's still getting through to Ravenscraig.

[More than halfway through the programme, after the Quebec siege, came the coal report with Lawley to camera and inset to right a still of pickets and coal lorries with caption 'Miners' strike'.]

Back home now, and to the dispute in the mining industry. Mounted police charged a picket line in Scotland today as miners tried to stop lorries of coal [cut to pictures of two lines of police, backs to camera, along edge of road facing big gathering of pickets on hillside above] destined for Ravenscraig steel plant. The mass picket was at the Hunterston coal terminal in Ayrshire. Sixty-five people were arrested. Mike Smartt was there.

[Then Smartt's voice over more pictures of two lines of police facing about 12 lines of pickets above them, police in ordinary uniform and pickets mostly in shirt sleeves.]

Switching from Ravenscraig yesterday to the Hunterston coal depot 40 miles away today, 1000 pickets gathered to meet lorries returning from their morning's successful run.

[Different camera on hilltop above pickets pans right to left over lorries approaching main road roundabout to section of terminal approach road now almost blocked by pickets who have pushed police back into the middle of road; as lorries draw near, moving fast, six mounted police charge through pickets from right to left, visibly knocking several over.]

As the convoy approached, the pickets charged – only to be met by the police mounted section. One horse fell – a picket pinned underneath – and there followed some of the most violent scenes of the dispute so far.

[Fierce scrum of police, horses and pickets to be seen below; lorries in convoy pass close – two to three feet? – to bulge of police line into road, as more pickets and police run downhill to join in.]

The police managed to take the sting out of the pickets' rush, but not out of their anger. And as the last lorries sped unimpeded into Hunterston [more convoy pictures], the fighting broke out again.

[Hilltop camera closes on fighting scrum at foot of hill; pause in commentary; road now blocked by pickets and police, but no lorries to be seen.]

Four pickets were hurt, and treated in hospital for superficial injuries. A total of 65 pickets were arrested. Although struggling violently [close-up of man being dragged away kicking in all directions], some of those arrested were photographed at the scene.

Tonight the police say there's been more violence. Pickets throwing stones at vehicles on a motorway back to Ravenscraig are in custody. When the convoy reemerged with more coal, most of the pickets had dispersed and there was no more violence [pictures of lorries passing, fast, on apparently clear road now with five lines of police along edge].

However, again the miners can console themselves that they delayed convoys long enough to prevent the full amount of coal needed at Ravenscraig getting there. [Lorries turning off motorway further on, no pickets or police in sight.] Now the best hope of compromise is the Scottish TUC's continuing effort to set up talks between the striking miners and the steel men.

[Time elapsed from start of item to here, 1 minute 34 seconds.] [Next Sue Lawley to camera reported briefly on an agreement reached in South Wales between miners and steelworkers on the supply of coke to Llanwern; then the report moved to John Thorne in Nottinghamshire, where 2000 pickets had been outside the Piehill colliery in the morning.]

It's still the Nottinghamshire coalfield that's the focus of daily mass picketing. [Pictures of police in ordinary uniform, mingled with pickets, and two mounted police with riot helmets.] It's a cat-and-mouse game between police and strikers. Today both sides flooded into the village of Underwood. [Pickets walking past camera: some smile, some cheer, some give fingers up sign.] The flying pickets tried to blockade Piehill pit. [Two police lines thinly spread along pavement, pickets massed behind.] About 2000 miners from Yorkshire evaded the road blocks and lined up along the High Street to barrack and abuse the day shift.

In the school yard [mother and child passing through mixed group of police and pickets] police advised parents to take their children home. They escorted them through the invasion of pickets. [NCB bus, edging through narrow space with police lining either side, much shouting and jeering.] Some vehicles were damaged, nine arrests were made and three police injured. But the heavy police presence kept Piehill open. Attendance was reduced, said the Board, but coal was still produced on all three faces.

Finally Sue Lawley to camera summarised the Energy Department report on North Sea oil.

Total duration, including Hunterston, 3 minutes 8 seconds.

News at Ten

[No headline was given to coal, and the item was well down in the running order. It came after the Quebec shooting, introduced by Sandy Gall to camera, with an inset still of a pithead and caption 'Miners' strike, week 9'.]

Here 5 miners' pickets were injured and 65 arrested when they clashed with police at the Hunterston coal terminal in Scotland today. Miners claimed that mounted police had deliberately tried to ride them down as they attempted to halt lorries taking coal to the Ravenscraig steel works. The coal convoys got through again, though tugboatmen said they'd black all ships bringing in further supplies.

[Mark Webster's voice over pictures of two thin lines of police and only a few pickets on the hill behind.]

More than 1000 police were called this afternoon to the British steel depot at Hunterston, which supplies coal to Ravenscraig. Hundreds of pickets had been bussed to the plant [close-up of group of pickets walking and shouting behind police] as part of a tactical war to outmanoeuvre them and stop the coal trucks reaching Ravenscraig. [Mounted police facing pickets at bottom of hill, one policeman leaning forward to speak to a miner.] But many had drifted away by the time today's second coal convoy roared out. [Lorries passing, plenty of space this time.]

Many lorries are now fitted with wire mesh grills after windscreens were shattered by stones thrown yesterday.

Earlier three pickets were taken to hospital [ambulance being loaded with casualty wrapped in red blanket] after some of the most violent clashes so far, when police horses were used for crowd control. [Man being marched off by large WPC and a constable.] More than 40 miners were arrested during the day.

At Ravenscraig less than 50 pickets turned up for the arrival of the coal convoy, despite threats of mass pickets by miners' leaders yesterday. Police called in extra men [group of policemen, three abreast, running up road outside Ravenscraig] just before lorries pulled in at the plant, and they were greeted with good-humoured jeering by the pickets. The miners are still confident [miners stripped to waist in sunshine watching lorries pass] that they can stop coal convoys with their lightning pickets; but talks are planned for later this week between the miners and the steel men which could resolve the deadlock over how much coal will be allowed into the plant. Mark Webster, at Hunterston . . .

Then Burnet to camera on a warning from the Board to miners in Derbyshire that deterioration may close their pits for good; and brief reports on the Piehill picketing, agreement in Wales on coke supplies for Llanwern, Mr Roy Hattersley saying that the government were treating the strike as a political convenience and calling Mrs Thatcher 'a suburban Boadicea', while Mrs Thatcher in the Commons was contradicting Mr Scargill's claim that coal stocks were down to eight weeks. She said that there was sufficient for 'many months yet'. Also short mention of Energy Department report on offshore oil reserves.

The item lasted 2 minutes and 51 seconds.

Commentary

There is an obvious contrast between Channel Four News's concentration on the offshore oil report and its implications for the coal industry, virtually disregarding the events at Hunterston and Underwood, and the intensity of the BBC's attention to the two mass pickets. Also, the BBC's reporting and its pictures were more obviously dramatic than ITN's lower-key reporting.

There is, however, one factor that emerged from our interviewing. Both the BBC's network crew in Scotland and ITN's were at first wrong-footed by indications from the NUM that the mass pickets were to be at the Ravenscraig steel works, not on the coast at Hunterston. So also, to some extent, were the Strathclyde police, who had comparatively few men at Hunterston early in the day. In fact, overnight the NUM had planned its switch. (The previous day the NUM had similarly outmanoeuvred the police by making them think that Hunterston was then to be the target; but the pickets in turn were then misled by the police into believing that the convoy would enter Ravenscraig by the main gates, whereas it went through the back gates instead.) On the Tuesday, however, while both the BBC and ITN network crews went to Ravenscraig in the morning, BBC Scotland also sent two crews to Hunterston. It was from one of them that the pictures of the cavalry charge came. The ITN crew, misled by the NUM, reached the coast too late to see the cavalry charge and their report was consequently muted.

For Channel Four News the pictures were a secondary factor. In the morning it had decided that the offshore oil report was worth an eight- or ten-minute item. That was in line with its policy of trying to explain the issues and the consequences. If Hunterston pictures such as the BBC's had come, they would certainly have been used, possibly before the oil report and with the whole item lengthened and promoted to a higher place in the running order.

The BBC's pictures from Hunterston were by far the most alarming seen anywhere until then, and among the most frightening of the whole year. The vantage point of one camera on the hill above the road gave a vivid impression of what happened. As the lorries approached, the pickets surged downhill and pushed the police line back into the middle of the road. At once the horses went in at a fast trot, knocking men over as they went. That stopped the surge, but with only a narrow gap left between the police lines on either side of the road and the lorries speeding onwards, there seemed a frightening possibility of sudden fatalities.

Again, we cannot know how much of the detail an audience

would absorb. My own reaction that evening was shock; and having looked at the recording a number of times since then, that impression remains. The pictures told their own story. The main event was an almost continuous sequence, lasting 31 seconds (the whole Hunterston item being only 1 minute and 34 seconds).

The commentary, however, calls for further study. At the Edinburgh Television Festival, parts of the audience jeered two or three times at Smartt's words – particularly when he referred to 1000 pickets gathering to meet lorries returning from their 'successful' morning run and when he said that the mounted police 'managed to take the sting out of the pickets' rush'. That reaction was understandable, even though Smartt's words were strictly accurate, but it was also unjust to Smartt because the extracts screened in Edinburgh stopped short of his later words. Omitted were his further words that 'the miners can console themselves that they delayed convoys long enough to prevent the full amount of coal needed at Ravenscraig getting there'; and short of his concluding words on the STUC's efforts to bring agreement between the striking miners and the steelworkers.

It should not be forgotten that the future jobs of steelworkers at Ravenscraig were at risk as much as the jobs of miners at Polmaise and Polkemmet; that the steelworkers at that stage were distressed and angry over the forceful tactics adopted by the NUM; and that both BBC and ITN had to try to report events as fairly as they could.

Looking further at the use of words, one of the usual tests is the frequency of adjectives, adverbs and epithets, and their nature. In the texts of Smartt, Thorne, Gall and Webster there are few. 'Successful' was an adjective, though a conveniently short way of saying that the morning convoy had delivered its coal. 'Some of the most violent scenes' was descriptive: they were violent, and Smartt did not attribute responsibility to either side. 'Struggling violently' was true enough, though it might have been more precise to say of the man in shot 'kicking in all directions'. Thorne's 'cat-and-mouse' as adjectival nouns to describe police and picket tactics in his opening was reasonable, and he did not say which was which. His 'heavy' police presence (second paragraph) was similarly an acceptable usage. Objection might also be taken to his use of the noun 'blockade' in his opening; but not to call a blockade is pussy-footing. Gall's 'deliberately' in his introduction is quoting the miners' claim that the police had deliberately tried to ride them down. Webster's use of 'violent' was both descriptive and relevant, as was his use of 'good-humoured' about the Ravenscraig pickets later.

On voice intonations, criticism may be made of Smartt's unemotional delivery in his account of alarming events at Hunterston. But suppose he had written and delivered a more emotive report, how much more criticism might have been heaped on him? He implied no judgement between any of the three parties – the pickets for surging forward as the lorries approached, putting police lives and their own at risk; the lorry drivers, led by a police car, for approaching so fast; or the mounted police for forcefully 'taking the sting' out of the pickets' forward rush. He left viewers to make their own judgements. In an incident as disturbing as this, he took the most expedient course.

When interviewed, he said he did not think about it in those terms anyway.[4] After they were all back in Glasgow, he talked to the two BBC Scotland reporters and to the hilltop cameraman, who had instinctively chosen the right location. He then prepared the clearest account he could, with only a short time before transmission.

THURSDAY 21 FEBRUARY 1985

Channel Four News

[Headline, Sissons to camera, with inset picture of pithead right.]

It's back to trench warfare in the pit strike. The union delegates say the strike goes on. Mrs Thatcher and her ministers say there will be no more talks. The Energy Secretary forecasts that more than half the miners will be back at work in the next few days.

Tonight – why the path to peace turned into a dead end; and we revisit Shirebrook – last year bitterly divided by the strike, this year coming to terms with the men going back.

[After other headlines, Sissons again to camera with still of miners in pit clothes inset on right.]

But first the coal dispute, where it looks very much as if it's back to the long slog. On the miners' side, last night's executive decision to reject what the Coal Board says is positively the last offer has been unanimously endorsed by a special delegate conference of the mineworkers' union. On the other side the Energy Secretary [still of Walker] Peter Walker was making it clear that there would be no new talks – all that was left, he told the House of Commons, was for the strike to be brought to an end by the drift back to work. And he predicted that in the next few days more than half Britain's miners would have returned.

[Whole screen now taken, with NCB logo at top and bold captions below: '129 "new faces" ' and '46% not on strike'.]

According to the Coal Board another 129 went back to work today, bringing the number of miners not on strike to about 46 per cent. Our industrial editor Ian Ross has been following today's events . . .

[Ross's voice over picture of taxis outside TUC offices, some shouting in background.]

As the miners' delegates left Transport House after the conference the gloomy faces [close-up pictures of delegates passing camera] revealed the gloomy prospect now that the executive has unceremoniously ditched the Coal Board's latest final proposals, worked out with the help of the TUC acting on the NUM's instructions.

[Cut to close-up of Peter Heathfield, looking partly sideways at reporter, caption 'Peter Heathfield, NUM General Secretary'.]

Well, we haven't been negotiating, have we? Only by proxy. It's an incredible way of seeking to resolve a major industrial dispute, that the main parties are not getting together; they're not sorting out a form of words that's acceptable to both. You're having to send messengers with documents.

[Cut to Sid Vincent close up, caption 'Sid Vincent, Lancs NUM'.]

We want immediate negotiations with the Board; ourselves, nobody else.

[Cut to Trevor Bell, caption 'Trevor Bell, NUM executive'.]

All these talks we've had over the last few days, all the talks that have been between the TUC and the Prime Minister and with the Coal Board isn't about getting the dispute settled. It's been about getting in to have talks to have the dispute settled.

[Ross's voice over artist's impression of ministers facing TUC members across table.]

Not so, Mr Bell. At Tuesday's meeting between the Prime Minister and the TUC, Mrs Thatcher had asked them if this was part of a final agreement. Mr Willis and his team assured her that it was an agreement and not an agenda. Norman Willis's meeting with the Coal Board yesterday morning had appeared to clear up [new artist's drawing of pithead and miner, caption 'NCB changes'] one or two areas of disagreement which the NUM leaders had asked the TUC leaders to pursue. The NCB had agreed to make it clear . . .

[A series of captions were now superimposed on the artist's drawing, each being slightly faded down as the next came up, with Ross's voice continuing to report them. To save space, only the captions are given here.]

- ALL pit closures to be reviewed under the new pit closure procedure
- NO disputed closures would be considered under the old procedure as long as the new review procedure was introduced by June

- The interests of ALL the NCB's employees are best served by the development of an economically sound industry

[The above captions are then wiped and the top caption changes to 'NCB wouldn't'.]

- Drop the word 'economically'
- Drop the concept of 'developing coal reserves' in line with the NCB's 'responsibility to the industry'

Next came pictures of a letter, the print too small for viewers to read, and Ross's voice saying that MacGregor had made clear that this was part of a final agreement, not an agenda, and that this was 'the final wording'. The TUC knew it and Mr Scargill knew it, he said. Then a short interview with Peter Walker on his expectation of a continuing return to work. Then pictures of Mr Scargill in the street with a big crowd around him, and Ross's voice over saying he had asked for the NUM not to be 'left isolated'. Finally a short interview with Mrs Thatcher in Washington, saying that the NUM had not moved its position, which was disappointing.

That had taken almost seven minutes; a further ten minutes followed, with Jane Corbin from the village of Shirebrook on the Derbyshire side of the Notts boundary. She drew a comparison with a report she had made from there in September, when only one in ten miners was back at work and there was bitterness and much violence in the village. Now nine out of ten were back at work and the village was peaceful; the police were no longer preoccupied with investigating attacks, intimidation and damage to property; trade in the shops was picking up again. For some people there were permanent changes – she interviewed again a family who had been building a new house which had been destroyed while the man was at work; the wife had been frightened to go through the village and the children frightened to go to school. Now they were living in rented premises some miles away, having lost their life savings, but the children were less distressed and settling down. The item was, however, on the whole optimistic about a return of good relations between those who had worked and those who had struck.

Nine o'clock News

[Headlines, voice of Julia Somerville over pictures of Scargill and McGahey leaving TUC headquarters.]

Miners' delegates reject the Coal Board proposals, so it's deadlock again.

[Somerville to camera, with inset still of pithead on right and caption 'NUM'.]

Good evening. Miners' delegates from all over the country have followed their executive's advice and thrown out the Coal Board's latest proposals to end the strike.

The terms had been negotiated for them by seven senior members of the TUC, and they are said to be furious at the rejection. The Energy Secretary Peter Walker [still] said the NUM had delivered a slap in the face to the TUC. He insisted that the terms were the Coal Board's final offer and he said that the miners' best interests now lay in returning to work.

Mrs Thatcher [still] said the union was acting differently to any other union in industrial history. Now it was up to the miners themselves. On the day's developments, Martin Adeney reports . . .

[Adeney's voice over pictures of Norman Willis approaching on foot, loud shouts and jeering in background.]

TUC General Secretary Norman Willis was booed by left-wing groups as he arrived at Congress House the morning after the failure of the TUC's peace initiative as go-betweens between the miners and the Coal Board. [Pictures of jeering crowd behind barriers.] A mixed bag of demonstrators met delegates arriving. They included contingents of miners, but also other groups [Young Socialist and other banners visible] backing a general strike.

Miners' leaders were looking for a united conference and also fresh support from other industrial unions. Union vice-president McGahey [close up of McGahey getting out of car] went so far as to speak at the conference of honourable and dishonourable men on the TUC general council. The meeting lasted 2½ hours but nobody backed the deal brought back as the Board's last word by the TUC team. They thought it had meant concessions; but the miners didn't [grim-faced delegates leaving, shouting heard] and it didn't seem to matter about the detail – they weren't having negotiations by proxy.

[Chadburn in foyer, caption 'Ray Chadburn, Nottinghamshire NUM'.]

Here we are: we're negotiating over pieces of paper. There's no clarification. No one understands what they're on with, and we're treated like a load of school children, and it's time the Coal Board realised their responsibility to the industry and to the people who work in it, and stopped negotiating by proxy.

[Vincent close-up, caption 'Sid Vincent, Lancashire NUM'.]

We want immediate negotiations with the Board – ourselves, nobody else.

[Scargill in lobby, crowd around him.]

We think the TUC have seen at first hand the duplicity of the Coal Board and the fact that the TUC representatives could be sitting with Mr MacGregor at the same time as the Coal Board were making a press statement rubbishing the efforts of the NUM to seek a solution to this dispute shows very clearly where they stand. But I only hope and wish that the TUC will now go over in a public way, campaigning for the decisions of the TUC Congress last year calling upon the trade union movement to support the National Union of Mineworkers.

[Adeney to camera outside Congress House, street now empty.]

As a result of today's conference, the prospects of an early end to the miners' dispute now look to be in tatters. If anything the line was harder against the Coal Board's new formula, regarded apparently by the miners here as an unacceptable ultimatum. That, of course, wasn't the view of the TUC group who talked to the Board and ministers and brought the formula to the NUM to consider. They're disappointed by the summary rejection of it by the executive and now by the conference – a decision some of them regard as perverse.

Julia Somerville then introduced an interview with Mrs Thatcher, in Washington, in which she said that the NUM hadn't budged an inch and were proud of it. It was sad. 'Now it's up to the miners themselves.'

That took 45 seconds, bringing the item as a whole to 3 minutes and 56 seconds.

News at Ten

[Headlines – Gall's voice over complex montage of stills of pithead, Westminster, Scargill and Walker, and with Big Ben 'bongs'.]

Bong. The miners and the government: a fight to the finish. Bong. One pit village thinks about life after the strike. Bong . . .

[Gall to camera, still of pithead left.]

Good evening. The miners' strike is to go on with no prospect of peace talks and with the NUM more isolated than ever. Its delegates unanimously rejected what the Coal Board called its final offer. The NUM executive had rejected it last night. Mr Norman Willis and other senior TUC men helped to negotiate the offer, so the miners' relations with the TUC are now strained. The NUM is urging its members to stand firm on strike, and the Energy Secretary [still] Mr Peter Walker told the Commons [caption 'talks have come to an end'] that the talks have come to an end and forecast more than half the miners would now be back at work within days.

[Giles Smith's voice over street pictures of police, banners and demonstrators.]

Although the TUC had made it clear overnight they were far from happy [caption, 'Giles Smith, TUC headquarters'] with the NUM's rejection of the peace plan they'd negotiated with the Board, there were still miners' supporters outside Congress House [banner 'Workers' Revolutionary Party' visible] calling on the TUC to organise a general strike. In contrast to the warm welcome [McGahey arriving, being patted on back] the miners' leaders got, the TUC's Norman Willis [Willis arriving, much shouting] got a far from enthusiastic reception. If they were to confirm the executive's rejection of the plan [delegates arriving, some giving thumbs up to demonstrators] the delegates knew that they'd be virtually on their own.

But 2½ hours later [Scargill seen pushing through crowd] the decision was confirmed by Mr Scargill in a chaotic press conference. But did he know [man puts sheet of paper in front of camera but it is pulled away] the TUC were saying it had been deceived by the miners?

'I agree absolutely.' [Scargill with group of reporters around him.] 'Yes, I agree the TUC have been deceived by the National Coal Board. I agree [Scargill turning away] with that.'

[Then voice of Smith, with pictures of Scargill still thrusting through crowd.]

Others from both sides of the union had more time to make it clear that the union was still united, determined and angry.

[Jack Taylor, close up, to camera; caption 'Jack Taylor, Yorkshire Miners' President'.]

I've never known a dispute where people representing workers have been unable to talk to employers. In this one there seems to be a block; now I can't understand that – the Coal Board must have some fear in their minds of meeting us. Perhaps [smiling] our case is a good one!

[Bell to camera, caption, 'Trevor Bell, Colliery Staffs'.]

To me the shocking indictment is that we have to accept a document like that in order to be able to get the Board to see us in the first place.

[Vincent, caption 'Sid Vincent, Lancs Miners' President'.]

We want immediate negotiations with the Board – ourselves, nobody else.

    Q. But you're prepared to stay out until . . . [words lost]?
    A. Yes, for ever.

[Pictures of other delegates leaving, then Smith to camera outside.]

As they left, the miners probably knew they were in for a fight to the finish – crucial to it, the rate of return to work next week. Significantly, the statement issued after the conference called on the TUC not to leave the NUM isolated; but TUC leaders, after the rejection of their painstakingly negotiated settlement last night, are in no mood to resurrect any support, industrial or otherwise for the NUM, even if they could. Giles Smith, News at Ten, at the TUC . . .

So far the item had lasted 2½ minutes. David Rose from Westminster came next, with reaction from ministers, Mrs Thatcher in Washington, a Labour MP during parliamentary questions saying the dispute would never be over until every miner dismissed was back at work, another Labour MP saying that the miners were loyal not to Scargill but to the union, Mr Kinnock staying silent, and Rose commenting 'not a comfortable afternoon for Labour'. Dr David Owen was also quoted, suggesting that the talks had only prolonged the strike. The Westminster element took just short of three minutes.

    Finally there was a shortened version of Jane Corbin's report from Shirebrook, taking 4¾ minutes. Total for the whole item: 10 minutes 16 seconds.

Commentary

Content, words and intonations – on this day, all were open to question. That may indicate battle fatigue among journalists, miners, the TUC and ministers after eleven months of conflict. Alternatively, it may only indicate that an exasperating situation was being described in appropriate terms.

Peter Sissons used such words as 'trench warfare', 'a dead end', 'back to the long slog' and described the NUM executive as having 'unceremoniously ditched' the Coal Board's proposals. The BBC's report said that senior members of the TUC were 'furious' at the rejection, that to NUM delegates 'it did not seem to matter about the detail' and that the TUC leaders thought the NUM decision 'perverse'. All strong stuff – but justifiable after the TUC's initiative had been summarily rejected. (Adeney, interviewed later, said that from his contacts there was no doubt whatever about TUC anger.)

Then there is the conflict of testimony over who misled whom. Trevor Bell said that the TUC's mediation was not about getting the dispute settled but about getting talks going. Ian Ross contradicted him, saying that the Prime Minister had asked the TUC team whether this was to be part of a final agreement and she had been assured that it was 'an agreement and not an agenda'. *The Times* that Thursday morning, before the NUM delegate meeting, published the full text of the NCB offer and details of the changes accepted and refused by the Board – and said that the TUC had been 'under an obligation' to tell the NUM that the terms could not be modified. Did they or didn't they? Both the *Guardian* and *The Times* said next day that there was some ambiguity about this, but that Mr Willis was upset by the way the NUM negotiators (Scargill, McGahey and Heathfield) had presented the proposal to their executive and the delegate meeting. The *Guardian* also said that Mr Scargill, in the private talks, had accepted that the NCB's draft 'would form part of the final agreement'.

News at Ten showed Mr Scargill replying on this point. He walked away from the question, physically and verbally. Did he know, he was asked, that the TUC was saying it had been deceived by the miners? 'Yes', he said 'I agree that the TUC have been deceived by the National Coal Board.' And he walked away.

His reply to the BBC's Martin Adeney, during those exchanges in the entrance hall, is also worth study. So is Jack

Taylor on the related question of why the Board would not meet the union, something that had angered most or all of the executive and the delegates. Taylor said 'I've never known a dispute where people representing workers have been unable to talk to employers'; and later, with a smile, 'perhaps our case is a good one'. Neither reporters nor their audiences were likely so soon to have forgotten the long sequence of NCB–NUM meetings in March, May, July (twice), October, January and on other occasions – all fruitless. Jack Taylor, however, had such an amiable and relaxed manner whenever interviewed that he could give misleading answers without causing offence.

In a written account such as this, verbal intonations cannot readily be conveyed. Some who have watched the 21 February sequences felt that Ross's voice was at times condescending; others thought it contained resigned endurance. Even Jane Corbin – winner of a Royal Television Society award for her 1984–5 reporting – did not escape disapproval. Her Shirebrook features were held by some to be too emotional, and to give too little attention to the sufferings of striking miners' families; others judged her to have added an extra dimension to the coverage, as Channel Four News intended. The objection to an emotional tone takes us full circle from the objection to Mike Smartt's cool delivery

To committed critics of the media the whole 21 February sequence may be further proof of bias and prejudice against the workers, in spite of the TUC's involvement. To journalists it is more likely to be recognised as yet another occasion when reporters, scriptwriters and others had to pick their way through conflicting evidence – sometimes drawing attention to half truths or untruths but more often letting them pass – and had to try to present as clear an account as they could, often under pressure of time.

Journalists must try to be dispassionate in their reporting, but must not hold back from stating the uncomfortable. Throughout the dispute Adeney, Ross, Sissons, Smith and many others maintained their detachment. If anything, they were too cautious about pointing to untruths or half truths; they tried, whenever possible, to let the antagonists speak for themselves. On the whole their audiences – the electorate – were well informed.

QUESTIONS NOT ASKED: ANSWERS NOT FOUND

Looking back, what was missed? In the early coverage, three omissions can be observed – the lack of challenge to the Coal Board's reasons for closing Polmaise and Cortonwood, the lack of attention to the changes that Mr MacGregor had made in the Board's top structure, and the failure fully to uncover Mr Scargill's 'domino' tactics. There was also very little, at first, about the implications of the closure policy for whole communities.

On Polmaise and Cortonwood, no serious questioning of the Coal Board's decisions to close those collieries was ever broadcast in national news bulletins in March. Apparently the relevant questions were never asked, both because the Board's case appeared at first sight to be strong and because the Board had a good reputation among journalists for giving reliable information – a better reputation, indeed, than most other public bodies. The Board's case was simply that more coal was being produced than could be sold, that losses were mounting at a rate unfair to the taxpayer, and that some of the older and more costly pits must be closed. In their place, the new and more efficient developments such as the Selby complex were to take over; and meanwhile no miner would be made compulsorily redundant. It looked reasonable, and was accepted as such. Mr Scargill's repeated rhetoric about 'butchery' of the industry made little impression on journalists.

Cortonwood, as an old pit with only a few more years of life, fitted this pattern. Polmaise, although also old, had lately been developed into virtually a new pit – with some £15 millions already invested, out of a planned £22 millions. But in October 1983, geological difficulties were reported, and in early 1984 the Board said that the pit must be shut.

A report in the *Guardian* on 8 March said that the BACM (British Association of Colliery Management), which included most of the senior management in the coalfields, had appealed against the closures at Polmaise in Scotland and Herrington in Durham. Polmaise, it said, ought to be 'mothballed' because it could provide valuable capacity when the markets improved. Its case on Herrington was that, again, markets could be identified for its particular grade of coking coal. Not long afterwards a letter appeared in the *Scotsman* saying that when the geological fault was encountered at Polmaise in October 1983 only one further bore hole was drilled, nine weeks later; that the geological difficulties were no greater than had been overcome often before; and that the ash content, another of the Board's reasons for closing the pit, was well below that of other collieries in Scotland.[5] Among journalists in Scotland there was at that time some speculation that Polmaise had been picked for reprisals because of its resistance, a year earlier, to the transfer of men from the Cardowan pit near Glasgow – the union at Polmaise arguing that this was a breach of the agreement that men previously laid off at Polmaise would be reemployed before any others were brought in.

The controversy was reported and discussed in the early evening regional television news, both on STV and on BBC Scotland. Not a word of it ever reached network television news through the main evening bulletins. Nor were the issues at Herrington ever aired. That particular 'snowball' failed to roll.

Cortonwood is a different case. As mentioned in Chapter 9, the NCB decision was abrupt. The colliery was to close within five weeks, although the appeal procedure required months. Among journalists working in Yorkshire, the belief grew that Cortonwood had been picked primarily because the Yorkshire area was required by the NCB planning to cut production by 400 000 tonnes, and closing Cortonwood fitted the requirement exactly. But a secondary reason was also discussed: the supposition, never tested, was that the Coal Board chairman knew that a confrontation with the NUM president must be coming, knew also that stocks were high and the summer near, and decided that a closure in Mr Scargill's home territory – almost on his doorstep – was expedient at that moment. It was an interesting speculation, conceivably correct, but none of that reached the main news programmes; and although the abruptness of the Cortonwood closure was mentioned, not much was made of it. John Thorne touched on it on 6 March, when explaining the Cortonwood men's resolute stand; Jane Corbin for Channel Four News did so in her account of the Yorkshire 'Alamo' (the Cortonwood men's own term) on 15 March; for News at Ten, with nobody on the ground in Yorkshire in the first week and preoccupation with pickets and court action in the second, such retrospect was squeezed out by immediate events.

So the Coal Board's reasons for closing these collieries were never adequately explored by television news. Possibly that was not of great moment, since the Board, if challenged by anything less absolute than the NUM's 'no closures', would have replied by asking the union where it proposed to reduce output and so reduce the deficit – which the union would have countered by demanding greater government financial backing. Nevertheless it remains a gap in the coverage.

The changes in the Board's top structures also went unnoted by television news. After taking over as chairman, Mr MacGregor had reduced the number of full-time executives on the board and added part-time directors, mainly from the City. He concentrated authority in his own office, that of chief executive, and within Hobart House there was greater secrecy about policy and decisions. One consequence was that those with whom the journalists had regular contact, both centrally and in their areas, knew less than before or were not authorised to talk. It took some time even for the industrial specialists to grasp what was happening. In March and April 1984 they tended to assume that the Board was being candid, and consequently they were less critically inquisitive than with other nationalised industries; by midsummer, at least some of them had come to believe that the Board's information was no longer as open and reliable as in the past.

On the other side, Mr Scargill's smokescreen to conceal his tactics was never fully penetrated. Asked by Adeney at the press conference on 6 March, after the NCB–NUM meeting, the direct question, 'How close are you now to balloting your members on all-out action?', Mr Scargill replied: 'We shall do everything in our power to bring Mr MacGregor to his senses and ask him to come back to the negotiating table – that's what we're after doing.' (That was followed by Mr McGahey's words, much quoted, 'We're not dealing with a nicety – we will not be constitutionalised out of action in defence of our jobs.') On Thursday 8 March on Channel Four News, Ian Ross explained the two routes to a strike that were feasible under the NUM constitution – a national ballot or area action approved by the national executive – and said that a 'domino' effect was possible. It could 'snowball' across the country. That was the day when the NUM executive gave approval for the area strikes in Yorkshire and Scotland. Further interviews with

Mr Scargill in the next few days failed to secure any clarification.

On Friday 9 March, all the bulletins said that the use of flying pickets from Monday was probable and that their illegality would not deter the union. Mr Scargill was explicit in saying that he believed every area had agreed that picket lines should not be crossed. The following week, with mass picketing by Yorkshire miners taking place in Nottinghamshire and Lancashire, both Peter Snow on *Newsnight* and Peter Sissons on Channel Four News tried to extract from Mr Scargill more information about union policy. Both were persistent but neither completely succeeded. The exchange with Sissons on Thursday 15 March lasted nearly seven minutes. It is too long to reproduce in full, but here is an extract.

Q: Will you respect the views of those areas which decide *not* to take action, and ballot accordingly?

A: As far as we are concerned we have given authority to those areas which have already declared that they want to take strike action. Areas will determine their own policy, but I understand that every single area has decided that when there's a picket line that picket line should be respected – and of course in saying and doing that they are carrying out the policy decision and the principle both of the NUM and the trade union movement.

Q: You mean the area leadership has decided?

A: The area leaderships have decided on the basis of conference decision, determined by individual members, and I don't think you can get better democracy than that – unless of course you've got a warped mind and declare a balloting system which puts Mrs Thatcher in power with 43 per cent of the votes, and that that's democracy.

Q: So if a pit of say 1500 men votes not to stop work and is faced with a picket line of six men, that pit stops none the less?

A: What happens, Mr Sissons, is that if we have a picket line at a pit I would expect the miners at that pit – or indeed the workers in any industry – to respect that picket line; and that is exactly what the area leaderships have said, in their individual areas of the NUM.

Q: Isn't that a travesty of democracy?

A: No, I don't think it's a travesty of democracy at all, I think that if you hold a principle as dear as the NUM and the trade union movement do, and that is the recognition of a picket line, then you should practise what you preach . . .

Q: So it doesn't matter a row of beans how many of these areas actually vote, if there's a picket on the front gate that's that?

A: As far as I'm concerned, if the areas of the NUM vote to oppose current union policy, then naturally as a leader and as an NEC member as well as being president I would look at the position very carefully and in line with the NEC decision we would then reconsider the position. But at the present time, with 90 per cent of our union members involved in strike action, it appears to me that a majority of our membership certainly support the views of our executive . . .

Q: But is that not going down the path of disenfranchising large areas of your membership?

A: No, it isn't. If we had a national ballot, for example, under rule 43, instead of sanctioning area action under rule 41, you could very well have a situation where certain areas which did not agree with the national policy decision would find themselves voting in a minority way; but under the national rules you would expect to see them abiding by the majority decision . . .

Q: But wouldn't a national ballot get you out of the present situation – after all, your union's respect for and use of the national secret ballot was legendary. Isn't that now being destroyed?

A: Not at all. And indeed our sanctioning of rule 43 selective action in areas is nothing new. We've done it before . . . You know, we never talk about balloting for Mr MacGregor's appointment as chairman of the National Coal Board and, far more important, Mr Sissons, we never seem to ballot to determine whether we accept Mr MacGregor's decision to close a pit and throw 1000 men on the scrap heap, to join the four million umemployed put there by the Tories.

The exchange goes on further; but in this extract, the outline of Mr Scargill's tactics begins to emerge, if not quite clearly. Having failed three times to get a strike through a national ballot, Mr Scargill and his supporters on the NEC knew that they could not count on the necessary 55 per cent vote. (His reply saying that 90 per cent of union members were involved in strike action was totally misleading.) So they had to find another way. It was to use the Yorkshire miners – his reliable home base – as the spearhead, and to create a snowball or domino effect so that one area's decision influenced others. It also relied on the use of flying pickets, not just to bring out the miners in Nottinghamshire, Derbyshire, Lancashire and the Midlands, but to give the spearhead such momentum that it would be extremely difficult to stop. It depended also on a calculated exploitation of the miners' traditional loyalty to one another, so that even those who would have voted against a strike on a national ballot would stand by the union once a confrontation with the NCB had been created.

By the weekend of 18–19 March, that strategy was on a knife-edge between success and failure. That was the only time in 100 or more interviews that Mr Scargill appeared at all ruffled. Nottinghamshire, the Midlands, North Derbyshire, South Derbyshire, Lancashire, Durham and Cumberland had all voted against a strike in separate ballots; only Northumberland had voted in favour. No ballots had been held in Yorkshire (the largest area), South Wales, Scotland and Kent. (In South Wales, however, 16 out of 28 pits had voted to stay at work.) Of those voting, who were less than half the total NUM membership, the aggregate was 63 per cent against a strike, and that figure did not include the dissidents in South Wales.

In television interviews on the Friday evening, officials in Nottinghamshire, Lancashire and the Midlands had each said separately that they now expected a national ballot. Mr Scargill was asked about this twice on the Saturday afternoon. Answering a BBC reporter he said this: 'I'm prepared to consider whatever my membership feels appropriate, but what I'm not prepared to consider is either ITV, BBC, or the jackals and hyenas of Fleet Street giving me advice. Of that you can rest assured.' And to an ITN reporter later he said: 'What we shall do is to press Mr Ian MacGregor to stop his thuggery and butchery of the industry and to maintain the jobs of our people.' To the ITN man he gave the same answer three times, both on a ballot and on pickets, and he told the reporter that it appeared that he just didn't want to listen to the NUM's case.

These were smokescreen answers, which of course Mr Scargill was entitled to give. They illustrate the difficulty that reporters and interviewers often have in getting a straight reply. Nevertheless, it is one of their primary tasks to try to cut through the camouflage and to show the reality behind. Simply by putting the replies by Mr MacGregor, Mr Scargill and others on the screen they went some way towards doing this, but the truth at times remained partly clouded.

PICKETS AND POLICE

Mass pickets became prominent in television news, because they were dramatic and pictorial. Some reporters were conscious that they were giving an incomplete impression. 'We were presenting a picture that wasn't quite right', one said. 'At most collieries there were only half a dozen men round a brazier, and for hours nothing happened. Violence was not general. There was nothing to show. It was boring.' At the bigger events reporters often put phrases into their narrative, saying that the violence lasted only a few minutes in many hours or that 'only a few were throwing bricks'; but the scenes of violence were memorable and the qualifying words probably made less impression.

The earliest scenes of violence came in Scotland – on Saturday 10 March at a pithead meeting at Bilston Glen, near Edinburgh, and again on the picket lines there on Monday 12 March and Tuesday 13 March. Not much was seen on television screens, though cameramen were roughed up twice – an STV man working for ITN on the Saturday and a BBC man on the Monday. On Friday 9 March BBC news had carried brief interviews with men coming off the early shift. They were short and pithy, against a strike and wanting a national ballot. At the pithead meeting next day, when they were refused a local vote, scuffles broke out among the miners. Some fighting was shown both on BBC news and on ITN that night.

On the Monday more punching and shoving were seen at Bilston Glen, with a large picket – many from Polmaise, 40 miles away – as the afternoon shift tried to go in. Mike Smartt on BBC news described the morning picket as having been 'good-humoured' but the afternoon as 'ugly'. Both channels carried pictures of the police cordon being pushed back and broken through, and both had 'vox pop' comments from men deterred from going through. 'It's either a brave man or an idiot that'll go through that', one said. The Coal Board was quoted as saying that 8000 miners in Nottinghamshire and Scotland had been 'scared off' by the pickets.

For the next two days, events at the pitheads took second place to the High Court. On Tuesday 13 March the Coal Board lodged its application to have flying pickets declared illegal, and next day the court ordered the Yorkshire NUM not to send them out. Two days later the Board decided to go back to the High Court to seek damages, but almost immediately, because of the many areas voting against a strike, it delayed further action.

Each day, however, in the later stages of the bulletins there were pictures of mass picketing. Access to the Harworth and Ollerton collieries in Notts could be seen to be physically blocked by ranks of miners, said to be from Yorkshire, at dawn and before the afternoon shifts were due. At Bilston Glen on the Tuesday, pickets were again seen breaking through the police cordon and manhandling men who wanted to work. The Agecroft colliery in Lancashire was blockaded by Yorkshire men on the Wednesday; and Kent men were reported to be in action, though not seen, in Leicestershire. At Ollerton the first fatality was reported, when a picket collapsed and died, apparently from chest injuries.

Although the pictures were less dramatic than many in later weeks, especially those from Orgreave and Hunterston, they were the first visible evidence of the effectiveness of mass pickets. The ability of massed strikers to block a road completely could be seen, and it was clear that the police forces were inadequate to control what was happening. It was clear also that the NUM leadership was not willing to comply with court orders based on 'Tory' legislation.

Was too much made of the early picketing and violence? Looking back, the reporting appears low key. At that stage neither BBC nor ITN had more than three reporters deployed in the coalfields on any one day; and each reporter rarely had more than two or three minutes of air time for his item. Ken Rees for ITN, for example, was in South Wales one day, Notts the next, Staffordshire the third day and then back to Harworth, Ollerton and Thorsby in Notts. The reporting was factual and adjectives were infrequent, but relevant when used. The mass pickets were taking place and had to be reported; the violence was treated as incidental, and in that week it was never headlined. The nearest thing to an inflammatory headline was Channel Four News's on the Thursday: 'Arthur Scargill says the flying pickets go on . . . The Home Secretary calls it mob rule . . . We talk to both.'

With that as the worst, there was not much to complain about. For viewers, it was clear enough where the violence originated – from pickets who were trying by force to stop men working in areas or at collieries which had voted to continue work. It was clear also, at that stage, that the police were frequently outnumbered and unable to keep roads open. Neither the violence nor the blockades were begun by the police. Television news had a responsibility to make this plain, and it did so without undue emphasis.

That Thursday (15 March), the Home Secretary appeared in all three evening bulletins, saying that the police had to ensure that those who wanted to work could do so. He had asked the Chief Inspector of Constabulary, Sir Lawrence Byford, to keep in touch with operations and to advise him. Next day the BBC's Bill Hamilton had a scoop on mobilisation of the National Reporting Centre at New Scotland Yard and the preparations for a major police reinforcement of the Midlands. Hamilton told us that he was at New Scotland Yard for a quite different purpose that day, but passed the rooms on the thirteenth floor where the NRC was located.[6] Because of the obvious activity, he asked whether he could bring in a crew to film there. The NRC had been activated before, in the 1981 riots and during the Pope's visit in 1982.

'We discovered that it was quite a sophisticated operation in there', he said, 'and the questions then had to be asked – who are these people, what rights do they have, are they managing the strike from the police side?' From that came Hamilton's short account of its function, with pictures of the operations board showing the back-up forces available from counties and an interview with the Chief Constable of Humberside, David Hall, who was in charge as coordinator. 'They were at great lengths to point out that this was not a national police force, that the operational decisions were still being taken by the five or six Chief Constables in the counties mainly involved in the strike.' In that and later interviews, Hamilton said, Hall had insisted that it was not a political operation and not under government direction. Nevertheless, in Hamilton's view, it had been necessary to go on asking whether the police were not overreacting and themselves creating intimidation.

Over the weekend there were news pictures of convoys of Metropolitan police heading north and of other contingents on their way to the Midlands – and from the Dartford tunnel, reports that Kent miners were already being intercepted and turned back. Monday's bulletins (19 March) brought not only cover of the huge police presence, leading to 42 pits being at work (ITN) or 44 (BBC) compared with Friday's 11, but also two ITN initiatives. For Channel Four News Jane Corbin set off at 3 a.m. with a group of Yorkshire pickets, having talked the Brodsworth strike centre into letting her go with them; and for the main ITN programmes, including News at Ten, Ken Rees did an early morning circuit of Harworth (4.30 a.m.), Ollerton (5 a.m.) and Thorsby (5.30 a.m.), to report on the return to work.

On Jane Corbin's run, the pickets were not intercepted until they reached Bevercotes colliery in Notts, though they passed various police patrols, but they had to leave their car and walk the last part of the way. Their picketing succeeded in turning 30 miners back – 'not enough to close the pit'. It was all quite peaceful, perhaps because the camera was there.

For many journalists it was the start of a series of midnight and early morning vigils. John Thorne, the BBC network newsman based in Leeds, reckoned that from then onwards his supposed five-day 42-hour week was at least doubled.[7] It was often necessary to be on the road, with his crew, soon after midnight. There was not only the question of where to go, but of a probably hostile reception when arriving at the location. Newspaper journalists could mingle with the crowd unobtrusively, provided they were not 'wearing middle-class green wellies'. With a camera, recorder and powerful lighting pack, television people could never be part of the scenery.

> We had to arrive early and be seen around for as long as we
> could before the action started, so that by the time you had
> to turn the light on – to get pictures of the buses coming
> through or the push and shove – they'd got used to the light

going on, and they'd gone through all that 'get that f—ing light out'; and those guys who loved to come up and 'eyeball to eyeball', they'd got all that out of their system.

How did they decide where to go? To begin with, Thorne said, it was impossible to get any indication either from the Notts police or from the miners as to where things would happen. 'The pickets were trying to fool the cops, and the police didn't like us being there.' Later it became easier, and the police in South Yorkshire were willing to say at what time the buses would go in to particular pits.

For the BBC men, breakfast television was an added complication. A despatch rider had to be on the way to Leeds or Nottingham or Glasgow with the first videotapes early enough for transmission at 7 a.m.; if possible, a second delivery had to be made for 8 a.m. Those pictures could still be used at lunchtime, but editors of the early evening and Nine o'clock News programmes usually decided that the public must have seen those pictures already. It meant that for evening audiences 'the real crunch action' was likely to disappear.

On the question of violence, Thorne believed it was sometimes brought about by 'foolish' police action – by a 'bolshy' inspector or superintendent saying 'I won't have this' or trying to move pickets without reason or by not concealing the presence of dogs, horses and reinforcements with riot gear. Unless hidden away, those were 'red rags to the bull'. Other reporters said much the same. But Thorne and others we interviewed were sure that the violence was more often started deliberately by striking miners.

An example was at the Orgreave coking plant on 18 June, a day of some of the most disagreeable scenes on television, with violence on both sides. As on previous days, Thorne said, the trouble began when the lorries arrived to load coke for the Scunthorpe steel plant, and it marked the miners' frustration at being unable to stop the lorries. There was a 'long and concentrated period' of picket violence, with attempts to punch and kick the front line of the police cordon and later a barrage of bricks and stones. (One such barrage was well seen on the ITN pictures, with some missiles falling close to the camera.) To relieve the pressure, Thorne said, the police put their horses in; they were followed by men in riot gear and others who used their truncheons. In the running chase one policeman 'went wild' and beat a miner repeatedly with his truncheon. That incident was recorded by an ITN camera, and it was the more horrifying because the man appeared already to have been injured; but to the 'mortification' of Thorne and his crew, their camera failed. It had developed a fault, running only seven seconds at a time, and had battery trouble. ITN that day had the advantage of extra cameras from YTV and Central.

Asked whether instructions were given from London about the treatment of particular events or the policy of coverage, Thorne said 'no, never'. He had received no general or specific instructions at any time. Other BBC and ITN reporters, when asked the same question, gave much the same reply.

Michael Crick of Channel Four News, who was almost as heavily involved in Notts and Yorkshire as Thorne, thought there had been a failure to tackle police violence adequately. That had created a sense of injustice among miners' families, who believed it was happening. The police, he said, were more careful than the miners about where and when they did it. When it was in police vans or at police stations it could not be filmed. But at Orgreave, he said, the police had had to put up with being pelted with stones and bottles – as indeed Channel Four News and News at Ten had shown.[8]

Crick and others thought it unfortunate that the cameras were so often behind the police lines and therefore appearing to present a 'police' view. The reason lay in the physical attacks on camera crews. They could not take pictures when being punched and jostled, and taking pictures was their job. Channel Four News cameramen, Crick said, were an exception – they carried Channel Four stickers on their equipment and because the miners believed they were getting a better deal from Channel Four, the crews were less likely to be assaulted.

Two of the ITN cameramen to whom we talked compared the picket lines with their experiences in Northern Ireland, with the difference that in Ireland the rioters and the security forces were preoccupied with each other and left the camera crews alone. The filming in Ireland had been with handheld cameras, whereas now they were using ENG (video cameras) linked to a heavy recorder by an umbilical cord. Both cameramen had been the victims of sudden physical attack, for no apparent reason.

Among the BBC cameramen often at Orgreave was Bernard Hesketh, who in 1982 provided most of the television pictures from San Carlos, Goose Green and battlefields beyond. Whatever one's view of the Falklands War, Hesketh's courage and stamina are beyond doubt. He was attacked at Orgreave, Markham Main and other sites. Once, when preparing to record an interview with Mr Scargill at Orgreave, he had the umbilical cord ripped out of his camera and the camera damaged.

> I was very angry [Hesketh said]. I confronted Arthur Scargill and asked him why we should be subject to this mindlessness – it didn't do his cause any good that we should be unable to interview him when his own men had damaged our camera. And he said something to the effect, 'well if you felt the way these men did and if you had suffered at the hands of the media in the way they did, you'd do the same thing.' In other words, he was condoning it and not condemning what they did.[9]

Another time, when trying to film at Orgreave from the pickets' side, Hesketh found the atmosphere fairly friendly at first. Then he was suddenly pulled to the ground, his camera with him. The police offered to arrest his attacker, who could be readily identified; Hesketh's answer was 'No thanks, we've got to come back here tomorrow.' At Markham Main colliery, where the NUM had agreed to send a team underground to deal with a fire, the television crew were set upon, punched, kicked, and told that if they didn't get out 'they'd have the living daylights beaten out of them'.

Thorne believed that many of the assaults on camera crews at many sites were the work of the same dozen or so men from Markham Main, who 'felt it was their job to be the hard nuts of the Yorkshire campaign'. They whipped up hostility among pickets whose confidence the crews had tried hard to win. They did it, he said, at Rossington, at Gascoigne Wood, at Harworth and at Orgreave. They kept it up right to the end of the dispute.

Mr Scargill himself at times induced attacks. Criticism of the press and television was part of his standard repertoire at rallies or meetings – often light-hearted and enjoyable even to the reporters, but sometimes not. One television man described the loneliness of having Arthur's finger pointed accusingly at the crew and then being surrounded by a group of hostile young miners, rather as by Paisley's 'bowlerhats' at meetings in Northern Ireland, he said. They were kicked and had to leave. Television journalists had no doubt that Mr Scargill must share responsibility for the physical attacks and the consequent restriction of coverage. Nevertheless, during the interviews we found that although the crews did not like the treatment they had received they were extraordinarily tolerant about it, generally having much sympathy for the miners and their families.

One other omission, apart from not often filming among the pickets, was that the news bulletins never reported the way the flying picket strategy was being coordinated and directed. This was done in Yorkshire apparently through four or five strike centres, one of them in a Barnsley pub, through which instructions were distributed each evening for next day's action. To outsiders it was obvious enough that the sudden arrival of hundreds of men at one pithead in the early morning was not spontaneous, but the mechanism of control was never revealed to television audiences. Thorne said it was because the time required to arrange it, if it could have been arranged at all, would have been too great.

Miners often complained to crews that police violence was not being reported. Mike Smartt, when trying to persuade a union official in Fife to let his crew travel on a pickets' bus so that they could film police road blocks at the Kincardine bridge, was told that they never filmed police action – such as the horses knocking men down at Hunterston. Had the official been there, Smartt asked? No: but he'd seen it on television.

As already observed in this chapter, viewers can draw opposite meanings from the same set of pictures. Even so, there can be little doubt that the sequences from picket and police lines from mid-March onwards attracted a great deal of attention among audiences. With the Hunterston, Orgreave and Llanwern episodes in May and June, and then with reports of attacks on working miners and their homes, that attention was held through the summer and into the autumn. Again, reactions could be of many kinds; but in England, Wales and Scotland, where physical violence was alien and abhorred, those scenes must have caused profound shock. There had been similar episodes in the Grunwick dispute and in the conflict between the NGA and Mr Eddie Shah, but never anything on the scale of the scenes from Nottinghamshire and from the steel or coke plants, nor of such prolonged duration.

This was an industrial dispute on a new scale and with a new dimension of violence – new, at any rate, since the arrival of television. It had to be reported. To many of the audience it must have carried the threat that, unless stemmed, it could bring industrial chaos and social disintegration; to others it must have been welcome evidence of trade union strength and evidence also of what they saw as the institutional violence of the state. For the broadcasters, the first requirement was to present the evidence as best they could.

POLICY, POLITICS AND SOCIETY

Moving forward to midsummer, the focus changes. In the first ten days of July, it was on negotiations between the NCB and NUM – the latest and most hopeful yet in a series of meetings. There was continuing trouble over coal, coke and iron ore deliveries to the big steel plants, and continuing disagreement between the miners and the steel unions. But the preparations for meetings between the NCB and NUM in London were the dominant news.

Channel Four News, the BBC's Nine o'clock News and News at Ten all carried substantial previews of the talks on Tuesday and Wednesday, 3 and 4 July. Headlines indicate the atmosphere:

Talking again – MacGregor and Scargill agree to meet (BBC, Tuesday).
Talks again this week – the NUM says 'yes' (ITN, Tuesday).

Ian Ross on Channel Four News was cautious: hopes were being pinned (not nailed, he said) on a new formula based on the Edinburgh talks in June. Martin Adeney also outlined the progress made in Edinburgh, with agreement on two out of

three categories of pits that might be closed. Giles Smith for
News at Ten said that the Board was ready to 'redefine' the
term 'uneconomic'.

Coincidentally, the ITN programmes had the first interview
given by the Energy Secretary, Mr Peter Walker, since the
start of the strike. Talking to Alastair Burnet, he said that
there would be no power cuts in the autumn and coal stocks
could last well into the new year. The strike, he said, was doing
'colossal damage' and the government was willing at any time
to meet the NCB and NUM together – if they could agree on a
new plan. It was also ready to review capital investment in the
industry.

Also coincidentally, BBC Nine o'clock News and *Newsnight*
carried a study by Bill Hamilton of what the strike was costing
local authorities in police pay and other extra expenditure, and
an interview with the chairman of the Police Committees of
Metropolitan Authorities; he said that the police authorities
were losing financial and other control, and the chief constables losing operational control – the Home Secretary was now
in charge. (Hamilton said that collecting all the information
from local authorities had taken him 12 hours of telephoning
and much other work.[10])

On Thursday 5 July the talks at the Rubens Hotel in London
lasted from 10.30 a.m. to 7 p.m., ending too late for Channel
Four News to say anything about the day's progress. The main
bulletins could say little, either, because secrecy was maintained by both sides. Adeney on the BBC believed that the two
sides had begun to bridge 'a yawning gap'; Giles Smith on ITN
said that 'some sort of breakthrough' had been achieved. Next
day the talks lasted a further five hours, ending with agreement
to meet again on Monday, in Edinburgh. Saturday's bulletins
showed Mr Scargill at a rally and march in Birmingham,
proclaiming 'No compromise, no sellout – we've come too far
for anything other than to win a victory.'

But Monday in Edinburgh brought a breakdown after eight
hours of talks. Mr Scargill, at a press conference before leaving
Scotland, blamed Mrs Thatcher: 'either MacGregor had his
hands tied behind his back or she's firmly holding his left
hand.' The Coal Board chairman, on return to London, said he
was disappointed but that they would meet again in nine days.
'We have made a major effort.' When told of Mr Scargill's

comment he laughed (in a rather forced way, it might be thought) and said that he ran the Coal Board without help from anyone.

On the wording that had led to the breakdown, only Channel Four News gave it precisely. The disagreement, Ian Ross said, was on whether or not to include the word 'beneficially' in a definition of one category of pit that could be closed: 'no further mineable reserves that are workable or can be beneficially developed'. The NUM wanted 'beneficially' deleted; the Board refused. The meeting nine days later, unfortunately, fared no better.

By any reasonable standard, the reporting of that phase of negotiations was factual, impartial and without bias. Each side was given the opportunity to state its view in its own words. Mr Scargill's assertion about Mrs Thatcher's 'intervention' was reported straightforwardly, with no added comment. Only Channel Four News gave the text of the key passage in dispute, but its bulletin was longer than the others. If there was a flaw, it was in the failure of the others to give the text; even for peak audiences it would have made the position plainer, and it needed only 20 seconds. ITN's interview with Mr Walker was useful – and, being his first in 18 weeks, evidence of the government's previous determination to keep a low profile. Hitherto he had been heard only in House of Commons exchanges or seen in public statements. He appeared more often after that.[11] The only person with any cause to complain – and not much of a cause at that – was Mr MacGregor, since all the bulletins in passing noted that his personal letter to miners the previous week had drawn no response. The return to work was only a 'trickle', contrary to confident forecasts from the Board.

Moving on to September and October, Mr Scargill and the striking miners can be seen to have received generous exposure first at the TUC and then at the Labour party conference. On Monday 3 September, television news was a bonanza for Mr Scargill – 'a day of personal triumph' according to the Nine o'clock News and the day of 'a hero's welcome' in News at Ten. Fresh talks with the NCB had been announced and there was an air of optimism. Some 3000 miners paraded outside the hall in Brighton – urged by Mr Scargill to be on their best behaviour – and the day passed off 'noisily but peacefully', as

ITN said. Mr Scargill received a standing ovation inside the hall as well as outside. The only cloud on the scene was the refusal of the electricians, power workers and steelmen to support the strike.

Next morning, with his flair for an occasion, Mr Scargill went live into the BBC's broadcast from the conference at 11 a.m. – diverting coverage from a debate on trade union legislation to his press conference in the foyer – to announce that the Coal Board had called off the talks. Mr MacGregor, interviewed later in London, said that Mr Scargill was 'lying in his teeth' and that the Board had not called off the talks. Reporters spent many hours before the evening bulletins in trying to piece together what had really happened. Such was the impact of Mr Scargill's announcement that Mr Kinnock's address to the TUC had to take a low place in the reports from Brighton. Once again, the reporters and specialists were doing their utmost to provide an accurate account of a confusing development.

A month later, at the opening of the Labour party conference in Blackpool, Mr Scargill and the miners again enjoyed triumphant publicity through television news. For the sake of brevity here, it is enough to say that he received a 'rapturous' reception from the conference and was seen on every channel achieving conference support for a resolution condemning police violence and demanding a ban on any police activity during industrial disputes. The bulletins also reported two or three opposing speeches at Blackpool and a reply from the Home Secretary saying that if there had been no violent mass pickets and no intimidation there would have been no need for a police presence. Next day Mr Kinnock made his own speech condemning violence, whether by stone-throwers or by cavalry charges; and the political staffs of BBC and ITN noted the anxious discussions, behind the scenes, aimed at dissuading the Transport and General Workers from taking the party further towards illegality through contempt of court over the coal dispute. Mr Kinnock, the BBC's John Cole said, was trying to educate his party and remind it of the previous year's election disaster. Also under discussion that day was the Nacod's initiative on a new procedure for reviewing pit closures – a possible road to peace. Altogether it was a day of complex industrial, political and legal cross-currents; and again a day on which a great deal of journalistic skill, knowledge and detachment went into providing intelligible reports.

In assessing reactions to the work of reporters, it has to be remembered that no two people will ever perceive an event in exactly the same way. Nor will any two take exactly the same meaning out of the kind of compressed summary and selected extracts from speeches that even the most skilled team of journalists can provide from a TUC or party conference. Those of the audience strongly sympathetic to Mr Scargill and his cause may possibly have thought, when viewing the TUC report, 'at last they are doing justice to Arthur on the tele'; about the reports from Labour at Blackpool they may have had more reservations, because in addition to giving a good showing to Mr Scargill, the bulletins reported the Home Secretary's comments and the speeches of trade unionists opposed to the NUM's line. At the same time it is probable that some committed Conservatives in the audience were angered by the TUC reports, believing that the BBC and ITN were again showing their left-wing bias, and those viewers may have been hardly less annoyed by the reports from Blackpool. In spite of such reactions, it is also quite probable that a majority of the audience accepted the reporting as fair and adequate – and drew their own personal conclusions, many and various, about the events.

Individual reactions are heavily conditioned by individual points of view; and as in earlier chapters, we should note the influence of 'sociocentralism'. It means that the media tend to reflect the society in which they live; anything which threatens the peace and well-being of that society is likely to bring an unfavourable reaction from much of the audience, unless there is already a tide of reformist feeling brought about by earlier events. It was not the media as such who made the actions of the striking miners unpopular. The media were only the messengers. It was the actions themselves and their implications for society as a whole that generated the unpopularity.

Before we leave policy and politics, one partial omission and one initiative ought to be noted. Television news in May and June gave less prominence than newspapers to Mr Scargill's political purposes, when he said at rallies that the miners would beat the Coal Board and the government and would bring Mrs

Thatcher down. At the Mansfield May Day rally (Monday 7 May) the BBC extracts from his speech concentrated on his message to the Notts miners, 'don't cross picket lines', while ITN gave first place to his demand to the steelworkers that they should stop production. A week later, at another much bigger rally at Mansfield, both presented the occasion as a cheerful carnival – which it was, until there was trouble in the late evening – and both headlined his promises 'We'll stay out until Christmas if we have to' and 'We're on to a winner.' They also reported his claim that coal stocks had 'dramatically deteriorated'.

The BBC's Nine o'clock News added later in the bulletin an extract from the electricians' union annual conference, with its general secretary criticising 'nursery revolutionaries' who wanted to bring the government down. News at Ten, at the end of its item, carried pictures of one of its cameramen being viciously attacked – the pictures having been taken by a second camera – but mentioned that incident only briefly. The preference in both programmes for emphasis on the carnival atmosphere and Mr Scargill's words directly related to the dispute, not to politics, is understandable. Those aspects must have seemed more immediately relevant.

The notable initiative was on policy, not politics, and it came in mid-June in Channel Four News. Channel Four News made identical offers to Mr MacGregor and Mr Scargill. Would each like to make a ten- or twelve-minute film stating his case? Each was provided with a camera crew, a journalist as adviser, access to ITN's film library and use of its computerised graphics. The two reports, each about twelve minutes long, were broadcast by Channel Four News on Monday 18 June – the day many thousands of pickets converged on Orgreave, and there was bitter fighting.[12] Mr MacGregor's film concentrated on the economics of the industry and the importance of investment in the new coalfields; Mr Scargill's portrayed the 'vandalism' by the Coal Board of mining communities and challenged the Board's concept of an 'uneconomic' pit. Neither man knew what the other had produced. They were two fascinating films, entirely different in content and style. More important, they were a model of how to let contending parties speak for themselves – an example that ought to be followed much more frequently.

MEASURING THE COVERAGE

Measurement of the time given to particular aspects of the NCB–NUM dispute is a useful element in the analysis of television coverage, but of no more than limited value as a guide to fairness. Like all such measurements, it is not and cannot be wholly objective. It can confirm, for example, that the NUM's national president received very much more time on television news than the Coal Board's chairman. But one must look elsewhere for the evidence that Mr Scargill enjoyed publicity while Mr MacGregor was, at best, a reluctant performer.

To make our measurements, we have looked in detail at one week in each of the first eight months – the first full week of the Yorkshire strike (12–16 March), and then the first full week in each month from April to October. The figures are for Mondays to Fridays each week on Channel Four News, the BBC's Nine o'clock News and ITN's News at Ten. Earlier, we had measured the three weeks from 5–23 March 1984, and the two sets of figures are consistent with each other. We had been advised that it was sociologically acceptable to use the first weeks of each month as a sample.

The use of the main evening bulletins does, however, have one unavoidable effect. As stated earlier in this chapter, the coming of the BBC breakfast-time programme – with an emphasis on news – meant that some of the most dramatic scenes from pitheads had been used there and at midday, and were therefore judged to be unsuitable for further repetition in the evening. Consequently the totals for pickets, whether non-violent or violent, are almost certainly lower than if earlier bulletins had been measured. Because TV-am does not carry ITN's service and is less attentive to news, ITN's bulletins were not so restricted.

The aggregate measurements are given at the end of this chapter. Here we summarise some points that stand out:

1. In those eight weeks the coal dispute took up almost one quarter of all news time. In 60 hours of television news, 14 hours and 20 minutes were devoted to the dispute. Apart from the Falklands War, there can be no precedent for such sustained and extensive cover. The dispute was mentioned in every one of 40 programmes on News at Ten, in 38 out of 40 by

the BBC's Nine o'clock News, and in 39 out of 40 on Channel Four News.

2. The extent of coverage varied greatly week by week, reflecting the pressure of other news rather than events in the coal industry. Programme editors must have been relieved when they could lead with other topics. The lowest figures were for 4 to 8 June, when President Reagan was in London and the D-Day anniversary was commemorated in Normandy – although that was also the week of the NUM's biggest demonstration in London, with fighting in Parliament Square, and of a meeting between Mr Scargill and Mr MacGregor. That week saw altogether only 19 minutes of Channel Four News, 19 on News at Ten and 18 on the Nine o'clock News.

Totals in the first week of May were also low, in spite of heavy picketing at Ravenscraig and Hunterston, but in that week the aftermath of the St James's Square siege took precedence, along with Russia's withdrawal from the Olympic Games. The weeks with longest coverage were in March and September, the latter coinciding with the TUC conference.

3. In the eight representative weeks, the total time given to NUM officials supporting the strike or to miners and their families in support was 1 hour and 29 minutes. The total given to NCB staff, including Mr MacGregor, was 36.5 minutes. The total for NUM officials opposing the strike or to miners and families against it was 12.5 minutes. Of the interviews with NUM officials, two-thirds were in studios or offices and one-third in public settings (an aspect measured because of past criticism that union officials and workers were interviewed in adverse surroundings while managements were interviewed in comfort). The figures for NCB officials were 31.5 minutes in studies or offices and 5 minutes in public settings.

4. Government ministers received 45 minutes for statements or interviews and Labour party members 35.5 minutes. For Alliance members the total was 1 minute and 22 seconds. Third-party interviews – CBI, trade unionists other than NUM, historians, legal advisers – came to 59 minutes. Police interviews or statements, other than on picket lines, took 8 minutes.

5. The time given to background or explanation was substantial – over 2.5 hours of Channel Four News's 6.5 hours

on the dispute; one hour out of News at Ten's 4.5 hours; and 28 minutes of the BBC Nine o'clock News's 3.5 hours. Admittedly the boundary between the day's events and any background explanation is often blurred, but the figures follow from an endeavour to pick out the explanatory elements.

6. The background items included in the early stages features of five minutes or more on Channel Four News on such topics as the mining community at Grimethorpe in Yorkshire, on miners' welfare provision at Knottingley in North Yorkshire, on the Ridley report of 1978 on how a future coal strike should be handled (a confidential report to the Conservative party, with the defeat of the Heath government in 1974 much in mind), and on allegations of police undercover operations with phone-tapping and infiltration of the NUM. News at Ten carried shortened versions of these reports. The BBC's Nine o'clock News included few such features, though *Newsnight* on BBC2 provided comparable background.

7. On the controversial issue of violence, measurements again depend on value judgements. Applying a strict standard – counting as violence only those scenes where there is physical assault or injury, the use of missiles which may cause injury, the use of truncheons or active use of police horses, or serious damage to property – then the total of violence attributed to pickets outside collieries is 4 minutes 8 seconds and the total attributed to pickets elsewhere (Orgreave, Hunterston, London, etc.) is 5 minutes 53 seconds. The total of all picketing seen outside collieries is just over 40 minutes and of picketing or demonstrations elsewhere a further 50 minutes. Violent scenes on a strict measurement therefore amount to just over one minute in nine of television news pictures of picketing or demonstrations; or well below one minute in each hour of television coverage of the dispute.

8. If, alternatively, the measurement is widened to include some of the turbulence leading up to violence or the arrests afterwards and any scene where pickets outnumber police and physically prevent men from going to work, then the totals double – to 9 minutes 26 seconds of violence outside collieries and to 10 minutes 48 seconds elsewhere. In total, the violent scenes then amount to about 1 minute in 4.5 of television news pictures of pickets or demonstrations; or 1 minute in every 43 minutes of television coverage of the dispute.

9. Violence attributed to police (not pickets) outside collieries came to 18 seconds, and violence elsewhere to 1 minute.

10. Violence reported but not seen amounted to 14 minutes attributed to miners and 1 minute attributed to police.

11. Taken together, these figures do not suggest either exaggeration of violence or undue concern with it by television news. As has been said elsewhere, television did not invent the violence, and had a duty to report it. Although numerically few, the scenes of violence were among the most memorable in the coverage of the dispute, whether through the shock caused by the physical blockading of pits at the start or through the police 'cavalry charges' at Hunterston and Orgreave in May and June. The fact that cameras were generally behind the police lines rather than among the pickets may have resulted in an underrepresentation of police violence, but that was a direct result of the assaults on cameramen and recordists, sometimes condoned by Mr Scargill himself and sometimes encouraged by him.

12. As to the style of interviews, we attempted to categorise them as 'friendly', 'neutral' or 'hostile' – though realising that such judgements are subjective. Nine out of ten were logged as 'neutral'. In any event, Mr Scargill responded more effectively than Mr MacGregor to sharp questioning, so where did the advantage lie? A close look at the interviews does not suggest that either man or either side was treated more leniently or more respectfully than the other.

CONCLUSIONS

In reading the transcript of a programme rather than watching the videotape, one loses the vividness of pictures and the nuances of speech. But in a printed book there is no alternative to transcripts and summaries. Those presented here have been designed so far as possible to let readers form their own judgements, helped by interviews with journalists. Without wishing to preempt anyone else's conclusions, let me state mine. They relate to the questions set out at the beginning of this chapter.

Was the reporting fair, accurate and non-partisan? The short answer is 'Yes'. The longer answer is that within the limitations of human frailty, mobility of equipment and shortage of time the reporters, scriptwriters, video editors and others tried hard to provide a reliable service. Whatever their personal views, television news journalists can be seen to have exerted themselves to provide an unprejudiced picture. No policy directions were given to them from above; and unlike some newspaper journalists, they were not required to find a particular 'angle' to a story. They were expected to provide a clear and compact account of events that were often complicated, to try not to be misled or let their audiences be misled by half truths or untruths, and to do it whenever possible through factual evidence. Reporters were also expected to work in close cooperation with their cameramen and recordists, with the aim of providing relevant and visually dynamic pictures. That inevitably meant a subjective choice of what to emphasise. On the whole, nevertheless, they served their audiences well.

Was the background to the news adequately explained? This question can be taken together with the one on future implications. Here the answer is more qualified. Some of the background and some of the future implications were explored, but the urgency and drama of each day's events – or of other events unconnected with the coal dispute – tended to leave little time for extra information. Channel Four News can be seen to have done more than the others, not only through having more time but by its imaginative approach to the historical background, the effect on communities and the presentation of economic aspects. It was also the first to show a reporter travelling with pickets and being intercepted by the police; others followed its lead.

Were the NCB's pit closure policy and the NUM's response fully covered? Here the answer must be 'No'. The apparent logic of the NCB's case was too readily accepted; and because Mr Scargill was so uncompromising about closures any detailed inquiry appeared likely to be unrewarding. The doubts about how and why the Polmaise decision was taken, expressed in the Scottish press and regional television news, never received a hearing on network news. Nor was the Cortonwood decision adequately investigated.

Was there excessive emphasis on violence? The physical violence that occurred on picket lines, in mining villages and at locations where no NUM members worked (such as Orgreave and Hunterston) was profoundly shocking to many people. That it was initiated by striking miners is beyond doubt, though when large numbers of police were brought into action the blame occasionally lay with them. The mass pickets and their violence were a new phenomenon (Grunwick and the Shah dispute apart) and it could not be covered up. The actual time given to it was small, but the pictures were the most memorable in the year's coverage. To have refrained from reporting the violence or to have played it down would have been to withhold evidence and to distort the truth. It could have served no public good.

Was there a tendency to play down anything damaging to the police? To some extent, yes. 'Sociocentralism' was at work here, in that journalists, like others, tended to believe that without the presence of the police even uglier events were likely to have followed, with industrial chaos and possibly greater rioting. That was not a reason to play down police violence; but in practice the assaults by striking miners on camera crews and reporters forced them to work mainly from behind the police lines. It is worth noting that the threat to civil liberties inherent in setting up police road blocks sometimes a hundred miles or more from the collieries was well covered in television news; so was the risk that central coordination at New Scotland Yard might pave the way for a national police force.

Did the immediate events exclude the reporting of longer-term trends? Yes, though the longer term is more appropriately covered by current affairs programmes, not by news.

What was missed? The failure to explore the NCB and NUM policies on pit closures has already been mentioned. On the political purposes of Mr Scargill and on the government's activities behind the scenes, when compared with press coverage television news was reticent. Apart from such gaps, at the time of writing we do not know of others.[13] The memoirs of participants published in the next few years, the research work of economists, sociologists and others, and government records released in the years 2014 and 2015 may reveal more.

No previous event taking place in Britain had had such extensive television coverage. Because the pictures of action were often so compelling, it is fairly safe to say that for the first time television news displaced the newspapers and radio news as the primary source of public information. Along with the action pictures went the reporting of attitudes, policies and negotiations. In all these aspects it was vital – and for the future will be vital – that television news retains and develops high standards of journalism and social responsibility.

MEASUREMENTS: THE NCB–NUM DISPUTE

TABLE 10.1 *Place in bulletins (1984–5 coal dispute)*

	C4N	BBC 9	NaT
First item in 68 out of 120 programmes (over half)	24	21	23
Second item in 23 out of 120 programmes (nearly one in five)	9	7	7
Lower place in 26 out of 120 programmes	6	10	10
No mention in 3 out of 120 programmes	1	2	0

Total of 14 hrs 18½ mins of coverage of coal dispute in 60 hours of TV news. Approx. 24 per cent of news time.
Total for C4N – 6 hrs 28 mins; for BBC 9 – 3 hrs 28 mins; for NaT – 4 hrs 23 mins.

NB: C4N=Channel Four News; NaT=News at Ten; BBC 9=BBC Nine o'clock News.

TABLE 10.2 *Hours of coverage in each week (hours, mins, secs)*

	C4N	BBC 9	NaT
12–16 March	1.07.44	21.54	36.57
2–6 April	47.48	26.57	44.00
7–11 May	27.04	21.21	26.49
4–8 June	18.49	17.43	19.10
2–6 July	42.30	23.35	29.07
6–10 August	58.09	21.50	21.13
3–7 September	1.10.58	35.02	44.19
1–5 October	54.53	39.45	40.54
Total	6.27.55	3.28.07	4.22.29

TABLE 10.3 *The reporting of press conferences, statements and interviews (in mins, secs)*

NCB, in studios or offices	31.37
NCB, in public settings	4.45
NUM officials, in studios or offices, pro-strike	49.58
NUM officials, in studios or offices, anti-strike	0.34
NUM officials, in public settings, pro-strike	21.00
NUM officials, in public settings, anti-strike	1.08
Miners, not officials, in studio or home, pro-strike	1.13
Miners, not officials, in studio or home, anti-strike	3.42
Miners, not officials, in public setting, pro-strike	15.18
Miners, not officials, in public setting, anti-strike	6.06
Miners' wives or families, pro-strike	1.22
Miners' wives or families, anti-strike	0.45
Third-party interviews (including CBI and other trade unions, historians and legal advisers)	59.08
Police, interviews or statements	7.57
Government, ministers' statements or interviews	44.49
Opposition statements or interviews, Labour party	35.37
Opposition statements or interviews, Alliance	1.22

Total of NCB: 36.5 mins
Total of NUM officials, miners and families pro-strike: 1 hr 29 mins
Total of NUM officials, miners and families against strike: 12.5 mins

TABLE 10.4 *The reporting of violence (in mins, secs)*

	Strict measure[a]	*Broader measure*
Non-violent pickets outside collieries	36.17	30.59
Violence outside collieries attr. to pickets	4.08	9.26
Violence outside collieries attr. to police	0.18	0.25
Non-violent pickets elsewhere (Orgreave, Hunterston, NUM headquarters, etc.)	29.18	27.23
Violence elsewhere, attr. to pickets	5.53	10.48
Violence elsewhere, attr. to police	1.00	1.18
Violence reported but not seen, attr. to pickets	9.28	14.08
Violence reported but not seen, attr. to police	1.01	1.01

Total of non-violent picketing (in 60 hours of TV news): 1 hr 5 mins 35 secs
Total of violence attributed to pickets (strict measure): 19 mins 29 secs
Total of violence attributed to police (strict measure): 2 mins 19 secs

[a] For explanation of 'strict' and 'broad' measurements, see text in Chapter 10.

TABLE 10.5 *Presentation (in hours, mins)*

Studio, including presenter, maps, graphics, reporters in studio, etc.	6.23
Location, including reporters on location, interviews not in studios, conference settings, etc.	7.10[a]

[a] includes one programme presented from Harworth, Notts, with 25 mins of miners and coal dispute coverage (C4N, Wednesday, 8 August).

11 War, Terrorism and Ourselves

War, civil war, espionage and kidnapping bring exceptional problems for journalists. Should they suspend normal practice, in the interests of saving life or national security, or should they 'publish and be damned'? The Falklands War of 1982, the long conflict in Northern Ireland, the sieges of the Iranian Embassy in 1980 and the Libyan Embassy in 1983: these and other episodes posed problems for editors and their staffs.

Starting with the Falklands, let us hear first from Peter Preston, editor of the *Guardian:*

> If your country is at war, your readers won't thank you, your country won't thank you and your paper won't thank you for a dramatic exclusive which manages to get 2000 British soldiers killed; that was clear, we all knew that and we all operated on that basis. But it didn't actually stop us trying to find out what the strategy was, what the likely stages of events were and so forth; but we were trying to behave as responsibly as we could.

No Fleet Street, provincial or television editor dissents from that reply: none knew where the landings were to take place, and most of the guesswork proved wrong, but if any editor had known beforehand that San Carlos was to be the beach-head he would not have published it. As Preston said, they still tried to find out as much as possible; but they tried also, in relation to military security, to 'behave responsibly'.

Mike Molloy, of the *Daily Mirror,* said that although war had not been declared, nearly all the information was being channelled through government sources or through Defence Ministry control. If, as a newspaper, they had been convinced that the government was embarking on 'an act of folly', it would have been their responsibility to reveal that. But journalists, he said, were not computers and when something on the Falklands scale was happening to their country they were naturally affected by it. William Deedes, editor of the *Daily Telegraph,* similarly said that the tone of reporting had to be watched because of its possible effect on families at home or on the fighting forces, who were hearing it relayed by radio programmes. It must not be treated as if it were a football match, where it did not matter who won. But that did not prevent the printing of facts; and if a disaster had appeared imminent the news would certainly not have been 'smothered'. (These replies all came in interviews with the author for a BBC Radio 3 documentary, soon after the campaign ended, and are reproduced with their consent.)

David Nicholas of ITN was sensitive about feelings among audiences:

It was a unique experience in broadcasting, for me anyway and for many of us in ITN, in that we were addressing an audience – after all, there were 25 000 servicemen involved and that means an awful lot of families and so on – so one had to be extremely careful how we presented the news, on what one said; and we consciously throughout had in mind the fact that we were addressing an audience greatly involved in an emotional way, perhaps as at no time since Suez.

Were there, then, any acute problems of taste with film coming back from the South Atlantic – for example, with casualties who might be identified?

Yes, particularly of course after Bluff Cove [the midway landings] when the raw material did show some pretty horrendous scenes, and they probably would have been identifiable. We made the judgement, rightly or wrongly, that we would not show in detail the worst of the casualties, and we certainly made it clear to everyone concerned in the editing here that we did not wish to identify any casualty – we did not want anyone to recognise a relative from our picture.

Those horrendous scenes, however, did not prevent the

courage and humour of the combatants from coming through. Thus one of the Welsh Guardsman, wading ashore wet and blackened from the burning ship *Sir Galahad,* growled as he passed the camera: 'Next time I want to paddle, I'll go to Blackpool.'

During the campaign, live reports from the Falklands were possible only by radio, and those were censored first by Defence Ministry men with the task force and then again when they reached London. Television tapes had to be flown to Ascension Island and transmitted from there, with the result that they were two weeks or more old by the time they were seen at home, and they too had been censored. (An account of the technical difficulties of transmission and of the erratic censorship is given in the book by Robert Harris, *Gotcha!.*) The delay made editorial decisions slightly easier. If live coverage had been possible, Nicholas still took the view that in addition to a security check it would have been essential to make sure first that no viewer could identify a husband or son being killed.

Peter Woon, then editor of BBC television news, concurred with that judgement – adding, however, that the audience as citizens ought to be told what was happening.

> I think we had a serious problem highlighted by the Bluff Cove pictures, though by the time we had those it was over. We considered whether or not some parts of that should be cut back further and were quite convinced that 'no they shouldn't', that people should see things as they actually happened. There was no doubt in our minds that horrifying as some of it was it was right that the public should see what had happened in their name.

'In their name' – that mattered, Woon thought. Again, others agreed. And in the debate that followed after the campaign – with some MPs arguing that television and radio had been allowed too much freedom during the fighting – there were those who replied that if Ypres or Loos or Passchendaele had been shown to British audiences in 1915 or 1916 or 1917 some of the British and French generals might have been sacked sooner. In 1916 or 1917 that would have been sheer gain.

For reporters with the task force, there was a host of

hazards – lack of suitable clothing, for the first group had left home at only a few hours' notice; lack of food when ashore; for some, lack of previous experience in military operations; the hostility or indifference of some of their Defence Ministry 'minders'; the unpredictable censorship, the danger, the distance between ground fighting and the ships from which messages could be sent and so on. Reporters quickly found that anything atmospheric or of a critical tone risked being delayed or stopped. At Bluff Cove, a voice report from Brian Hanrahan to the BBC which described survivors as badly shaken was delayed; one from Michael Nicholson to ITN, with a more optimistic tone, went through. Even the weather could not be mentioned until well on in the campaign – nor the fact that any mention of the weather was prevented. The word 'censored' itself was censored.

Max Hastings of the *Evening Standard* was the most successful of the print journalists both in getting information and in transmitting it. It was his tenth or eleventh war, but this was the first where he had felt any personal commitment. He had 'an affection and admiration' for the British armed forces. His respect for their competence and endurance was made plain.

> In this case one's principal interest was to write in a way that would first of all help and encourage those at home as much as possible; and secondly help, or if not help, at least not impede what the landing force were trying to do; and if, for instance, one had a day like that on which *Coventry* and *Atlantic Conveyer* were sunk, when obviously everybody wasn't feeling at their absolute best, it scarcely seemed helpful to our cause and our task force to tell the Argentinians that morale was pretty low in the beach-head.
>
> I felt that the moment that our war ended a different set of standards applied in that literally the day that the Argentinians surrendered I wrote an article for the *Evening Standard* which was the first one I'd written that was not subject to censorship, in which I said 'now that it's over I can tell the truth about certain things,' for instance, the differences of opinion between Admiral Woodward and the landing force at times – for instance the difficulties that 5 Brigade suffered in the south. And in fact some of the

senior officers involved turned on me and said 'How could you after supporting us all through the war suddenly write something like this'; and I said 'Because while the war was on I felt my first duty was to you and to the force to which one was attached, but once the war was over then one went back to being a journalist in the good old revelatory investigative tradition'; and that's the spirit in which one would go to any other war fought by any other country.

Hanrahan felt that his lack of previous military experience, except in Northern Ireland, was no disadvantage. It was a fresh experience to him, and he described it as best he could. Listening to the BBC's World Service, he had a fair idea of how much from his messages was being used, as almost everything was – 'even a cough'. He said that he went through a number of phases, thinking about what to do and how to do it.

The first one was in fact leaving Portsmouth, when I thought it was necessary to point out in fairly stark terms that this had at the end of it the possibility of a real war; and that however much it might seem a bit of jape or a bit of an adventure or whatever the people back home thought it might be, it was time to start spelling out that there were men here who might get killed. Indeed at that stage I was at odds with the naval authorities who would have preferred that all of us had been a bit less bloody in some of our choice of words . . .

As we went further south, as it got closer and closer to becoming a real situation, it seemed to me there was less and less need to attempt to point out the consequences – the consequences would come through themselves – and I made a deliberate decision to go more and more unemotional and flatter and report in a very flat way what I saw and heard and not get too tied up into saying that it was dreadful or brave or anything else; it seemed to me that the adjectives could be filled in from the descriptions.

For those who were listening at the time, his calm and unemotional reports became memorable.

This is not the place for a more detailed study either of the war or of the way it was covered, though for both purposes the books by Max Hastings (jointly with Simon Jenkins) and Robert Harris can be commended. The former reveals a great deal that was not known or reported at the time, of the politics and of the campaign; and the latter reminds the reader of 'eyewitness' accounts by journalists of events that never took place, and of at least five occasions when official information deliberately misled the press and public.

The purpose of including even this much about the Falklands War is in order to consider three questions. Ought journalists to accept government censorship in war or near-war? Ought they to temper their reporting to surges of public feeling such as swept through the country after the Argentine invasion of the Falklands? And ought they to suspend their normal practice of inquiry and of revealing as much as possible? The three are, of course, interlocked.

On censorship, in practice they have no option. If the government with the backing of Parliament imposes censorship, they have to comply. Mike Molloy of the *Mirror* found it 'a most frustrating time', with only a trickle of information, no certainty about whether official information given in London was reliable, and with the censorship of messages from the South Atlantic. William Deedes at the *Telegraph* was more tolerant, relying on his defence correspondent (a retired general) as 'anchor man' and accepting his ability to interpret the available news. With Preston of the *Guardian* he found the regular private briefing of editors by Sir Frank Cooper, permanent secretary at the Defence Ministry, of only limited value. Preston found the advice 'misty', especially in the period just before the landings. One of the biggest complaints was that much of the copy, delayed by censorship and by the volume of radio traffic from the South Atlantic, was arriving only between 11 p.m. and midnight, making it difficult to handle. Such matters were taken up with Sir Frank Cooper every week, to little or no effect.

That British governments are unlikely in future to follow the more open information policy of the Americans in Vietnam was confirmed in the autumn of 1983. An exercise was held in Germany to test press relations. For the press and television it was a fiasco: journalists were required to sign undertakings that effectively prevented any useful reporting, and no censors were present. The general in charge, Sir Martin Farndale, said that no television cameras would be permitted in the event of real action. Thus even the limited cover achieved by Hanrahan, Nicholson and Hesketh from the Falklands would be prevented.

That extreme caution derives partly from the belief that the Americans were defeated in Vietnam because of television coverage – a misreading of what happened. US television in the end (though not at the beginning) showed the American public that a war which should never have been undertaken was being fought at a human cost that was unacceptable; and that it was not being won. Public opinion turned strongly against the war. More extensive coverage from the Falklands would have brought credit to the British forces, whatever political judgements might have been formed about its validity and its cost. Our generals and admirals drew the wrong conclusions from Vietnam and from the controversy over coverage of the Falklands campaign.

As to bending by journalists before the tidal wave of public feeling, to some extent they themselves were responsible for that tide – particularly through the jingoism of the *Express, Mail, Sun* and *Star*. But it was being felt even before the newspapers had had much effect. The tone of the emergency debate in the House of Commons on the Saturday after the invasion was evidence of that. Labour's front bench and all but a handful of members took a strongly 'patriotic' line with the government; after that, the launching of the task force was unstoppable. At Suez in 1956 events moved more slowly, though more secretly. Then the *Guardian* and the *Mirror* took a strong stand against the government; over the Falklands there was no such opposition. There was not even any adequate analysis of alternative policies. It is hard to escape the conclusion that the Commons debate stampeded possible opponents in the press, and the broadcasters were then left with no substantial dissent that they could report.

Preston said that on the Sunday he believed that the best the *Guardian* could do was to try to dispel some of the euphoria among MPs who felt that the House had 'spoken for Britain'. Molloy at the *Mirror* at first thought the whole thing a storm in a teacup – an 'Ealing comedy' or a 'Peter Sellers film' – but soon realised that it was not. The *Mirror,* however, had not forgotten its loss of sales over Suez, and readers' letters

showed a huge majority on the 'patriotic' side. The BBC's
Panorama, somewhat later, tried to look at the dissenting case.
It was thrashed by MPs as a result. To recall this is not to say
that press and broadcasters were at fault in taking account of
public feeling. It is to say that they failed to explore the
alternative policies.

On whether and how far to suspend normal journalism, the
main test that emerges from the Falklands experience is
whether or not casualties may be increased. It is hard to apply.
Governments are too ready to invoke 'national security' to
keep control over the flow of news; journalists are too often
uncomprehending of operational restraints. There was much
criticism, for example, of the delay in announcing the loss of
the *Coventry*. Fleet headquarters believed that an announcement could bring an immediate change of Argentinian tactics,
with three Type 42 destroyers and their Sea Dart missiles out
of action. That would have put more lives at risk. They had
good cause to hold back the news. Journalists are justified in
asking questions and distrusting official information, but they
must temper their decisions on what to publish.

Judgements about covering the long conflict in Northern
Ireland have been as hazardous. Until the Derry disturbances
of October 1968, the mainland press and broadcasters ignored
Ulster. After that, they were often too cautious in challenging
official restriction and manipulation of information.

The dilemma is illustrated by the opposing views of two
liberals. Dr Conor Cruise O'Brien – academic, politician and
journalist, having served in the Irish Cabinet and later been
editor-in-chief of the *Observer* – said that liberalism must be
'relevant to the dangers of the day' and ought to 'support and
strengthen the principle of authority under the law'. As
Minister of Posts and Telegraphs he banned interviews with
members of the Provisional Sinn Fein and kept a close control
on broadcasting. Richard Francis – formerly the BBC's Controller Northern Ireland (1973–7), then its director of news and
current affairs and latterly managing director, BBC Radio –
took a more open view. He believed that the media must
'contribute to the maintenance of the democracy which is
under threat', both by providing a forum where 'the harshest
differences of opinion' could be aired and by courageous
investigation and reporting. (Both views are more fully

explored in *Televising Terrorism,* by Schlesinger, Murdock and Elliot, 1983; an alternative is provided by Richard Clutterbuck's *The Media and Political Violence,* 1981.)

The case for an open policy is that unless reporters talk to the IRA, INLA and Protestant UVF they cannot discover their motives, intentions and likely action. To talk directly to them, difficult and dangerous though it can be, is essential – and their stance must be reported. The case against an open policy is that publicity is important to them, that it may give a false authenticity to their cause and that it may bring further violence. After 1968 some mainland editors had a sense of guilt for their previous failure to report the discrimination against Catholics and the gerrymandering which led to the civil rights movement, and their failure to report the activities of the B Specials in the police. From then onwards there was friction with the authorities in Northern Ireland over what it was or was not expedient to report.

The problems were greatest for the broadcasters, who had to decide whether to put representatives of the IRA, INLA, UVF and other forms of terrorism on television screens or live on radio. They did it very rarely, and there was bitter criticism from politicians every time they did. A BBC interview with an INLA man in July 1979 brought the public wrath of Mrs Thatcher, the Attorney-General and many others – and was eventually blamed by some for the murder of Lord Mountbatten two months later. Even such thoughtful explorations of alternative policies as the BBC's 1972 programme *The Question of Ulster* (Chapter 2) were damned.

Inevitably, the BBC has insisted on strict application of its rules about 'reference up', which in this case means reference up to the Director-General; and since 1979, so far as is known, no interview with a Provisional IRA or INLA man has been recorded or broadcast. The IBA has been almost as restrictive, banning or delaying documentary or current affairs programmes made by the companies or demanding deletions in them. Little account seems to have been taken of the likelihood that Provo and other such appearances would do nothing to enhance the standing of terrorists, though it might lead to greater understanding of their tactics. In 1981 Granada was required by the IBA to delete 30 seconds of an IRA man's funeral – the clearest evidence of the way the Provos were exploiting a hunger striker's death – but the company then chose not to show the programme at all. In such ways there have been serious losses to public knowledge and understanding.

Sieges such as Balcombe Street (1975), the Iranian Embassy (1980) and the Libyan Embassy (1983) have been handled with substantial agreement between the Metropolitan police and the broadcasters. The foundations of such agreement were laid while Sir Robert Mark was Metropolitan Commissioner, for he applied an intelligent and liberal policy to press access. At Balcombe Street, in central London, IRA men were holding an elderly couple as hostages. They were able to watch television news and hear radio news. By agreement with the police, television cameras showed how completely escape routes had been blocked, and radio news reported the presence of an SAS squad at the scene. After four days the gunmen gave up – largely because, Sir Robert said afterwards, they feared a fatal shoot-out.

Much the same techniques were used in coverage of the embassy sieges, though at the Iranian Embassy precautions were taken not to show the SAS preparations for an assault lest hostages were killed. (One was killed in the first seconds of the assault.) There was agreement not to broadcast live pictures of the assault, though ITN had it on the air within minutes.

CONCLUSIONS

These are exceptional occasions, whether in civil emergencies or in wartime. If lives can be protected or saved, broadcasters and newspapers are well justified in agreeing to exceptional arrangements. But even when journalists agree to withhold or delay publication, they themselves ought to find out as much as they can and monitor the action of authorities; and they should never knowingly publish any false information. At an event such as a siege or kidnap it may be expedient for the detail of arrangements between authorities and the media to remain confidential at the time; but the fact that such arrangements are being made ought to be acknowledged publicly, as generally they are. As to wartime censorship, the fact that it is taking place ought always to be stated.

12 A Personal Postscript

While the last part of this book was being written, a student from a reputable polytechnic came to consult me. He had been thinking of a career in journalism but had concluded that newspaper journalists were corrupted by commercial ownership and broadcasters too much influenced by the government of the day. He was intelligent, and his words made me wonder what sort of teaching he had had and how much time he had spent reading newspapers, listening to radio news or watching television news.

He and others who read this book will, I hope, gain a different impression. Some of the best newspapers in the world are published in Britain – and some of the worst. Our standards of broadcasting are among the highest in the world. Anyone living in this country is exceptionally fortunate in having available to him or her a choice of newspapers such as (in no special order) the *Financial Times,* the *Daily Telegraph,* the *Guardian* and *The Times.* He or she is no less fortunate in having access to the radio and television news provided by the BBC, ITN, the regional ITV companies and ILR. Among the non-metropolitan and weekly newspapers, the majority try to serve their readers honestly and well.

The quality of journalism attained by many newspapers and nearly all broadcast news is not an accident. It is the result of a tradition built up over many years, especially through the work of men such as Delane at *The Times* and C. P. Scott at the *Manchester Guardian,* and in broadcasting by the inspiration of men such as Reith, Haley, Hugh Greene and Geoffrey Cox and women such as Grace Wyndham Goldie. It owes a great deal also to certain proprietors and institutions. The Walter family began the building of *The Times,* which could have been wrecked by Northcliffe but survived, to be carried forward by the Astors. Successive proprietors kept it going in spite of losing large sums of money. C. P. Scott and his family did as much for the *Guardian* and its journalism, ultimately handing

292

it over to a self-perpetuating and non-commercial trust. Newspapers such as the *Scotsman* and the *Glasgow Herald* have, by different routes and with lesser resources, adopted a similar discipline.

The structures and ownership of the BBC and ITV are separate and distinct. Over the past 60 years the BBC has grown into a vast corporation, making and broadcasting an extraordinary range of programmes. In its daily operations it is free from government intervention, but its money depends on the level at which the government sets the television licence fee. It is vulnerable to private pressure from ministers, though that is only infrequently exercised. Its news services suffer at the top from being subordinate to a management that is preoccupied with other matters, often nervous and at times insensitive to the need for freedom to make fast decisions in a news organisation. In spite of that, BBC radio news and BBC television news are generally reliable, comprehensive, politically non-partisan and sometimes brilliant (for example over the Ethiopian famine of 1984–5 and at the bombing of the Grand Hotel in Brighton).

For ITV, its federal structure has meant the creation of a separate television news company, ITN. That company enjoys the managerial freedom that BBC news lacks, and its top executive are wholly concerned with news. It is free from commercial or political pressure. (One curiosity during the coal dispute was that the Energy Secretary, Peter Walker, often talked in private to senior people in ITN who did not feel under any pressure from him, whereas he never talked privately to their counterparts at BBC television news, who might have felt under pressure.) ITN output can stand comparison with any news service in North America, Europe or other advanced societies, and the innovations brought by Channel Four News have been of ITN's own making.

Britain's broadcast news and its quality newspapers are social assets that ought to be protected and preserved. They will not be protected if Mr Rupert Murdoch's style of journalism becomes more prevalant – particularly through his influence at *The Times* and *Sunday Times* – nor if the government gives him and other newspaper tycoons the opportunity, through restructuring the BBC, to take over some of its programme services. In the early months of 1985 there were worrying signs that Mr Murdoch's interests were beginning to influence editorial standards at *The Times,* which embarked on a vendetta against the BBC in leaders, news stories and features and showed a disinclination to publish letters critical of its position. If, from the start of its campaign, it had declared its proprietor's interest, its position would have been more honest. Its conduct was reminiscent of the Northcliffe period; but Murdoch is a younger man and as proprietor may last longer.

How long the BBC will continue in its present form is an open question. Its size and managerial style make it vulnerable, and there is a case for structural reorganisation. A federal system remains one model, possibly with an independent unit running news and some parts of current affairs; and there is the more radical solution of breaking up the BBC, rejected by the Annan Committee of 1974–7. Currently (1985) its financial base is being examined by the Peacock Committee, appointed by the Home Secretary to consider alternative sources of revenue.

Whatever option is put forward, the direct and indirect consequences for the BBC's news and current affairs programmes will have to be examined, including the implications for its integrity, independence and finance – and for those of its competitors. Its strongest protection lies in the loyalty of audiences, for many would be outraged by any further reduction in standards.

The BBC is not alone as a target for reform. On the ITV side, there has long been a demand for revision of the relationship between the IBA, the programme companies, Channel Four and ITN over programme and editorial control. The IBA is at times seen by its charges as a fussy and interfering nanny. Controversy has been simmering over programmes on Northern Ireland for years; and the IBA's banning of the 20/20 Vision documentary on MI5 for Channel Four in February 1984 brought it back into the open. The Authority believed, on the basis of legal advice, that under the 1954 Broadcasting Act it had no alternative. It could not broadcast a programme known to be in breach of the Official Secrets Act. That led to a call – supported among others by the heads of news and current affairs in many of the programme companies – for the Broadcasting Acts to be amended so that legal responsibility lay with the companies and ITN, not with the IBA. It is a sensible suggestion, for it would diminish the IBA's need to intervene and would leave responsibility where it ought to be. Especially over Northern Ireland, it would give the companies greater freedom.

Changes of management, ownership and the law will influence the environment in which all journalists – including young newcomers – work in future. So will trade union agreements, both on the introduction of new technology and on recruitment. Until the 1960s, direct entry to national newspapers and to the larger non-metropolitan papers was possible; now it is blocked by the NUJ. Preliminary years in a smaller paper or a weekly can be a stimulating experience, especially where new technologies are in use, but the routes of entry for young graduates to print journalism have narrowed. In the end that is bound to be a loss to newspapers; the brightest and best young entrants now tend to look first towards radio or television. The training available through the BBC's schemes, ITN's and local radio is attractive, with shorter cuts to responsibility than in local newspapers.

The ways in which newspapers and broadcasting units condition new arrivals to their requirements have been mentioned briefly in this book. The differing ways in which the *Daily Mail* and the *Guardian,* for example, set them to work are touched on in Chapters 6 and 7. In both, the news editor plays an important part in acclimatising young reporters, testing their talents with a variety of stories and commenting on their copy. But just as Neville Cardus, joining the old *Manchester Guardian* reporters' room 70 years ago, was told to use his first day to 'absorb the atmosphere', so the prevailing atmosphere matters in every newsroom. At the *Mail,* David English's 'creative tension' reaches down to spur the newest recruit, as does the intensive system of postmortems at *The Times.* At the *Guardian,* critical chat among colleagues seems to matter about as much. But it is above all through reading the paper and studying its style and interests, through listening to broadcasts and noting what the programme editors like and dislike, and through responding to daily advice that recruits learn most readily.

As to news values – the core of editorial decisions – my primitive listing of seven categories in Chapter 1 has stood up well to examination. It remains as practical a means as any of testing whether an event is likely to make news and the nearest approximation to formulating the elements in a journalist's instinctive judgements. The added factors of flair and originality, nevertheless, ought not be be neglected; nor should the journalist's distaste for being pinned down as to how he makes his decisions. Here are three more replies to my questioning about the 'seismic scale', two from *Mail* men and one from *The Times*.

It's the wrong question. You cannot play news into a computer. You need news sense. It's like a camel – you can't define it, but you know it when you see it. If you could define it, every film producer or editor or thriller writer would have a best seller every time. Anyway, the answer isn't the same every day. The ratings have to be competitive.

News judgements are primarily about what will make a talking point at the breakfast table. There are no standard ratings. They are a denial of the journalist's skill. It's different every day.

The one word missing on that list, perhaps a rather boring word but important to us, is sheer information. First and foremost we set out to inform our readers, telling the news as it is, where it happens, as it happens. Information is the touchstone. Information relevant to our readers and potential readers.

'Telling the news as it is, where it happens' inevitably implies a host of unstated assumptions. These assumptions have been explored in preceding chapters, especially Chapters 4 to 7, and they are nearly all bound up with the journalist's perception of what is important to his viewers or readers, what will interest them and what will excite or entertain them. Those assumptions also govern the way staff are deployed. There are no fixed answers. In newspaper and broadcast news, a great number of separate and individual judgements go into making up the final pattern of the day's output.

The individual approach of editors is another significant factor in news, news judgements and success. Whether it is the quiet guidance of David Nicholas at ITN or the extrovert leadership of David English at the *Mail,* the editor's view is influential. Any newspaper or broadcasting unit where it is not creative is heading for trouble. Styles and attitudes differ, as shown in earlier chapters, but without an effective lead a newspaper or a programme will lack force and character.

On the language of news, especially in broadcasting, there is a common test. Is it simple, clear and concise? If you sometimes feel that an item has an institutional tone, try rephrasing it yourself. When your version is more clear or conversational, and still concise, then you are doing better than the BBC or ITN.

The coming of Channel Four, as observed in Chapters 4 and 8, has added a new dimension to television news. It has also brought the only regular programme giving the public a 'right to reply'. In the mid-1970s BBC2 used to carry on Sundays a programme called *Write On* – one that gave a wide range of people from all parts of the country the opportunity to express their own views, whether with one minute to camera or with a longer item, filmed on location. It was a valuable innovation but was killed off. The BBC's community programmes unit still produces an interesting diversity of items; and Channel Four, apart from the Friday programme *Right to Reply,* has also developed other opportunities for minorities. All that is welcome, but in broadcasting generally it remains an under-developed area.

Among newspapers, the *Guardian*'s Agenda pages are the nearest equivalent, along with letters to the editor. The quality papers – and occasionally the populars – have allowed a wider range of opinions in their pages than they did in the 1960s. That is partly because they are more prosperous and have more space. But it is again an underdeveloped area. In their own interests newspapers ought to be readier to publish factual corrections and to allow a wider debate. Legislation on rights of reply ought not to be needed; but if newspapers do not play fair, it will come.

One regret in this book is that, through lack of space, the study of the *Daily Record, Glasgow Herald* and *Scotsman* together with the early evening news on BBC Scotland and STV has been squeezed out. It showed that good journalism is to be found far from London and Manchester, with a pleasing variety of attitudes and a strong Scottish flavour.

Newspapers and news broadcasting are part of the society in
which they live. They influence it and they reflect it. Whether
commercially owned or non-commercially controlled, they
provide a vital public service. They are the foremost means of
communication between authorities at all levels and the
electorate – a two-way communication in a healthy society. It
will be at the peril of their souls and at the peril of their
communities if 'the unclouded face of truth suffers wrong'.
Fairness and accuracy are prime requirements. Dishonesty and
distortion exist in Fleet Street, as in the community at large.
Fortunately the unscrupulous are outnumbered by those intent
on honest journalism.

Appendix A: The National Newspapers

HEAVIES

Sales figures: daily average July–December 1984. (Figures in brackets give position in July–December 1983.)

Daily Telegraph

Conservative. Sales 1 235 500 (1 245 000)   23p (20p)
Stoppages on 16 days in half-year (12).
Owned by private company; controlling interest held by Lord Hartwell (Michael Berry). Other holdings with his elder brother (Viscount Camrose) and members of Berry family.
Inspiration: Lord Hartwell and his father, 1st Lord Camrose.
Other newspapers in group: *Sunday Telegraph*. Printed London and Manchester.

Financial Times

Independent. Sales 218 500 (211 000), one-fifth abroad. 35p (unchanged)
Stoppages on 20 days in half-year (44).
Owned by Pearson Longman Group which has wide interests in newspapers, publishing and television.
Inspiration: partly Lord Cowdray, but mainly Sir Gordon Newton, editor 1950–72.
Other newspapers in group: many provincial papers, managed through *Westminster Press*.
Printed in London and Frankfurt.

The Guardian

Independent   (left-of-centre). Sales 471 700   (445 100)
    25p (23p)
Stoppages on 31 days in half-year (20).
Owned by the Scott Trust which ploughs all group profits back
    into the business or distributes to charity.
Inspiration: C. P. Scott, editor of *Manchester Guardian* 1872–
    1929 and principal proprietor 1907–31. The Scott Trust was
    established by his family in 1936.
Other newspapers in group: *Manchester Evening News, Roch-
    dale Observer, Surrey Newspapers* and some weeklies. Owns
    20% of Anglia TV.
Printed in London and Manchester.

The Times

Independent   (right-of-centre) Sales 456 500   (369 400)
    23p (20p)
Stoppages on 13 days in half-year (12).
Owned by Rupert Murdoch who has extensive interests in
    Australia, US and UK – in newspapers, TV, satellite TV,
    travel and aviation.
Inspiration: a long tradition stretching through a series of great
    editors in nineteenth century; and ownership by Walter
    family, Lord Northcliffe, the Astor family (Astors of Hever)
    and Roy Thomson (Lord Thomson of Fleet, Canadian).
    Sold to Murdoch by Thomson family in 1981.
Other newspapers in group: *Sunday Times, News of the World,
    Sun.*
Prints in London only.

POPULARS

Daily Express

Conservative.   Sales 2 002 000 (2 054 400)   20p (18p)
Stoppages on 8 days in half-year (4).

Owned by Fleet Holdings; Chairman Lord Matthews (Victor Matthews). Fleet was hived off by Trafalgar House 1983. (There were two major takeover bids in 1984–5, one by the Australian Mr Holmes a' Court, the other by the large provincial group, United Newspapers.)

Inspiration: Lord Beaverbrook (Max Aitken, Canadian), chief proprietor 1916–64 and effectively editor-in-chief for most of that time. Editor, Sir Larry Lamb since spring 1983.

Others in group: *Sunday Express, Daily Star, The Standard* (London evening, half owned by Associated Newspapers, see below).

Prints London and Manchester. (Used to print also in Glasgow.)

Daily Mail

Conservative. Sales   1 846 500 (1 850 000)   20p (18p)
Stoppages on 5 days (2).

Owned by Associated Newspapers; Rothermere and Harmsworth families are the major shareholders. Interests in travel, hotels, television and other activities.

Inspiration: Lord Northcliffe (Alfred Harmsworth), founder and chief proprietor 1896–1914. Also Sir David English, editor since 1971, who has greatly changed it.

Others in group: a number of English provincial papers and half share in the *Standard* (London).

Prints London and Manchester. (Used to print also in Edinburgh.)

Daily Mirror

Labour. Sales   3 493 800 (3 354 750)   18p (16p)
Stoppages on 4 days (4).

Owned by Robert Maxwell since July 1984 when IPC Group was sold by Reed International. Maxwell is also proprietor of Pergamon Press and BPCC, household goods and television.

Inspiration: Cecil King, a director of Mirror Newspapers 1929–68 and latterly chairman and Hugh Cudlipp (Lord Cudlipp),

trained by Beaverbrook but with Mirror Group 1937–68.
Others in group: *Sunday Mirror, Daily Record, Sunday Mail.*
Prints in London and Manchester (and was printed Belfast
until Provos blew up the plant).

Daily Star

Sales   1 623 000 (1 407 200)   18p (16p)
Stoppages on 3 days (3).
Owned by Fleet Holdings (see *Express* above). Created 1978.
Prints Manchester only.

Morning Star

Communist.   Sales about 125 000?   30p (25p)
Prints London only.

Sun

Conservative.   Sales   4 083 000 (4 127 600)   18p (15p)
Stoppages on 22 days (12).
Owned by Rupert Murdoch (see *The Times*).
Inspiration: Rupert Murdoch and Sir Larry Lamb (editor
    1969–79, then in Australia, now editor, *Daily Express*).
Printed London only but owns premises in Glasgow.

Appendix B: Staffing – Journalists

These figures include journalists only, not clerical and ancillary staff.

BBC TELEVISION NEWS

Editor, deputy and chief assistant	3
Programme editors	5
Senior duty editors	8[a]
Producers/sub-editors	63[b]
News desk	15
Presenters/specialists and foreign correspondents	30
Reporters	16
Total	140

NOT included: regional television news staffs; Ceefax

[a] includes 2 breakfast news editors, and editor 'News Review'
[b] includes those on Breakfast Time news

ITN

	Channel 1	Channel 4
Programme editors	6	4[a]
News desk	23	3[b]
Chief sub-editors and deputies	9	3
Scriptwriters and sub-editors	27	10
Presenters and specialists	19	8[c]

ITN—*continued*

Reporters $\dfrac{22}{106}$ $\dfrac{7}{35}$

Managers $\dfrac{5}{111}$ $\dfrac{1}{36}$

NOT included: David Nicholas; two administrative managers; Oracle – manager/editor and 7 journalists; press office – manager and 2 contract journalists.

---

[a] includes two managers *not* counted under 'managers' below
[b] also includes two managers not counted below; and 8 'news desk assistants' doing journalistic work
[c] includes all newscasters

DAILY MAIL

The editorial staff comprises 221 journalists in London and 120 in Manchester.

London

Editor, assistant editors, leader writers, cartoonists   13
Night production executives   11
Sub-editors' table (21) and provincial desk (5)   26
Newsroom executives (8), specialists (13), reporters (25)
 and regional (2)   48
Features executives (6), sub-editors (11), feature art
 editors (2), staff artist (1) and columnists and writers
 (8)   29
Entertainments ('showbiz') executives (3) and reporters
 (7): not including non-staff critics   10
Femail executives (4) and writers (3)   7
Diary, including N. Dempster   5
Sport executives (4), sub-editors (14) including racing and
 writers (13) including racing   31
Foreign executives (3), correspondents (2 New York,
 1 Washington), assistants (2) and diplomatic correspon-
 dent (1): not including one columnist (Purgavie)   9

Pictures executives (3), assistants (8), night make-up (4)
and photographers (13) including one Birmingham, one
Bristol   28
City executives (3), subs (2) and reporters (7)   12

Manchester

Editorial director, editor and deputy   3
Night production executives (10) and sub-editors (25)   35
Newsroom executives (6), reporters (17) and district
reporters (11): the districts include Belfast, Glasgow,
Edinburgh and other centres   34
Features   2
Sports executives (5), sub-editors (11) and writers (11): of
the writers 2 are in Glasgow, 1 Belfast, 1 Leeds and
1 Newcastle   27
Pictures executives (6), assistants (2) and photographers
(11)   19

THE GUARDIAN

Editorial establishment: 216 (186 London, 30 Manchester)
Senior staff and leader writers   11
Specialists and reporters   46 (Manchester 12)
Sub-editors   25
Features   28 (Manchester 10)
Foreign   26
City   22
Pictures   7 (Manchester 2)
Sport   20 (Manchester 4)
Special features   1
Guardian Weekly   (Manchester 2)

THE TIMES

Editorial establishment: 240 journalists
Management (includes editor, deputy and senior executives)   11
Associate editors (includes four leader writers, letters
editors and obituaries editor)   9

Home news (includes specialists, reporters and regional
    men – one each in Midlands, Wales and Scotland)   51
Foreign news   19
Arts   6
Books page   1
Business news   20
Design, maps   3
Diary   2
Features   4
Law reports   1
Parliamentary   10
Pictures   10
Saturday   4
Social   2
Special reports   6
Spectrum   1
Sport   22
News production (sub-editors)
Backbench and production   9
Business news   10
Features   7
Foreign news   15
Home news   17

Glossary

ABS Association of Broadcasting and Allied Staff (BBC staff union)

ACTT Association of Cinematograph, Television and Allied Technicians (ITV and independent film and video union)

agency news agency, such as Press Association, Reuter or United Press International

agency copy news coming from an agency or agencies

animated graphics graphs, charts, maps and other illustrations on TV, now normally generated by computer

backgrounder article or feature filling in background to an event

basement story placed across bottom of newspaper front page or other page

BARB Broadcasting Audience Research Board, now measures audiences both for BBC and ITV

BBC British Broadcasting Corporation, publicly financed

BCC Broadcasting Complaints Commission

'bongs' headlines in ITN's News at Ten, punctuated by 'bongs' from Big Ben.

caption TV: name or wording superimposed at foot of screen, or elsewhere; newspaper: wording under picture

caption generator machine to supply captions in TV studio

centre spread centre pages of a newspaper

chapel sub-branch of a newspaper trade union. (Father of chapel, chairman; Imperial father, chairman of federated chapels in newspaper composing room.)

City pages pages of financial news

composing room where newspaper type is set and pages made up

comps compositors who set type

computer graphics as animated graphics, above

contempt of court legal hazard for journalists. See *Essential Law for Journalists* or other such textbook.

copy manuscript or typescript of a story, written by journalist

copy-taker telephonist who receives copy

copy-taster sub-editor who decides which stories are likely to be used

crosshead subordinate headline used to break up appearance of story or mark new section

DBS direct broadcast by satellite

editions newspapers print three, four or more editions each day, changing a number of pages for each

edition time time that last page must be ready

ENG electronic news-gathering, or use of portable video cameras and recorders in place of film

'exclusives' or 'scoops'. Stories that a newspaper or news programme believes it has to itself

flash (or news flash) short, urgent message, usually from agency

follow-up further exploration of an event

foundry where completed newspaper page goes for casting of metal plate

freelance journalist not on staff

ground floor ('in on . . .') being in at the beginning of an event

'heavy newspapers' sometimes called 'quality' or 'serious' – *Times, Guardian, Financial Times* and others of that character.

hyped artificially dramatised

IBA Independent Broadcasting Authority, supervising ITV and ILR

ILR Independent local radio (commercially financed radio stations)

intercut film or tape edited to go from one interview to another and back

intro opening passage in a news story

ITCA Independent Television Companies Association – the ITV programme companies
ITV Independent Television, counterpart of BBC

lead foremost story on newspaper front page ('splash') or other page
leader article expressing the newspaper's opinion
libel statement injurious to a person's reputation
live television item broadcast as it happens

masthead newspaper title, as displayed on front page
monitor TV set for watching a recording or other output

NGA National Graphical Association, trade union of newspaper compositors and other print workers
NUJ National Union of Journalists

OB outside broadcast
off stone page fully made up in the composing room
off-stone time time when a newspaper page must be fully made up

PA Press Association, biggest British home news agency
'popular' newspapers counterpart of 'heavies'. Usually tabloid (half size sheets)
phone-in radio or television programmes where audience telephone questions or answers from home

rejig revise a story to bring a different aspect to the top
'revise' man senior sub-editor who revises the work of others
RTS Royal Television Society
'rush' a brief message, more urgent than a 'flash'
'rushes' first prints of unedited film

satellite transmission relay by space satellite, now generally used for international links and some local links. Also now available to broadcast complete programmes
scanner outside broadcast vehicle which carries mobile control room
scoop exclusive story

slip page   a page revised and 'slipped' on to presses as soon as convenient, between editions

sociocentralism   the tendency to coherence in a society

Sogat (or Sogat 82)   trade union of printers – numerically the largest, but its members are generally less well paid than NGA

spike   sharp metal spike on wooden base, on which rejected copy is impaled. To 'spike' a story is to kill it

splash   the foremost story on the front page. To 'splash' a story is to make it the front page lead

stereo   newspaper production process by which a flexible impression of a whole page is made before it goes to foundry

stereotype   simplified and often inaccurate representation of a group of people or action

stone   metal plate on which columns of type and 'blocks' of pictures are made up into complete pages

stringer   journalist not on staff but with contract to supply news

sub   sub-editor, who edits copy. To 'sub' is to edit

sub-editor   as above

subtitle   secondary title displayed on screen

tabloid   newspaper printed on half-size sheets

teleprompt   mechanism that projects text through mirror below camera lens

timehands   term used for men who make up and correct newspaper pages, though it is derived from distinction between those paid by the hours worked and those paid by amount composed

title or title sequence   opening sequence of a programme

VDU   video display unit, used in electronic newsrooms

video   recording on electronic tape

VHS   video home system, the most popular of home video systems

wipe   visual change where one image wipes out another

wrap   end of a day's filming or recording

wrapping it up   in newspapers, writing a concise summary; in TV studios, bringing an item to an end

Bibliography

Manuel Alvarado, *Teaching the Media* (London: Macmillan, 1984)
David Ayerst, *Garvin of the Observer* (London: Croom Helm, 1985)
——, *Guardian – Biography of a Newspaper* (London: Collins 1971)
Cyril Bainbridge (ed), *One Hundred Years of Journalism* (London: Macmillan, 1984)
BBC Annual Report and Handbook 1985 (London: BBC, 1984)
Arthur A. Berger, *Media Analysis Techniques* (Beverley Hills and London: Sage, 1982)
Asa Briggs, *Governing the BBC* (London: BBC, 1979)
Tom Burns, *The BBC – Public Institution and Private World* (London: Macmillan, 1977)
Neville Cardus, *Autobiography* (London: Collins, 1947)
Arthur Christiansen, *Headlines All My Life* (London: Heinemann, 1952)
Richard Clutterbuck, *The Media and Political Violence* (London: Macmillan, 1981)
S. Cohen and J. Young (eds), *The Manufacture of News* (London: Constable, 1973)
M. Cockerell, P. Hennessy and D. Walker, *Sources Close to the Prime Minister* (London: Macmillan, 1985)
Geoffrey Cox, *See it Happen* (London: Bodley Head, 1983)
Hugh Cudlipp, *The Prerogative of the Harlot* (London: Bodley Head, 1980)
——, *Publish and be Damned* (London: Dakers, 1953)
James Curran (ed), *The British Press* (London: Macmillan, 1978)
Harold Evans, *Good Times, Bad Times* (London: Weidenfeld & Nicolson, 1983)
John Fiske and John Hartley, *Reading Television* (London: Methuen, 1978)
Johan Galtun and Mari Ruge, 'Structuring and Selecting News' in Cohen and Young, *Manufacture of News*.
Herbert J. Gans, *Deciding What's News* (London: Constable, 1980)
Peter Golding and Philip Elliot, *Making the News* (London: Longman, 1979)
Grace Wyndham Goldie, *Facing the Nation* (London: Bodley Head, 1977)
M. Gurevitch, T. Bennett *et al.* (eds), *Culture, Society and the Media* (London: Methuen, 1982)
Glasgow University Media Group, *Bad News* (London: Routledge & Kegan Paul, 1976)
——, *More Bad News* (London: Routledge & Kegan Paul, 1980)
——, *Really Bad News* (London: Writers and Readers, 1982)
Robert Harris, *Gotcha!* (London: Faber & Faber, 1983)
John Hartley, *Understanding News* (London: Methuen, 1982)
Max Hastings and Simon Jenkins, *The Battle for the Falklands* (London: Michael Joseph, 1983)

311

Alastair Hetherington, *Guardian Years* (London: Chatto, 1981)
R. Hoggart and J. Morgan (eds), *The Future of Broadcasting* (London: Macmillan, 1982)
David Hubback, *No Ordinary Press Baron* (London: Weidenfeld & Nicolson, 1985)
IBA, *Television and Radio 1985* (London: IBA, 1984)
Simon Jenkins, *Newspapers – the Power and the Money* (London: Faber, 1979)
Stephen Koss, *The Rise and Fall of the British Political Press,* vol. 2 (London: Hamish Hamilton, 1984)
Iverach McDonald, *The Times 1939–66* (London: Times Books, 1984)
Denis McQuail (ed), *Sociology of Mass Communications* (Harmondsworth: Penguin, 1972)
——, *Review of Sociological Writing on the Press,* Working Paper no. 2 for the Royal Commission on the Press (London: HMSO, 1976)
T. O'Sullivan, J. Hartley *et al.* (eds), *Key Concepts in Communication* (London: Methuen, 1983)
Henry Porter, *Lies, Damned Lies and Some Exclusives* (London: Chatto, 1984)
The Press Council, *Press Conduct in the Sutcliffe Case* (London: Press Council, 1983)
Report of the Committee on the Future of Broadcasting (the Annan Committee) (London: HMSO, 1977)
Royal Commission on the Press, 1947–9, *Report* (London: HMSO, 1949)
Royal Commission on the Press, 1974–7, *Final Report* (London: HMSO, 1977)
Philip Schlesinger, *Putting 'Reality' Together* (London: Constable, 1978)
——, G. Murdock and P. Elliot, *Televising 'Terrorism'* (London: Comedia, 1983)
Colin Seymour-Ure, 'Policy-making in the Press', *Government and Opposition,* 4,4 (1969)
——, *The Political Impact of the Mass Media* (London: Constable, 1974)
Anthony Smith, *The Politics of Information* (London: Macmillan, 1972)
The Times, *The History of the Times,* 5 vols (London: Times Books, 1935, 1939, 1947, 1952 and 1984)
Jeremy Tunstall, *The Media in Britain* (London: Constable, 1983)
——, *Journalists at Work* (London: Constable, 1971)
A. P. Wadsworth (ed), *C. P. Scott 1846–1932: The Making of the Manchester Guardian* (London: Muller, 1946)
Martin Walker, *Powers of the Press* (London: Quartet, 1982)
James Watson and Anne Hill, *A Dictionary of Communication and Media Studies* (London: Arnold, 1984)
John Whale, *The Politics of the Media* (London: Fontana/ Collins, 1977)
Lord Windlesham, *Broadcasting in a Free Society* (Oxford: Basil Blackwell, 1980)
Charles Wintour, *Pressures on the Press* (London: André Deutsch, 1972)

Notes and References

CHAPTER 1: WHAT'S NEWS? WHO MAKES NEWS?

1. Galtung and Ruge themselves provide a footnote, double-edged, which illustrates both the 'positive' approach to news and attitudes in developing countries towards elite nations. They summarise three months' systematic reading of the Moroccan newspaper *Le Petit Marocain*. Usually the first· page, they say, contained news about progress in Morocco and the second about decadence, murder, rape and violence in France – 'so that anybody could draw his conclusion'.

2. The *Guardian*'s 'Advice to staff' is described more fully in my book *Guardian Years* (1981) pp. 29–30. It was never intended to be more than a general guide and was written only because of the sudden recruitment of additional staff in preparation for printing in London. Among its priorities it put home policy and home politics first, the international setting second, and the economic, financial and industrial aspects third. It called for special attention to the social climate – including care of the old, slum clearance and changing social habits – and to books and the Arts, science and medicine, and to outdoor activities, the countryside and conservation. Perhaps it is not entirely a coincidence that these were the topics which mainly interested me.

3. In Geoffrey Cox, *See it Happen,* published by Bodley Head in 1983. Value of visuals: pp. 24–5, 37–45, 211–12 and others. Suez and Hungary: pp. 86–94. The BBC hits back: pp. 136–8. Note also Cox's 'oyster' theory, pp. 144–5, suggesting that the public mind is like an oyster which, under the pressure of dramatic news, is wide open for additional information. That, therefore, is the time to fill in the background quickly while people's interest is aroused. Relevant to news values is Cox's view that cameras can bring to life ordinary daily affairs more readily than print.

4. The news values summarised by Herbert Gans, however exactly observed, may be open to Anna Coote's criticism (*New Statesman,* 2 January 1981) of prevailing sexist news values in the UK: 'They have been developed, of course, by white, middle-class men, generation upon generation of them, forming opinions, imposing them, learning them and passing them on as Holy Writ.'

5. *Coronation Street, Crossroads, Take the High Road, Brookside* and others of that genre – along with the American *Dallas* and *Dynasty* – are more truly 'the opium of the people', and they provide some of the leading television personalities in the news. 'Len in Street shock' was a popular newspaper splash headline on one of the days we studied, and

313

'Len sacked' on a later one. Both referred to Len Fairclough of Coronation Street. In fairness to the British soap serials, we should note that they are much closer than the American imports to the real world as British audiences know it, and to British life as it appears in television news.

6. Gans, in letter to author January 1985.

7. I am conscious that I have so far quoted only a limited part of much useful sociological writing. Golding and Elliott's *Making the News* (1979), although based on research in Sweden, Nigeria and Ireland, contains much of direct application in the UK. Schlesinger's *Putting 'Reality' Together* (1978) contains an admirable account and analysis of the work of BBC radio and television newsrooms, which will be quoted later. Watson and Hill's *A Dictionary of Communication and Media Studies* (1984) is a helpful guide to terminology and much else. Cohen and Young's *The Manufacture of News* (1973) draws together extracts from a wide range of sociological writing. Tunstall's *Journalists at Work* (1971) deals with specialist writers (and if he had not preempted that title I would have used it). The McGregor Commission's 'Studies on the Press', Working Paper No. 3 prepared by Boyd-Barrett, Seymour-Ure and Tunstall (1977), includes observation inside newspaper offices. Please see also the bibliography at the end of this book.

8. For evidence see Henry Porter's funny and painful, *Lies, Damned Lies and Some Exclusives* (1984); and the Press Council report, *Press Conduct in the Sutcliffe Case* (1983).

9. For various communication models see Watson and Hill's *Dictionary* (1984), mentioned above, particularly the entries under Andersch and others, Barnlund, Berlo, Dance and Gerbner.

10. Fiske and Hartley, *Reading Television* (1978); the Northern Irish element is partly repeated in Hartley's *Understanding News* (1982).

11. In O'Sullivan and others, *Key Concepts in Communication* (1983) pp. 154–5.

12. For detail, see Martin Harrison's *Whose Bias?*, Keele Research Paper no. 19 (Department of Politics, University of Keele, 1984). See also Hetherington, review of *More Bad News* in *Glasgow Herald* (24 April 1980), and reply in letter to editor on 2 May 1980.

13. 'Almost random reactions' comes from John Whale in *The Listener* of 15 October 1970, but he himself qualified the comment in that and later articles. 'An artificial human construct' comes from Philip Schlesinger's study of BBC newsrooms (1978), but he goes on to explain the BBC's systems of editorial control and its advice to keep individual feelings out of news judgements (pp. 144–54).

CHAPTER 2: OWNERS, EDITORS AND AUDIENCES

1. R. C. K. Ensor, *England 1870–1914,* Oxford History Series (1936) p. 311.

2. Colin Seymour-Ure, *The Political Impact of Mass Media* (1974) pp.

48–50. See also Simon Jenkins, *Newspapers – the Power and the Money* (1979) pp. 19–24; Hamilton Fyfe, *Northcliffe* (1930); and The Times, *The History of The Times*, Vol. IV (1952).

3. The 'Chief' sent one to the editor of *The Times* in May 1918 instructing him to be more critical of the government in which Northcliffe himself was then serving in a minor capacity. See *The History of The Times*, vol. IV, part 1 (1952) p. 354.

4. Charles Wintour, *Pressures on the Press* (1972) pp. 177–82; A. J. P. Taylor, *Beaverbrook* (1972); and Arthur Christiansen, *Headlines All My Life* (1952).

5. *Report of the Royal Commission on the Press, 1947–9* (1949) paras 87 and 149.

6. *The History of The Times*, vols I to V; and Martin Walker, *Powers of the Press* (1982) ch. 2.

7. David Ayerst, *Guardian – Biography of a Newspaper* (1971); and A. P. Wadsworth (ed), *C. P. Scott and the Making of the Manchester Guardian* (1946).

8. For an account of the work of Philips Price and others in Russia, of Scott's initial hesitation over publishing the reports from Philips Price, of the heavy pressure from the British government against doing so, and of Scott's eventual confidence in Price, see Ayerst's *Guardian,* pp. 400–9. (Philips Price was later an MP, first Liberal and then Labour.) Similarly on MG reporting from Ireland see Ayerst, ibid., pp. 419–24.

9. Scott Trust members at present (1985) are Alastair Hetherington (author of this book and former editor) as chairman; Louis Blom-Cooper, QC; Peter Gibbings, chairman of G&MEN plc; Victor Keegan, economist and journalist on the *Guardian*; Peter Newsam, chairman of the Equal Opportunities Commission; Peter Preston, editor of the *Guardian*; Charles Scott, grandson of C. P. Scott and former personnel director of the company; and G. P. Taylor, former managing-director of the *Guardian.*

10. Harold Evans, *Good Times, Bad Times* (1983).

11. Thames Television programme on the bicentenary of *The Times*, broadcast 2 January 1985.

12. Richard Davy in BBC2 programme on the bicentenary, broadcast 30 December 1984.

13. *Daily Mail* editors: Guy Schofield, 1950–4; Arthur Wareham, 1955–9; William Hardcastle, 1959–63; Mike Randall, 1963–6; Arthur Brittenden, 1967–71; David English, 1971– . *Daily Express* editors: Derek Marks, 1965–71; Ian McColl, 1971–4; Alastair Burnet, 1974; Roy Wright, 1975–7; Derek Jameson, 1977–80; Arthur Firth, 1980–1; Chris Ward, 1981–3; Sir Larry Lamb, 1983– .

14. Jenkins, *Newspapers – The Power and the Money,* pp. 38–40; Wintour, *Pressures on the Press,* pp. 186–7; and Cecil King, *Strictly Personal* (1969).

15. *Sunday Telegraph,* 2 September 1984; see also *Sunday Times,* 21 October 1984 – 'Maxwell's first 100 days'.

16. Interview with author, December 1983.

17. Asa Briggs, *Governing the BBC* (1979) pp. 206–9.

18. Grace Wyndham Goldie, *Facing the Nation* (1977) pp. 156–60.
19. Alastair Hetherington, *Guardian Years* (1981) p. 11.
20. Briggs, *Governing the BBC*, pp. 227–31.
21. The meeting of 12 May was widely reported in the press next day. An account of it appears in the book by Robert Harris, *Gotcha!* (1983) pp. 83–6.
22. In the autumn of 1984 the chairman of the Conservative Party, Mr John Gummer, had a wrangle with the BBC over a *Panorama* programme on infiltration of the party by right-wing extremists. This hardly counts as pressure, however, because as chairman of the party he was fully entitled to state his view forcefully and in public. The BBC rebutted his criticisms.
23. Philip Schlesinger, *Putting 'Reality' Together* (1978) pp. 212 and 242.
24. Ibid., pp. 168 and 180.
25. Interview with author, January 1984.
26. Briggs, *Governing the BBC*, p. 83.
27. Schlesinger, *Putting 'Reality' Together*, pp. 106–34.
28. Gans (1980) p. 234.

CHAPTER 3: GOING TO PRESS AND GOING ON AIR

1. For a more detailed account, see the author's *Guardian Years*, pp. 144–6.
2. This passage happened to be written at a time when the *Guardian* had been delivered in central Scotland on no more than three days in either of the two preceding weeks; in the previous six months there had been comparable failings of delivery of both *The Times* and the *Financial Times*, because of guerrilla warfare by or among their printing unions.
3. The most serious delays in television have been in the introduction of ENG – electronic news-gathering. It was held up for two or three years because of union problems. ITN succeeded in bringing it into use in advance of the BBC.
4. Sir William Haley, editor-in-chief, BBC, 1943–44; Director-General, BBC, 1944–52; editor, *The Times*, 1952–66.
5. *The History of the Times*, vol. IV; *Struggles in War and Peace, 1939–66* (1984) pp. 214–16.

CHAPTER 9: THE 1984–5 COAL DISPUTE: NEWSPAPERS (Macbeath)

1. Ernest Dimnet, *The Art of Thinking* (New York: Simon and Schuster, 1928): 'Newspapers are historical documents prepared by men and women generally ignorant of, and indifferent to, history' (Arrow paperback edition, 1964, p. 156).
2. James K. Feibleman, *The Institutions of Society*, 2nd edn (London: George Allen & Unwin, 1956) p. 129. Feibleman contends that there can be no more than these three categories of language and that none exists

in a pure state. It is worth noting that the ideal assignment as outlined in this paragraph is most closely approached in formal, arranged events like ceremonies of state and games. Perhaps that explains the constant temptation to reduce complex unarranged events to simple contests.

3. When the first Aldermaston march against nuclear weapons reached Trafalgar Square in 1957, *The Times* report began by saying that the leaders of the Campaign for Nuclear Disarmament looked down with satisfaction on the crowd that filled Trafalgar Square. Although this was true, and the reporter was simply trying to find an introduction that was not too repetitive, Canon Collins, one of the leaders, wrote an angry letter saying that the paper was accusing them of elitism and demagoguery. The reporter was a member of CND.

4. Most union officers are relatively sophisticated in their view of the press, and recognise that there are reporters who are friendly or at least fair on some of the papers most hostile to the unions. Some of the arguments between journalists and embattled workers have a quality all their own; for example, a picket agreeing that the *Financial Times* was reporting fairly added: 'But it's just because the bosses want to know what's going on.'

5. When Sir Anthony Eden's successor as Prime Minister was being chosen in 1957 Dick Eccleston, a *Times* reporter keeping watch in Downing Street, came back to the news room and told the night news editor: 'It's Macmillan.' The night news editor was sceptical; everyone was saying it was Butler. Eccleston explained that Macmillan had come out for a walk in the park. 'He was as cheerful as a pig at its victuals. He danced a little jig on the bridge and made loud remarks about ducks. If ever I've seen a man who's got the job, it's him.' Eccleston was right and everyone else was wrong except Randolph Churchill, who was told by his father in confidence and broke it next day in the *Evening Standard*, just before Macmillan's appointment was announced. Eccleston's observation was not published.

6. 'Fame' is the credit given for meritorious achievement; 'notoriety' falls to someone who has behaved badly and been found out; 'celebrity' is neutral, fuelled by the human desire to have someone or something to talk about. As long ago as 1863 Matthew Arnold made the distinction in *Macmillan's Magazine*: 'They [Spinoza's successors] had celebrity, Spinoza had fame.'

7. By the end of the year the stoppage of work in the coal industry had attracted many superlatives – 'longest', 'biggest', 'most expensive'. In fact it was difficult to define. Did it constitute a national strike, as the courts held and most people seemed to believe, or a coincidence of area strikes, as the union leadership claimed? If it was a national strike, when did it begin? The 1912 strike involved more men: there were about a million miners then, and the South Wales union were out for eighteen months that time. Comparing expense is notoriously difficult, especially between different industries and over a lapse of time.

8. See below for the change between editions of *The Times* of 18 October. The temptation to arrogance of the office-bound is naively illustrated in Harold Evans's *Good Times, Bad Times* (London: Coronet, 1984) p.

313: 'Everyone played it safe, which meant giving space to a story from a *Times* staff man at the expense too frequently of a more important agency story arriving late or unexpectedly. There was little attempt on either the home or foreign desks to make the best out of several reports.' Evans gives no indication of how he decides what is 'best'.

9. Ecclesiastes 1, ix: 'That which is done, is that which shall be done; and there is no new thing under the sun.' An editor in the News International stable once misheard this as 'There is no news in the *Sun*', and protested vigorously.

10. This can be an extremely serious problem. Not only must a journalist avoid being 'told' in confidence what he may with reasonable effort discover for himself, but he may be gagged because a superior has been told in confidence what he has found out for himself. Sometimes this is to make a 'secret' of the obvious, which is silly. Sometimes it wrecks a carefully developed approach to policy: for example, both Geoffrey Goodman and I – I was labour editor of *The Times* – were 'warned off' incomes policy when the government imposed a pay pause in 1972 after calling in the editors of our and other newspapers for personal briefings. Even more seriously, Iverach McDonald recalls in the fifth volume of *The Times* history (London: Times Books, 1984) that he and Sir William Haley, foreign editor and editor respectively, were told so much in confidence by the government during the Suez affair in 1956 that they were obliged to keep their closest colleagues in the dark. They also became parties to deceiving the public.

11. Internal litigation has been a feature of trade union history, often initiated by left-wingers. Scargill and his colleagues in Kent and South Wales twice went to law in 1977 to try to prevent the introduction of incentive schemes, and lost. However, particularly in challenging election results, left-wingers have often been successful. Until 1972, when the Conservative Industrial Relations Act came into force, no British trade union had ever disobeyed a court order. By the end of 1973 the two biggest had done so and been fined for contempt of court. Even then, the distinction between acceptable and unacceptable jurisdiction was clear; what was unacceptable was recent legislation curbing union activities, not settled law of contract in respect of union rules.

12. It was reported also in the regional news programmes both of BBC Scotland and of STV.

13. Although natural enough, this gave a strange and abstract quality to their statements. For example: 'The suggestion that NCB management does not possess the necessary financial reporting information to assess the viability of individual collieries is incorrect. Accounts are produced at monthly intervals based on a sophisticated computer analysis of expenditure/income, a by-product of which is a profit/loss account for every activity operated in the coalfield. Also a detailed analysis of all assets is maintained to the point where individual items of plant are identified by individual numbers and thereby controlled where they are located . . .' (Albert A. Wheeler, Scottish area director, in a letter to the *Scotsman* on 2 February 1985). There was about twice as much again of such exposition.

CHAPTER 10: THE 1984–5 COAL DISPUTE: TELEVISION NEWS

1. Nicholas Jones in *The Listener* 29 March 1984; also on Mr Scargill's
   'calculated decision' to attack the news media, *The Listener* 26 July 1984;
   and summing up on the importance of media presentation, *The Listener*
   21 February 1985.
2. There were, of course, many other critics of television news – not least
   among academics. Rightly or wrongly, journalists in our experience
   tended to regard these critics as either more biased than any television
   reporter could afford to be or simply ignorant of the obstacles a
   journalist must overcome. A senior ITN man put it this way: 'I'm one of
   those old-fashioned journalists who happen to believe that you can tell
   any story in half an hour, ten minutes, two minutes or 30 seconds . . . I'd
   like to see some of them doing the interviews and putting it all together.'
3. Interview, June 1984.
4. Interview, June 1984.
5. Letter in *Scotsman* 10 April 1984 from chairman of Scottish Colliery
   Enginemen, Boilermen and Tradesmen's Association.
6. Interview, June 1984.
7. Interview, March 1985
8. Interview, June 1984.
9. Interview, June 1985.
10. Interview, March 1985.
11. Mr Walker is said later to have conceded to a friendly journalist that he
    could have settled the dispute in July or August. Why, then, had he not
    gone ahead and done so, telling Mrs Thatcher afterwards? Because, he is
    reputed to have replied, he could think of more pleasant ways to commit
    political suicide.
12. Channel Four News had consulted Mr MacGregor and Mr Scargill the
    previous Friday, asking whether the Monday would be a convenient day
    for transmission. Both agreed. Mr Scargill told Channel Four News that
    they could be sure the dispute would be in the news that evening. He
    must have known of the picketing planned for Orgreave on the Monday.
13. Some time after the dispute ended, CEGB sources expressed relief that
    so little notice had been taken of the importing of coal from the
    Continent through small and little-used ports on the east and west coasts,
    and of the midnight convoys taking coal into some of the power stations.
    The coastal shipping had been reported once by Channel Four News, but
    not much was made of it.

Thanks

Warm thanks, first to the University of Stirling for making the research project possible, and to the Economic and Social Research Council, the Television Fund (ITCA) and the BBC for funding it.

Secondly, to Howard Tumber and Innis Macbeath for working with me, especially to Innis for writing the whole of Chapter 9; and to Janet Morgan and Philip Schlesinger for reading some of the first drafts and for other consultation. And to Pauline Snelson at Macmillan and Anne Beech for their handling of the manuscript.

Next, to the editors and staff of BBC television news, ITN, the *Daily Mail, Daily Mirror, Guardian* and *Times* for allowing such free access to their newsrooms and for tolerating so much questioning.

Also to colleagues at Stirling for frequent advice and encouragement; to my wife Sheila for reading every chapter as it was written and for critical comment; and to Anna Buchanan for typing most of it and for much other assistance.

And to a number of Stirling University students for help with content analysis and measurement, particularly to Mathilda Hogg and Vicki Smith; to my daughter Lucy for assistance during the pilot project; and to stepdaughter Bridget Cameron and stepson Angus Cameron for much other help.

None of them, however, are to be blamed for any shortcomings in the book; which was nevertheless a pleasure to write.

Alastair Hetherington

Index

321